Learners'
Companion Series

Writing
in English

George Stern

LEARNERS
PUBLISHING

© 2003 Dr George Stern

This edition first published 2003 by
Learners Publishing Pte Ltd
222 Tagore Lane
#03-01 TG Building
Singapore 787603
Email: learnpub@learners.com.sg
Website: http://www.learners.com.sg

By arrangement with R.I.C. Publications Pty Ltd
Perth, Western Australia

ISBN 981 4107 03 4

Printed by Seng Lee Press Pte Ltd, Singapore

Contents

Preface

My aim in this book is to present you, the reader, with a writer's compendium. You can dip into the book for help on just about any topic in language use—from writing job applications to writing speeches, and from writing articles and essays to writing grant applications, business letters and more.

The book also doesn't leave you high and dry on how to write. It has twenty-two sections on good usage and a section dealing with 140 confusable pairs—pairs such as *affect* and *effect, complement* and *compliment, all together* and *altogether*. Oh, yes, and the book also deals with the vexing *who—whom* and *which—that* problems.

And there is more. A chapter on English grammar, so that you can bandy coordinating conjunctions with the best of them, and another chapter on punctuation so that you will be able to choose confidently between colons and semicolons. Best of all—and first of all—a chapter on style, so that everything you write has both panache and clarity.

I hope the book leaves you as satisfied in the reading as it has done me in the writing. If there is anything that I haven't explained fully enough or clearly enough, please write and tell me so care of the publisher's address.

Now, dip in and enjoy.

George Stern
Canberra, 2002

Style: writing in your natural voice

Can style be defined as what grammar leaves out?

(GW Turner, *Stylistics*.)

1

Style: writing in your natural voice

1.1 Style and Turner's question

GW Turner asks whether style can be defined as "what grammar leaves out". I believe that the answer to Turner's question is a qualified yes. Style may be defined as the choices you can make within the constraints of grammar. Choices such as word selection: "I am fond of you", "I like you", "I love you." And choices of word sequences: "Really, I love you", "I really love you", "I love you really." But not "Love really you I"—such are the constraints of grammar.

There are other choices as well. Together, the accumulated choices that you make give your language its style.

Let's take a look at two texts, separated by three centuries and by different styles.

> Amidst the hymns and hallelujahs of saints, some one may perhaps be heard offering at high strains in new and lofty measure to sing and celebrate thy divine mercies and marvellous judgements in this land throughout all ages; whereby this great and warlike nation, instructed and inured to the fervent and continual practice of truth and righteousness, and casting far from her the rags of her whole vices, may press on hard to that high and happy emulation to be found the soberest, wisest and most Christian people at that day, when thou, the eternal and shortly expected King, shalt open the clouds to judge the several kingdoms of the world, and distributing national honours and rewards to religious and just commonwealths, shalt put an end to all earthly tyrannies, proclaiming thy universal and mild monarchy through heaven and earth; where they undoubtedly, that by their labours, counsels and prayers, have been earnest for the common good of religion and their country, shall receive above the inferior orders of the blessed, the regal addition of principalities, legions and thrones into their glorious titles, and in supereminence of beatific vision, progressing the dateless and irrevoluble circle of eternity, shall clasp inseparable hands with joy and bliss, in overmeasure forever.
>
> (John Milton, "Of Reformation in England", 1641.)

All in one sentence! And what was Milton trying to say? Probably something like the following:

Thanks to the religious reformation now in progress in England, this country will receive divine honours and rewards at the end of days.

In the 1940s, George Orwell was writing like this:

> So far as writing goes, all one can attempt is a process of simplification. The first step is to find out which of the abstract words habitually used by politicians are really understood by large numbers of people. If phrases like "unprincipled violation of declared pledges" or "insidious threat to the basic principles of democracy" don't mean anything to the average man, then it is stupid to use them.
>
> Secondly, in writing one can keep the spoken word constantly in mind. To get genuinely spoken English onto paper is a complicated matter. But if you habitually say to yourself, "Could I simplify this? Could I make it more like speech?" you are not likely to produce language like that quoted above, nor are you likely to say "eliminate" when you mean "kill".
>
> (George Orwell, *Collected Essays, Journalism and Letters.*)

You might think that the difference between Milton and Orwell lies in the different centuries in which they were writing. But this is not so. Here are two poems, both of them acknowledged masterpieces, written by two poets who were contemporaries and who were writing on the same topic.

> **On His Blindness**
>
> When I consider how my light is spent,
>   E're half my days, in this dark world and wide,
>   And that one Talent which is death to hide,
>   Lodg'd with me useless, though my soul more bent
> To serve therewith my Maker, and present
>   My true account, lest he returning chide.
>   Doth God exact day-labour, light deny'd,
>   I fondly ask; but patience to prevent
> That murmur soon replies, God doth not need
>   Either man's work or his own gifts; who best
>   Bear his mild yoke, they serve him best; his State
> Is Kingly. Thousands at his bidding speed
>   And post o'er Land and Ocean without rest:
> They also serve who only stand and wait.
>
> (John Milton, 1608–74.)

> **On Blindness**
>
> I begin to wane in sight;
> Shortly I shall bid goodnight.
> Then no gazing more about,
> When the candles once are out.
>
> (Robert Herrick, 1591–1674.)

So what is the difference between the writings of Milton on the one hand, and those of Orwell and Herrick on the other? It is a difference in the choice of vocabulary and of sentence structures. These two elements, in turn, determine the register—the level—of the texts. On the one hand, Milton's writing is elevated, dazzling, impressive; the writings of Orwell and Herrick are direct, down-to-earth, almost casual.

The difference, ultimately, emerges from an attitude to writing. What is it that you want to do: make a show of your mastery of big words and complex language structures, or get your ideas across to the reader in the most immediate, most accessible form possible?

If, like Orwell and Herrick, you want to do the latter, then you can achieve this by applying a range of techniques to your writing. Interestingly, these techniques are as sophisticated as the techniques for writing in elevated language. Orwell, in the passage quoted above, hinted at this when he said, "To get genuinely spoken English onto paper is a complicated matter." It takes an effort on the writer's part to make it easy on the reader, but the effort is worth the result— readability.

Before we look at the elements of style, two disclaimers:

First, if you have already developed your own style, this chapter is not for you. But if you are groping towards a style, or if you think that yours is corrupted by bad example or instruction, then this chapter might help you find a style. Of necessity, I will have to make my advice on style sound formulaic, perhaps even mechanical. That is the penalty I pay for presenting a large topic in a short span.

Second, you should feel free not to follow my advice. Indeed, I suggest that once you have read and assimilated my advice, you should break free of it and follow your own instincts.

But now, on with the discourse on style. Below, we look at the separate techniques involved, and we then discuss how to integrate the techniques into a whole. The techniques we discuss are the following:

1   sentence length
2   sentence structures
3   choice of words
4   appropriateness
5   use of capitals
6   first and second person pronouns
7   active and passive.

1.2   Sentence length

Keep your sentences to an average length of one-and-a-half printed lines—some fifteen words—but vary the sentence lengths.

In the twenty-first century, people are no longer used to reading long, involved sentences. You may have the skill to write them, but it is no use doing that if the prose fatigues your readers and they give up trying to understand your prose. My recommendation, therefore, is that you restrict yourself to sentences that average one-and-a-half printed lines—fifteen words or so.

Here are the first ten sentences from an article in a magazine.

Jenifer and Gary Troxel see themselves as pretty typical grandparents. They like to go to their ten grandchildren's recitals and soccer games. They take the kids out to eat and invite them to their home to cook and do crafts together. The youngsters love to take turbo bubble baths in the jacuzzi. But the Troxels' experiences with two of their grandkids, Natalie and Isabelle, are frozen in time.

Though they all live about an hour north of Seattle, the Troxels haven't seen these granddaughters in almost a year because of a dispute with the girls' mother that started after the Troxels' son Brad died. The couple hadn't married and were estranged at the time of Brad's death. The Troxels had bonded with the girls during weekly visits with their father. Later their mother married, and her husband adopted the girls. Despite these complications, the Troxels' heartache is all too common.

(Amy Dickinson, *Time*, 1 January 2000.)

A hundred and fifty words in ten sentences: an average of fifteen words a sentence.

If you do a word count, you will see that the sentences are not uniformly long. They vary in length from ten words to thirty-six. This is the second secret of sentence length: vary the length—anything from single words to forty words in a sentence.

Even single words? Yes! (The last two paragraphs above contain sixty words in four sentences.)

Some writers, even very eminent ones, prefer ultra-short sentences. Here, for example, is an excerpt from the opening of a judgement rendered by Lord Denning in a case, *Lloyds Bank Ltd v Bundy*, before the Law Lords of the House of Lords. The average sentence length is ten words.

Broadchalk is one of the most pleasing villages in England. Old Herbert Bundy was a farmer there. His home was at Yew Tree Farm. It went back for 300 years. His family had been there for generations. It was his only asset. But he did a very foolish thing. He mortgaged it to the bank. Not to borrow money for himself, but for the sake of his son.

Now the bank have come down on him. They want him to get out of Yew Tree Farm and sell it. They have brought this action against him for possession. Going out means ruin for him. He was granted legal aid. His lawyers put in a defence. They said that when he executed the charge to the bank he did not know what he was doing; or at any rate the circumstances were such that he ought not to be bound by it.

At the trial his plight was plain. Yet the judge felt he could do nothing for him. There is nothing, he said, "which takes this out of the vast range of commercial transactions". He ordered Bundy to give up possession of Yew Tree Farm to the bank. Now there is an appeal to this court. The ground is that the circumstances were so exceptional that Herbert Bundy should not be held bound.

(Lord Denning, 30 July 1974.)

On the other hand, from time to time, you can—and should—go for an extra-long sentence if you have an extra-good reason. Here are the last two paragraphs from a review of a book about how men can and should attend to their own creature comforts.

Along with the hilarity—and it is a very funny book—there goes a lot of sound and applicable advice on how to make your hard-boiled eggs easily shellable (bung the hot pot with the boiled egg under a cold water tap); how to avoid bed-making chores (use fitted sheets and a duvet); when to defrost your fridge (once a fortnight or when the ice is half a centimetre thick); what to mix with Campari (grapefruit juice and lots of ice); the uses of a waistcoat (it provides extra pockets and hides the wrinkles in your unironed shirt); what to do with children who want to eat on the floor in front of the telly (put a newspaper under them); what to do about overweight (exercise as well as diet); how to give up smoking and drinking (if you actually want to); how to shop (around); how to seduce a damsel (with old-fashioned courtesy and consideration); how to pack for travelling (in one large suitcase rather than in three small ones); what your rights are as a tenant (and as a landlord); whether you ought to get insurance (yes, some); and what to do with your indoor plants when you leave home for a week (leave them in a bathtub with two centimetres of water).

But these snippets oversimplify and fail to do justice to Rushton. His is a book to buy, to savour and to chortle over. As a manual for the single man who is determined to remain single, the book is witty, useful and civilised.

(Author's text in *The Canberra Times*, 1970.)

This passage works for two reasons. First, the long sentence is in a simple, repeated pattern. Second, the long sentence is offset by short ones.

1.3   Sentence structures

English lends itself to variation in word order. Make use of this to avoid monotony and to introduce a variety of nuances and emphases in your prose.

a   Switching the words within a clause or sentence

The beginning of a sentence is the most prominent. So if you want to focus the reader's attention on a particular idea, bring it up front. Look, for example, at the varying structures you can use in a sentence about taking a friend to the movies.

I took a friend to the movies in town last night. [Focus on me.]

Last night, I took a friend to the movies in town. [Focus on last night.]

It was in town last night that I took a friend to the movies. [Focus on town.]

My friend it was that, last night, I took to the movies in town. [Focus on my friend.]

It was my friend that I took to the movies in town last night. [Focus on my friend.]

It was in town last night that I took my friend to the movies. [Focus on town and last night.]

And a live example: some sentences from an article in a magazine, under the title "The millennium in 825 words". Note the different positions in which the dates occur in the sentences.

China in 1024 issued the first paper money.

A Swedish bank followed suit in 1661.

The Black Death in 1347–49 killed millions in Asia and North Africa, and maybe one European in three.

The first European book was published in 1457.

In 1553 the Muscovy Company of London issued the first equity shares.

The first limited-liability law came in 1811 from New York state.

(*The Economist*, 31 December 1999.)

It is good style to vary the sequence of words in your sentences.

b   Switching the sequence of clauses

Many sentences consist of two or more sub-sentences (called "clauses"), each with its own subject (the doer) and predicate (what is said about the subject). In such sentences there is a stand-alone "main clause" and one (sometimes more than one) other clause.

You can identify the main clause from the fact that it can stand alone as a sentence. You can identify the other clause from the fact that it starts with a conjunction—a word that joins it to the main clause. (See chapter 5.14.)

In such multi-clause sentences, you can often put the main clause (without the conjunction) first, and the subordinate clause (with the conjunction) last. Or you can reverse the sequence. In the examples below, the main clauses are in a different colour.

MAIN CLAUSE FIRST	SUBORDINATE CLAUSE FIRST
I will help you if you help me.	If you help me *I will help you*.
They had dinner when they came home.	When they came home *they had dinner*.
You can have whatever you want.	Whatever you want *you can have*.

The difference between the pairs of sentences is one of focus. In the sentences on the left, the focus is on the information in the main clauses; in the sentences on the right, the focus is on the information in the subordinate clauses.

Here is a collection of five sentences from a magazine. The sentences show variation in clause sequence. Three sentences start with subordinate clauses (each headed by a conjunction); two start with main clauses (in blue).

Though Earth has no shortage of vivid scenes, *ease of travel is gradually turning the exotic into the mundane.* [Subordinate clause first]

Soon there'll be nowhere intrepid left to go, unless you are prepared to hike a little farther than most sightseers. [Main clause first]

If you travelled much farther, to Jupiter's moon Io, *you could witness one of the most extraordinary sights in the Solar System.* [Subordinate clause first]

Wherever there's a weakness in Io's crust, *lava erupts, squirting jets of dust and sulphur dioxide gas high into space.* [Subordinate clause first]

It was long believed that Io had little atmosphere to speak of. [Main clause first]

(Ben Crystal, *New Scientist*, 8 January 2000.)

You could, if you liked, easily reverse the sequence.

Ease of travel is gradually turning the exotic into the mundane, though Earth has no shortage of vivid scenes.

Unless you are prepared to hike a little farther than most sightseers, **there'll soon be nowhere intrepid left to go.**

You could witness one of the most extraordinary sights in the Solar System if you travelled much farther, to Jupiter's moon Io.

Lava erupts, squirting jets of dust and sulphur dioxide gas high into space wherever there's a weakness in Io's crust.

That Io had little atmosphere to speak of was long believed.

It is good style to vary the sequence of clauses in your sentences.

1.4 Choice of words

Before you start writing, think of your mother (or anyone else you are fond of) as the person you are writing to, and then start writing. I call this the "Dear Mum" principle.

Writing in "Dear Mum" style does not mean that your writing should be simple or stupid, slang or silly. Far from it. My mum was a highly intelligent and sophisticated person, so I would never write to her in a condescending or otherwise improper way.

What "Dear Mum" writing means is writing in a way that is normal, everyday, decent, respectful.

The opposite of "Dear Mum" writing I call "Yes, Minister" writing—after a popular TV comedy series. The programme spoofed British government practices in two ways.

- One was by showing up the tricks and dodges of government ministers and of their senior bureaucrats.

- The other was by showing up the convoluted and impenetrable language in which these people, especially the public servants, would couch the simplest of concepts.

So, for example, if the minister asked his head of department when a plan of action might get under way, the head might reply:

> The answer to that, with all due respect, Minister, and after due consideration of all the factors involved, is that the proposed date for the implementation of your proposal—taking all things into account and weighing up both the favourable and unfavourable consequences of the enterprise in hand—is, as far as can be ascertained at this point in time, yet to be determined or, rather, established, with any degree of certainty, given the circumstances under which its implementation might be considered.
>
> (Author's text.)

Which is another way of saying, "I don't like the plan, so I'm trying to stall it for as long as I can."

The text in the last box above might seem to be an exaggeration—and it is, for comic effect—but the spirit of "Yes, Minister" language lives on in some public service writing.

Here are some expressions that officials love to use. Next to them are the "Dear Mum" substitutes that I recommend.

"YES, MINISTER" LANGUAGE	"DEAR MUM" LANGUAGE
I refer to your letter of 10 October.	Thank you for your letter of 10 October.
I would appreciate an early response.	Please answer soon.
This is further to my last letter.	I am writing to you again.
I am grateful for your assistance.	Thank you for your help.
The project will proceed providing you agree.	The project will go ahead if you agree.
You wrote to me concerning the grant.	You wrote to me about the grant.
I will inform you of the committee's decision.	I will let you know what the committee decided.
Please do not hesitate to telephone me.	Please ring me up, if you like.
I trust this addresses your concerns.	I hope this answers your points (questions).

Here, by way of a real example, is the text of a letter sent by an official to a member of the public.

Dear Mrs Surname

I refer to your letter of 10 April 2001 to the Secretary of the Department of This and That concerning State Government Land Taxes. The Secretary has asked me to respond on his behalf.

You would appreciate that the issue of land tax by the State Government is entirely for the State administration. It is one of those matters which do not fall within the portfolio responsibilities of the Minister for This and That. Unfortunately I cannot assist you on this occasion.

Yours sincerely

This is haughty and intimidating. The letter leaves no doubt in Mrs Surname's mind that she is dealing with a Very Important Public Official.

Here is my translation of the letter into "Dear Mum" language.

Dear Mrs Surname

Many thanks for your letter of 10 April 2001 to the secretary. He has asked me to answer your letter. You ask whether this department can help you get an exemption from state government land taxes.

These taxes are a state matter, not one that my department deals with. So, unfortunately, I cannot offer you help with this. The phone number of the state government office that handles this is (02) 2000 0000.

Yours sincerely

No longer haughty and intimidating—just normal, everyday, decent, respectful.

What goes for official writing goes also for school and university assignments. It is a misconception that you prove yourself a worthy scholar by dazzling the readers with elevated prose. It doesn't impress them; it either bores or confuses them. If you really want to impress your readers, you should try doing it, not with fancy language, but with clearly expressed, fresh ideas.

In an appendix to this book, starting at page 279, you will find an extensive list of "Yes, Minister" terms changed into "Dear Mum" terms.

1.5 Appropriateness

Suit the language to the nature and the background knowledge of the reader.

No one has ever put it better than GW Turner.

> "Hello, darling," says a man to his wife. He says "Hello, darling" to his neighbour's wife. He says "Hello, dear" to his wife. An old lady says "Hello, dear" to her pussy cat. I write to the Commissioner of Taxes, beginning "Dear Sir". A young man says "Hello, darling" to another young man. I call you "Dear Reader". I address the Commissioner of Taxes as "Darling Sir". A young man says "Hello, dear" to another young man. A man says "Hello, dear" to his neighbour's wife. I call you "Darling Reader". An old lady says "Hello, darling" to her pussy cat.
>
> All very friendly. But we know that not all these events are equally likely to happen.
>
> (GW Turner, *Stylistics*.)

Suiting the register to the reader does not mean being obsequious to one's superior and arrogant to everybody else. It means making the necessary adjustments—and only the necessary ones—to the "Dear Mum" principle, accommodating the text to the nature and to the background knowledge of the reader. By way of example, here are two extracts from actual letters: one to an eight-year-old; another to a bank manager.

> Today I got a letter from Mummy with some photos of you at a party. You looked like a very funny clown—handsome, too. It will soon be your birthday, and I wonder what surprises Mummy and Daddy have in store for you. Whatever it is, it's sure to be good, and I hope you have a great time.
>
> -
>
> Mrs So-and-so has told me by phone that she is receiving some papers from your bank, but that the papers are going to the wrong address. She has asked me to remind you that you should send all correspondence and statements about her banking matters to me, as I am dealing with her income tax and other financial affairs.
>
> (Author's texts.)

Both of the above texts are normal, everyday, decent, respectful—"Dear Mum" style—but each suits the person it addresses.

1.6   Use of capitals

For the titles of institutions and of office-bearers, use initial capital letters if you write the full formal titles; use initial lower-case letters if you use short informal titles.

You might have noticed, in my version of the letter to Mrs Surname above, that I wrote the words "secretary", "department", "state government" and "land taxes" with initial lower-case letters. In the original letter, these words had initial capital letters. The original letter was wrong: just another way of trying to impress and intimidate the reader.

Let us take a closer look at the matter of capital letters. Here is an extract from the instructions to Captain Cook for his first voyage in 1768.

> Whereas we have in Obedience to the King's Commands, caused His Majesty's Bark, the *Endeavour*, whereof you are Commander, to be fitted out in a proper manner for receiving such Persons as the Royal Society should think fit to observe the Passage of the Planet Venus over the Disk of the Sun, ... you are to make the best of your way to Plymouth Sound, where we have order'd the Crew of the Bark to be paid two Months' wages in Advance.

In current English, twelve of the words (in blue) in the above text would start with initial lower-case letters in accordance with the rule: full formal up; short informal down.

In accordance with this rule, the following words should start with lower-case letters, whether or not you put the word "the" in front of them.

act (legislative)	chairperson	embassy	parliament
ambassador	church	federal	parliamentary
authority	clause (legislative)	federation	presidential
bar (judicial)	commission	government	press
bench (judicial)	company	leader	royal
bill (legislative)	constitution	legislature	secretary
board	corporation	local council	shire council
budget	court	manager	state government
bureau	department	minister	tax office
cabinet	director	opposition	university

I lifted this list straight out of *Spot On! Correspondence and Report Writing*, a publication of the Australian Government Publishing Service (1996). So it has official sanction. More importantly, this is the spelling you will see in the real world—in newspapers and magazines, and also in such government publications as the *Commonwealth Hansard* (Australia).

Please note that you actually do use initial capital letters if you:

- use the full formal title—*the Minister for Whatever*
- attach the short title to a person's name—*Ambassador So-and-So.*
- use the short title as a form of address—*Dear Minister* (the salutation of a letter).

Following are words that commonly start with initial capitals, even though they are not full formal titles; and there are others that some publications print with capitals, and others with lower-case letters. The main words in these two categories are currently the following.

Commonwealth	*North (sociopolitical)*
Crown	*Parliament House*
Democrats (party)	*premier / Premier*
East (sociopolitical)	*president / President*
governor / Governor	*prime minister / Prime Minister*
Greens (party)	*Queen, King*
High Court	*South (sociopolitical)*
house / House (legislative)	*speaker / Speaker (parliamentary)*
Independents (party)	*Supreme Court*
Labour (party)	*treasurer / Treasurer*
Liberals (party)	*West (sociopolitical)*
Nationals (party)	*whip / Whip (parliamentary)*

"North", "South", "East", "West" are special cases.

- These words start with lower-case letters when they refer to points of the compass: "We travelled north on the north-south highway."
- They start with capital letters when they appear in a sociopolitical sense: "The developing South is catching up with the developed North."

The above list features the main exceptions to the rule that full formal titles start with capital letters, and short informal titles with lower-case letters.

The practice of overcapitalizing "important" words is simply wrong. The use of upper- and lower-case letters has nothing to do with importance. All it has to do with is current spelling conventions. In English,

"January" starts with a capital letter, "spring" doesn't. Who is to say that the name of a month is more important than that of a season?

1.7   First and second person pronouns

- The first person pronouns are: *I, me, mine, myself, we, us, ours, ourselves.*
- The second person pronouns are: *you, yours, yourself, yourselves.*

Within reasonable bounds, feel free to use first and second person pronouns. This will make your writing more personal and, therefore, more reader friendly.

The opposite view—put about by some teachers, lecturers and office managers—is that one's writing should be objective and impersonal, especially in a technical or a professional text. But surely this cannot be right. The text does not come from nowhere, addressed to no one: it comes from me, and it is addressed to you. Consequently, and without overdoing it, I allow myself the occasional use of first and second person pronouns.

The following examples, written by professional scientists, show this principle in action.

As far as I am able to judge, after long attending to the subject, the conditions of life appear to act in two ways ... Granting whatever instincts you please, it seems at first quite inconceivable how they can make all the necessary angles and planes. (Charles Darwin, *On the Origin of Species.*)

My purpose is to examine the biology of selfishness and altruism ... If you wish, as I do, to build a society in which individuals cooperate generously and unselfishly towards a common good, you can expect little help from biological nature. (Richard Dawkins, *The Selfish Gene.*)

Jupiter's auroras are very bright—between a hundred and a thousand times more intense than the ones we have on Earth. (Ben Crystal, *New Scientist*, 8 January 2000.)

If you have a particularly tough calculation to perform, it pays to wait until a better computer comes along. (Marcus Chown, *New Scientist*, 8 January 2000.)

1.8 Active and passive

In the main: active, good; passive, bad.

The active and passive are different ways of structuring a sentence.

In the active, the structure is agent–action–target. In the passive, target–action–agent.

ACTIVE	PASSIVE
The manager has received your letter.	_Your letter has been received by the manager._
AGENT ACTION TARGET	TARGET ACTION AGENT

The active is better than the passive for two reasons.

- The active expresses the unfolding of an event in the sequence in which it actually occurs: first comes the agent (the doer of the action), then the action, finally the target (the done-to of the action).

- The active does not allow you to omit the agent from the sentence, but the passive does. In the active, therefore, we always know who is responsible for the action; in the passive, we don't.

ACTIVE NEEDS AN AGENT	PASSIVE DOESN'T NEED AN AGENT
~~_The manager_~~ _Has received your letter._	_Your letter has been received ~~by the manager~~._
AGENT ACTION TARGET	TARGET ACTION AGENT

The left-hand (active) sentence is not possible without an agent; the right-hand (passive) sentence is possible. If writers leave out the agent in a passive, they are leaving their readers in the dark as to who is responsible for the action. In many cases, this can be an irresponsible, unethical way of writing. Consider the following examples of passive sentences without agents.

> _Your cheque has been mailed._
>   TARGET   ACTION
>
> [Tell me who is responsible for mailing it so that I can complain if it doesn't reach me.]

The job has been completed.
   TARGET   ACTION

[Who completed it? I may want to give the agent praise or blame.]

I therefore recommend that, in the main, you use the active instead of the passive.

There are three steps in converting a passive sentence into an active one.

Step one: identify the passive.

You identify the passive from the fact it always consists of a form of the verb *be* + a past participle. A past participle is a verb that, typically, ends in –*n*, –*d* or –*t*.

FORMS OF THE VERB *BE*   +   PAST PARTICIPLES

am is are was were be being been	a verb + –*n* (*seen, taken, known, eaten, done, …*) a verb + –*d* (*noted, said, showed, played, made, …*) a verb + –*t* (*meant, sent, learnt, spoilt, kept, …*)

Each of the following sentences is passive, because each has a form of the verb *be* + a past participle.

1   *Your letter was received.*

2   *It is being processed.*

3   *The cheque has been sent.*

4   *The deed was well done.*

In the above examples, we see two additional, important points about identifying the passive. One is that a sentence (2 above) may have two forms of the verb *be* (*is* and *being*). If so, you simply ignore the first of the two (*is*) and count the second (*being*).

Second, there can be a word or two between the form of the verb *be* and the past participle. In sentence 4, the word *well* separates the two elements (*was* and *done*), and the sentence is still passive.

Step two: add *by* + an agent after the action.

1   *Your letter was received by the manager.*

2   *It is being processed by Robin Surname.*

3   *The cheque has been sent by the pay office.*

4   *The deed was well done by you.*

There are two things to note about the above examples.

- You can designate the agent using a title (sentence 1) or a name (sentence 2) or a corporate entity (sentence 3) or a pronoun (sentence 4).

- If the original passive sentence already contains an agent (say, if sentence 1 had read *Your letter was received by the manager*) you simply omit step two.

Step three: switch from the sequence target–action–agent to agent–action–target.

PASSIVE	ACTIVE

1 *Your letter was received by the manager.*
    TARGET   ACTION   AGENT
	The manager received your letter.
	    AGENT ACTION TARGET

2   *It   is being processed by Robin Surname.*
  TARGET   ACTION   AGENT
	Robin Surname is processing it.
	    AGENT ACTION TARGET

3 *The cheque has been sent by the pay office.*
    TARGET   ACTION   AGENT
	The pay office has sent the cheque.
	    AGENT ACTION TARGET

4 *The deed was well done by you.*
    TARGET   ACTION   AGENT
	You did the deed well.
	  AGENT ACTION TARGET

You can see that, when you effect the switch, the form of the verb (which expresses the action) also changes:

PASSIVE	ACTIVE
… was received …	*… received …*
… is being processed …	*… is processing …*
… has been sent …	*… has sent …*
… was done …	*… did …*

A live example from an official document:

> Progress reports are to be completed by the recruits after the seventh week
> of training. These will enable a suitable programme to be devised for a recall
> session. The recall sessions are being organized to allow for further
> discussion. You will be notified of the time, date and place of the session
> you are to attend.

Step one: identify the passive.

*Progress reports are to be completed by the recruits after the seventh week
of training. These will enable a suitable programme to be devised for a
recall session. The recall sessions are being organized to allow for further
discussion. You will be notified of the time, date and place of the session
you are to attend.*

There are two things to note:

- in the third sentence, there are two forms of the verb *be—are* and *being*. We ignore the first and mark the second.
- in the last line, the words *are* and *attend* do not constitute a passive. This is because the *–d* at the end of *attend* is part of the word itself: it is not a past participle *–d*.

Step two: add *by* + an agent after the action.

We see that, for the first passive (*be completed*), we don't need to add an agent, because there is already one in the text: *by the recruits*. For the other passives, we do need to add agents.

*Progress reports are to be completed **by the recruits** after the seventh
week of training. These will enable a suitable programme to be devised*
by the training officer   *by your supervisor*
⋀ *for a recall session. The recall sessions are being organized* ⋀ *to allow*
                                by me
for further discussion. You will be notified ⋀ *of the time, date and place of
the session you are to attend.*

For all but the first of the four passives, I have had to guess at the agents—and I might have guessed wrong! This is the plague of the passive, especially the agentless passive. The reader never knows who is responsible for what.

Step three: switch from the sequence target–action–agent to agent–action–target.

> *The recruits* *are to complete progress reports after the seventh week of training. These will enable* *the training officer* *to devise a suitable programme for a recall session.* *Your supervisor* *is organizing the recall sessions to allow for further discussion.* *I* *will notify you of the time, date and place of the session you are to attend.*

The agents (in bold italics) in the sentences above tell me who is responsible for the action in each case.

One more point about the passive. As far as possible you should avoid the passive. Occasionally, though, there may be a good reason to use it. Here are three examples where the use of passives is justified.

> *I* *was born* *in November.*
> [I could add "by my mother". But that is too obvious to mention.]
>
> *The tea room* *is located* *in the east block.*
> [I don't need to know who located it there.]
>
> *A house* *was burgled* *in town last night.*
> [I haven't a clue as to who the agent might be.]

1.9 Putting it all together

The actual technique for writing in an accessible and communicative way is to focus:

a   during the writing, on getting it down on paper in short, "Dear Mum" sentences

b   in the revision, on checking the text for each of the seven principles of good style—

- sentence length
- sentence structures
- "Dear Mum" language
- appropriateness
- use of capitals
- first and second person pronouns
- active and passive.

Here is a beautiful and especially noteworthy example of the seven techniques that we have discussed so far. The example is especially noteworthy because (a) it comes from a government publication, and (b) the authors are high-level professionals. If they can write in such clear and reader-friendly terms, so can you and I.

> Ordinary Australians seem to have the best science understanding in the world. Are there any clues why this is so? There is one revealing fragment of evidence. We were able to compare the distribution of scores for Australians and people in the European Union. Roughly 1 per cent of both Australians and Europeans scored zero in the test. About 10 per cent got 40 per cent right in the test in both countries.
>
> But then as we start to look at the higher scoring people, a divergent pattern begins. For example, about 2 per cent of Europeans score 100 per cent. In Australia it is over 6 per cent. The simplest explanation is that highly educated people in Australia are more aware of science than their European counterparts.
>
> (Dr Ralph Lattimore and Dr Brett Wilkinson. 1995. *Science understanding and awareness: How Australia ranks in international surveys.* Canberra: AGPS.)

The above passage repays close analysis. For example, you may note the following.

- There are ten sentences containing, in all, 125 words. The sentences range in length from seven words to nineteen.
- The sentences vary not only in length but also in their structures.
- The second sentence ("Are there any clues why this is so?") is the "Dear Mum" equivalent of the "Yes, Minister" formulation: "What are the indices that would account for this phenomenon?"

- The authors twice avoid using the elevated "approximately" and use, instead, "roughly" and "about".
- There are two occurrences of the first person pronoun "we".
- There are no passives and no superfluous capitals.
- The text is appropriate for any adult reader.

There is one other important point to note in the above passage. It is that, where a technical term is necessary, the authors simply use it—for example, "distribution of scores". Similarly, Lord Denning (section 1.2) uses the technical terms "action for possession" and "mortgaged".

The reason I point this out is to highlight the fact that writing in plain language does not mean using baby language. On the contrary: writing in plain language is a highly sophisticated technique that involves the writer in much more work, in much more thought and care, than does the routine use of officialese, legalese or academese.

To illustrate the above principles I take another actual departmental letter to a client. First the original, and then my rewrite.

Dear Mrs Other

You recently wrote to the Secretary of the Department of This and That regarding the manner in which your pension is calculated and the availability of a wheelchair for your husband.

I have forwarded a copy of your letter to the Regional Office of the Department with the request that you be contacted in order that the manner in which your pension is calculated can be explained to you and the availability of a wheelchair for your husband can be discussed.

An officer of the Department will contact you shortly. The telephone number for the Office is 1 800 000 000, which is a toll-free number.

Yours sincerely

Overall, the above text is unfriendly, difficult to read and, to some extent, confusing. Here are the reasons.

1 **Sentence length.** The first two paragraphs are each a single sentence giving a number of disparate ideas that are hard to disentangle.

2   **Sentence structures.** All the sentences are uniform in structure: *You did this. I will do that. Somebody will do such-and-such. This is so-and-so.*

3   **Choice of words.** The writer uses such fancy words as "regarding", "request", "availability", instead of everyday words that are clearer and that do exactly the same job.

4   **Appropriateness.** The language sounds about right for a stuffed shirt—certainly not for an elderly person who is worried about her pension and about getting a wheelchair for her husband.

5   **Use of capitals.** There are three superfluous capitals in the second paragraph; another two in the third.

6   **Use of first and second person pronouns.** The letter is all right in this department.

7   **Active and passive.** The first paragraph has one agentless passive; the second has four. Let us look at just one of these: *your pension is calculated*. Without the official telling Mrs Other who it is that calculates the pension, Mrs Other might wonder whether she has to pay a tax agent or an accountant to calculate the pension, or whether the department will do this for her.

Below is my rewrite of the letter.

Dear Mrs Other

Thank you for your recent letter to the secretary. I am answering on his behalf. You wrote about two matters. One was about how the department calculates your pension. The other was about a wheelchair for your husband.

I have sent a copy of your letter to the regional office of the department. I have asked them to get in touch with you and explain how the department calculates your pension. You can also discuss the wheelchair matter with them. The toll free number of the regional office is 1800 000 000.

Somebody from that office will get in touch with you soon. Please give them a week or so.

Yours sincerely

I am not alone in thinking that a straightforward, unfussy style is the best. Here is what some other people have had to say on the matter.

It takes a lot of experience to make things simple. It is a real art form. (Professor Allan Snyder, *ANU Reporter*, June 1997.)

The government is committed to greater use of plain English in legislation. Laws that are simpler to understand and administer will reduce unnecessary conflict and expensive litigation. (Australian Prime Minister Paul Keating, *Social Justice Strategy*, 1993.)

A scrupulous writer will always ask in every sentence: what am I trying to say; what words will express it; have I said anything that is ugly; could I put it more shortly? (George Orwell, *Collected Essays, Journalism and Letters*.)

Many ministers are now realizing that they've got to get better presentation by departmental material. Just take, for example, the simple letter to a pensioner advising of changes. Some of those letters have been absolutely barbaric in their phraseology. (Allan Morris, MHR, on ABC Radio, 31 October 1988.)

You can't beat plain English. I wish all my officers would use it. Then I wouldn't have to ask, "What does this mean?" (ACT Minister for Education and Training, Bill Stefaniak, LLB, 11 November 1997.)

Why do lawyers insist on using nonsense language? It is not impressive—at least, not in the way they think. Reaction to it varies from a desire to slit the solicitor's throat to hilarious contempt. (*New Scientist*, 11 March 1989.)

A touch of humour, carefully controlled, can properly find a place in judicial writing. It can be useful in deflating an overblown argument. (Justice Wallach, in *The Australian Law Journal*, November 1990.)

Brevity, simplicity and clarity. These are the hallmarks of good judgement writing. But the greatest of these is clarity. (Justice Michael Kirby, in *The Australian Law Journal*, November 1990.)

My suggestion for the elimination of unreadable scientific papers is, first, to omit needless words and, second, to write as you would speak. (Dr Martin W Gregory, *Nature*, 5 November 1992.)

I very purposely write short chapters, short paragraphs and short sentences. (Nicholas Negroponte, *Scientific American*, September 1995.)

Tossing off unusual words may seem a put-down, a way of saying, "I know more than you." ... Don't be afraid to use "I" if it fits your subject and purpose. (TS Kane, *The New Oxford Guide to Writing*.)

> Obscurity in thought inexorably leads to obscurity in language. (Lord Denning, *The Discipline of Law*.)
>
> Little people use big words; big people use little words. (Roman Emperor, Justinian, sixth century AD.)

1.10 A complete guide to style

Here is a complete ten-point guide to style—the seven points we discussed above and three more.

1 Keep your sentences to an average length of one-and-a-half printed lines—some fifteen words. But vary the sentence lengths. Occasionally, allow yourself long sentences or really short ones, even one-word sentences.

2 Take advantage of the flexibility that English allows in word and clause sequences, and vary:

 a the word order in clauses and sentences: *Now I will see you. I will see you now. I will now see you.*

 b the sequence of main and subordinate clauses: *I'll help you if you help me. If you help me I'll help you.*

3 Use the "Dear Mum" principle. Before you start writing, think of your mother (or anyone else you are fond of) as the person you are writing to, and then start writing. By all means, use technical words for technical things but, for the rest, use language that is normal, everyday, decent, respectful: *I refer to your letter of* ... *with regard to* ... *Thank you for your letter of* ... *about* ...

4 Make your language appropriate. While still keeping your language normal, everyday, decent, respectful, you should also take into account the nature and the background knowledge of the person you are addressing.

5 Use capitals only where modern spelling requires them. Start full formal titles with capital letters (*the Department of Whatever*); short

informal ones with lower-case letters (*the department*). Remember, though, that there are some exceptions to this rule (*Crown, Labour, Liberals, Commonwealth, Aboriginals* ...).

6   Within reasonable bounds, use first person pronouns (*I, me, myself, we, us, ours* ...) and second person pronouns (*you, yours, yourself* ...). This will make your writing more personal and, therefore, more reader-friendly.

7   The passive is all right in some contexts but, for most cases, activate the passive in three steps.

   a   Identify the passive: a form of the verb *be* + a past participle (a form of a verb that ends in *–n, –d* or *–t*).

   b   After the verb, add *by* + an agent. (Omit this step if the passive already has an agent.)

   c   Switch the sequence from target–action–agent to agent–action–target.

8   There are several good reasons why we should use plain language, especially if we are writing on behalf of a public or a private organization. Plain language—

   a   for government agencies, accords with official policy

   b   creates a friendlier relationship between the office and its client

   c   is what experts recommend (see the box above) and what great writers use

   d   makes it easier for people to understand what we write

   e   improves the organization's corporate image

   f   improves the writer's work satisfaction.

9   The matter of style is not mainly one of technique; it is more a matter of mental attitude. The attitude you should adopt is one of wanting to communicate with your readers rather than to impress them.

10   The ultimate secret of style is not to adopt one at all—it is just to write in your natural voice. The techniques discussed above are there to help you recover that voice in case you have lost it through wrong training or wrong example.

Finally, here are six techniques for acquiring a good style.

First, second and third: read, read and read. It matters little what you read: popular magazines, novels, collections of essays, poetry, newspaper articles, biography, science fiction—whatever you fancy. The important thing is that you should enjoy what you read so that reading becomes an ongoing pleasure for you.

Fourth, from time to time, backtrack on what you have read and pay close attention to the features of style in a paragraph or two or on a page or two. Look at the sentence length and structures, at the vocabulary and at the other features we have discussed above. Fifth, put the principles of style into practice in your own writing. Sixth, diverge from my advice on style in any way you like; develop and foster your own style—write in your own voice.

Good usage: the split infinitive and all that

The facts of usage are what they are and it is not the place of grammarians to legislate.

(Noam Chomsky, *Language and Mind*.)

2

Good usage: the split infinitive and all that

2.1 So who decides?

We need to determine what "good usage" is and against what standard we can check usage. But before we determine that, let us first look at what standard we can't appeal to—authority.

Many nations have established language academies: official bodies that lay down rules and regulations for what is good and what is not good in a language. The Italians were the first to establish such an academy (1582). They called it the "Chaff Academy", suggesting that it was designed to separate the wheat of good Italian from the chaff of bad Italian. Next in line were the French (1635), with their Academy of the French Language.

Jonathan Swift, the author of *Gulliver's Travels* was so impressed with the French model that he wrote a letter (1712) to the British prime minister of the day, pleading for the establishment of a similar institution in England. Swift's aim was to "fix" the English language for ever—ignoring the fact that English (indeed, all living languages) are in a continual state of flux and change. Swift's proposal came to nothing. Thank goodness! For who wants a government body to tell us how to write in English?

So, what is there in English that sets standards and establishes what is and what is not currently good English? There is a two-part answer to that.

The first is your native language intuition.

You don't have to have a degree in linguistics to be able to tell that "I some chocolate want" is bad usage and "I want some chocolate" is good usage. Your innate language sense does the job for you—unconsciously, automatically.

The second is common usage.

This does not mean that anything goes. Locutions such as "We was ready" and "We never done nothing" are not current good English, no matter how common they are. So we need to refine our notion of "common usage" a little: good English is the common usage of good users of the language—people such as authors, editors, broadcasters and writers for the quality press.

As Simeon Potter wrote: "Custom and usage are the final measure of linguistic correctness" (1950). That may sound a little vague, but that's all we have in English. That, and our native intuition for what is good and what isn't. By and large, then, we can take as good usage anything that:

a　we intuitively feel to be good usage, and

b　is in common use among good users of the language.

If any expert tells you "This is good English" or "That is bad English" don't ask for logical or grammatical reasons. Instead, (a) see whether you intuitively agree, and (b) ask the "expert" to show you a wide range of supporting texts.

With these two criteria in mind, let us examine some questions of usage.

2.2　Is it wrong to split an infinitive?

Let's first find out what an infinitive is and how to split it. Then we'll see whether good authors split theirs.

An infinitive is the word *to* followed by a verb: *to go, to run, to take, to be* … A split infinitive is an infinitive with one or more words inserted between the *to* element and the verb element.

> *to* suddenly **go**　　*to honestly and truly* **be**
> *to* unjustly **take**　　*to really and fully* **understand**.

If you look at the writings of good authors and quality journals, you will see that they sometimes allow themselves to split their infinitives.

31

He waited as if he expected the enemy to suddenly stop. (Stephen Crane, *The Red Badge of Courage.*)

I wasn't trying to write a moral story, but to simply look at the social factors involved. (Elaine Pagels, *A World of Ideas.*)

We're talking about whether kids have sufficient protein to properly nourish growing brains. (*National Geographic*, January 1999.)

Mary Leakey preferred to carefully evaluate scientific evidence before reaching any conclusions. (*Time*, 10 April 1999.)

We want to empower state and local governments to better serve their citizens. (Al Gore, *Presidents & Prime Ministers* magazine, January–February 1995.)

The government discussion paper will focus on how to change the unemployment insurance system to better help people get jobs. (Jean Chretien, *Presidents & Prime Ministers*, January–February 1995.)

Act in such a way as to really control decision making. (Noam Chomsky, *A World of Ideas.*)

The last example sentence comes from one of the world's leading experts on language. There are many more examples of split infinitives by many more writers in many more texts. The fact that these writers choose *to* occasionally *split* their infinitives validates the practice for you and me—occasionally.

2.3 Can you start a sentence with *and, but, because* or *if*?

These (and scores of similar words) are conjunctions. There has never been a book written in English that doesn't have sentences starting with conjunctions. The Bible has thousands of sentences starting, "<u>And</u> the Lord said to Moses …" and the like. Here are some more textual examples.

But wherefore do not you a mightier way
Make war upon this bloody tyrant Time?
And fortify your self in your decay
With means more blessed than my barren rhyme?

(Shakespeare, the first four lines of "Sonnet 16".)

This dialogue had been held in so very low a whisper, that not a word of it had reached the young lady's ears. **But**, by this time she trembled under such strong emotion, that Mr Lorry felt it incumbent on him to speak a word or two of reassurance … She did indeed start. **And** she caught his wrist with both her hands. (Charles Dickens, *A Tale of Two Cities*.)

A writer should be prepared even to fight in civil wars if it seems necessary. **But** whatever else he does in the service of his party, he should never write for it. He should make it clear that his writing is a thing apart. **And** he should be able to act cooperatively while, if he chooses, completely rejecting the official ideology. (George Orwell, *The Collected Essays, Journalism and Letters*.)

Because of these biases, the researchers rejected the six studies. (*New Scientist*, 15 January 2000.)

Because black holes swallow light, they can only be observed indirectly. (*The Economist*, 28 January 2000.)

If you have a particularly tough calculation to perform, it pays to wait until a better computer comes along. (*New Scientist*, 8 January 2000.)

We in Britain remember especially the heroism of all those who fought against the tyrannies in Europe.

But we must also remember the small bands of brave men and women who resisted from within. **And** we should not forget that, in the second world war especially, civilians were both victims as well as courageous contributors to the war effort. (Queen Elizabeth, *Presidents & Prime Ministers*, July–August 1995.)

The last example reassures us that the practice we are discussing is the Queen's English.

Even grammarians who command us to stop using conjunctions at the start of sentences breach their own commands. Edward Down, for example, writes in *Mastering Grammar*: "Starting a sentence with a joining word is awkward and amateurish. Hide your joining word well inside your sentence" (Melbourne: Longman Cheshire, 1991: 36). But Down ignores his own rule in many instances, among them the following:

And so the conversation continued … (98)
As you mark their essays, … (viii)
When you return their essays, … (viii)
If nothing else, … (ix).

2.4   Can you end a sentence with a preposition?

A preposition is a "positional" word such as *in, on, with, about*. Here is a range of citations from reputable sources, showing that it is all right to end sentences with prepositions (in blue).

I will not leave thee, until I have done that which I have spoken to thee of. (Genesis 28:15.)

The iron bit he crushes 'tween his teeth, / Controlling what he was controlled with. (William Shakespeare, *Venus and Adonis.*)

A mail journey from London in winter was an achievement to congratulate an adventurous traveller upon. (Charles Dickens, *A Tale of Two Cities.*)

In my own teaching, I'm at my best when I have something that I feel passionate about but that I can find a way of presenting the play in. (Sara Lawrence Lightfoot, *A World of Ideas.*)

What are you going to say or add or write that has not been said or written about? (Vartan Gregorian, *A World of Ideas.*)

When this novel first appeared in book form a notion got about that I had been bolted away with. (Joseph Conrad, *Lord Jim.*)

It was long believed that Io had little atmosphere to speak of. (*New Scientist*, 8 January 2000.)

Telling the truth, BEING my own truth—that's a right worth standing up for. (Donna Britt, *National Geographic*, February 2000.)

Finally, this is what Winston Churchill said about the ban on ending sentences with prepositions:

This is the sort of pedantry up with which I will not put!

2.5   Can you use *can* in the sense of "have permission"?

Many people strictly distinguish between *can* (meaning "be able") and *may* (meaning "have permission"). They say that it is wrong to say, "You *can* do whatever you like." It should be "You *may* do whatever you like."

The Oxford English Dictionary agrees that the primary meaning of *can* is "be able". But the *OED* also cites texts, going back to 1879, that show the use of *can* in the sense of "have permission". As one of the definitions of *can*, the *OED* gives, "To be allowed to, to be given permission to; = may", and it cites Alfred Lord Tennyson: "Can I speak with the Count?" as an example of this meaning of the word.

Following are some other citations I have found where *can* has the meaning of "have permission".

What **can** I do for you, sir? (Charles Dickens, *David Copperfield*.)

Can I speak confidentially? (Arthur Conan Doyle, "Black Peter".)

You **can** have whatever allowance you like, and live where you choose. (Oscar Wilde, *A Woman of No Importance*.)

You **can** talk as much as you like. (LM Montgomery, *Anne of Green Gables*.)

While the old man and I out-knowledge the beaver, you **can** fish, and knock down the deer, to keep body and soul together. (James Fenimore Cooper, *The Deerslayer*.)

If the Washington statute is overturned, states could give parents more control over when and how grandparents **can** visit the kids. (Amy Dickinson, *Time*, 1 January 2000.)

2.6 Can you use *hopefully* in the sense of "it is to be hoped that"?

Some people contend that *hopefully* can only mean "in a hopeful manner"—just as *quickly* means "in a quick manner". In support of this contention, people cite Robert Louis Stevenson (1850–94): "To travel hopefully is a better thing than to arrive" (*El Dorado*). In the Stevenson citation and also in the following two citations *hopefully* does indeed mean "in a hopeful manner".

He watched the dawn's growing hopefully, yet sometimes afraid. (Lew Wallace, *Ben Hur*.)

Johnny looked hopefully at his father. (Stephen Crane, "The Blue Hotel".)

But *hopefully* can also mean "it is to be hoped"—as in the following texts.

> **Hopefully**, this book will prove of interest to anyone concerned with words. (Jean Aitchison, *Words in the Mind: An Introduction to the Mental Lexicon*.)
>
> Men with fully developed emotional lives will be better husbands, fathers and friends—while **hopefully** remaining just Martian enough to keep things interesting. (Amy Dickinson, *TIME*, 17 January 2000.)
>
> **Hopefully**, you want to be able to say that you're working on something that's important now—not something that was important in the past. (James Watson, *TIME*, 23 March 1999.)

We can see that *hopefully* doesn't always have to mean "in a hopeful manner", by comparing it with *normally*, which similarly doesn't always have to mean "in a normal manner": "I <u>normally</u> eat breakfast at 8.00 am." The use of an adverb (such as *hopefully* or *normally*) to modify a sentence is called the adjunctive use of an adverb. (See chapter 5.10.)

To quote Professor Paul Brians (of Washington State University) on the matter: "*Hopefully* has meant 'it is to be hoped' for a very long time, and those who insist it can only mean 'in a hopeful manner' display more hopefulness than realism."

2.7   Is it all right to use the word *get* or *got*?

I have often heard it said that *get* and *got* are "childish" words. This is a strange myth if ever there was one. The word *get* must be important: *The Oxford English Dictionary* devotes some thirty pages to it, giving some 300 meanings of the word. Here are some citations with *get*.

> And Shechem spake unto his father Hamor, saying, "**Get** me this damsel to wife." (Genesis 34:4.)
>
> **Get** thee to a nunnery! (William Shakespeare, *Hamlet*.)
>
> The passenger would then lower the window to **get** the reality of mist and rain. (Charles Dickens, *A Tale of Two Cities*.)
>
> Every president is also trying to make things happen, to **get** policy enacted. (Sissela Bok, in *Bill Moyers: A World of Ideas*.)
>
> It would have been all the better if she had **got** someone else to dress her. (Lewis Carroll, *Through the Looking-Glass*.)

> To play a leading part in the world the British have **got** to know what they are doing, and they have **got** to retain their vitality. (George Orwell, *Collected Essays, Journalism and Letters.*)
>
> You **get** everything just as you like it when, guess what, it's time to upgrade. (*New Scientist*, 8 May 1999.)
>
> Americans **get** most of their complex carbohydrates from refined grains. (*Time*, 10 May 1999.)
>
> All of Europe's banks face pressures to **get** bigger. (*The Economist*, 7 May 1999.)

If the above reputable authors (and many more) can get away with it, so can you and I.

2.8 Is it true that, after *if*, *then* is redundant?

Yes. But that doesn't mean to say that you mustn't use it. Good speech and good writing are full of redundancies. I have never understood why, out of all the redundancies, people pick on the poor defenceless word *then*. Neither, apparently, have the writers of the following texts.

> **If** thou wilt take the left hand, **then** I will go to the right; or **if** thou depart to the right hand, **then** I will go to the left. (Genesis 13:9.)
>
> **If** ten of thine ten times refigur'd thee,
> **Then** what could death do, if thou shouldst depart,
> Leaving thee living in posterity? (William Shakespeare, *Venus and Adonis.*)
>
> **If** his wife had implored the king for any tidings of him and all quite in vain, **then** the history of your father would have been the history of this unfortunate gentleman. (Charles Dickens, *A Tale of Two Cities.*)
>
> **If** you had to define humour in a single phrase, **then** you might define it as dignity sitting on a tin tack. (George Orwell, *Collected Essays, Journalism and Letters.*)
>
> **If** organic beings vary at all in the several parts of their organization; **if** there be at some age, season or year, a severe struggle for life, **then** it would be a most extraordinary fact if no variation ever had occurred useful to some being's own welfare. (Charles Darwin, *The Origin of Species.*)
>
> **If** humans and their descendants remain sufficiently motivated (that may be a big "if"), **then** technology will be bounded only by the laws of physics. (Paul Davies, *The Last Three Minutes.*)

> If you could introduce tests at, say, the age of three, then you could intervene early and reduce the long-term suffering of many people. (*New Scientist*, 24 April 1999.)
>
> If the questioner cannot determine by the responses to queries posed to them which is the human and which the computer, then the computer can be said to be "thinking" as well as the human. (*Time*, 29 March 1999.)

Of course, you don't have to use *then* after *if*. The point is that you may, if you feel like it.

2.9   After the word *different* do you use *from, to* or *than?*

The Oxford English Dictionary answers this question as follows. "The usual construction is now with *from*. [The construction] with *to* is found in writers of all ages, and is frequent colloquially, but is by many considered incorrect." *Different than* also occurs but is also, by many, considered incorrect.

> Music is strange stuff. It is clearly different from language. (*The Economist*, 18 February 2000.)
>
> "We're not just different from *Lifetime*," says Laybourne. "We're different from all TV." (James Poniewozik, *Time*, 31 January 2000.)
>
> The past 20 years are different from the previous 30. (*National Geographic*, March 1999.)
>
> The smear on your nightgown might have a meaning entirely different to the meaning which I had given to it up to that time. (Wilkie Collins, *Moonstone*.)
>
> Such fickleness! How different to your brother and to mine! (Jane Austen, *Northanger Abbey*.)
>
> It could be that video images appear unstable to them, almost stroboscopic, because birds have a different flicker fusion rate than humans do. (Irene Pepperberg, *New Scientist*, 15 January 2000.)

2.10 Can you use *I have gotten* or must it be *I have got?*

Both forms can—at a stretch—be used as the past participle (that is, the form used after *have, has* or *had*) of *get*. So there is nothing ungrammatical in saying either "I <u>have got</u> your letter" or "I <u>have gotten</u> your letter."

Gotten is the older form of the past participle, and *got* is the modern abbreviated form—much as *pram* is the modern abbreviation of *perambulator*. Nowadays, *gotten* (like *perambulator*) is hardly ever used, except with *ill-* as in *ill-gotten gains*.

The texts below divide into old and new.

> Jack Cade hath **gotten** London Bridge. (William Shakespeare, 1591. *King Henry the VI.*)
>
> The wine had **gotten** a little into his head. (Edgar Allan Poe, 1832. "Bon Bon".)
>
> I had **gotten** used to it. (Sir Walter Scott, 1896. *The Chronicles of Cannongate.*)
>
> The activists have **got** their acts together. (Walter Korn, TIME, 24 April 2000.)
>
> If the new-paradigmists have **got** it wrong, the danger is clear. (*The Economist*, 21 April 2000.)
>
> Wittgenstein returned to England in 1929 to declare dramatically that he had **got** it all wrong the first time … We have **got** on to slippery ice. (TIME, 29 March 1999.)

2.11 What is the etymological fallacy?

It is the false notion that the non-English meaning of a loan word keeps its original meaning when it comes into English. I became aware of this fallacy when someone chided me for using the expression "very true". You can't say "very true", the self-appointed language expert told me, because *very* comes from the Latin "verus", which means "true", and it's nonsense to say "true true".

Well, I checked the literature, and I found that some pretty good authors used this supposedly nonsense expression.

POLONIUS: That's **very true**, my lord. (William Shakespeare, *Hamlet*.)

Indeed this is a **very true** proposition. (John Locke, *An Essay Concerning Human Understanding*.)

Some of the old poets said that the gods were at first created by human fear, which is **very true**. (Thomas Hobbes, *Leviathan*.)

Simple they were, not savage; and their rifles,
Though **very true**, were not yet used for trifles. (Lord Byron, *Don Juan*.)

I said to Miss Mills that this was **very true**. (Charles Dickens, *David Copperfield*.)

I crossed some white fantails, which breed **very true**, with some black barbs. (Charles Darwin, *The Origin of Species*.)

"That is **very true**," replied Elizabeth, "and I could easily forgive his pride." (Jane Austen, *Pride and Prejudice*.)

It was **very true**, that this kingdom was not in a flourishing state. (Thomas Paine, *The American Crisis*.)

"**Very true**," said the Duchess, "flamingoes and mustard both bite." (Lewis Carroll, *Alice's Adventures in Wonderland*.)

This letter is from your **very true** friend. (Mark Twain, *Life on the Mississippi*.)

"It is **very true**," Winterbourne pursued, "that Daisy and her mamma have not yet risen to that stage of culture." (Henry James, *Daisy Miller*.)

Another occasion, another chiding. Thou shalt not use *terrific* in the sense of "wonderful", because the word comes from a Latin root that means "frightening". Well, not in English, it doesn't: it means "wonderful". And if you want to express "frightening" with a word from the same Latin root, you can always use *terrifying*.

Spanish-language radio is booming, and it has proven to be a **terrific** [wonderful] launching pad for Latin crossover artists. (*Time*, 24 May 1999.)

No wonder many of them are asking themselves whether e-business is the most exciting opportunity or the most **terrifying** [frightening] challenge they have ever faced. (*The Economist*, 2 July 1999.)

Some words do, and some words don't, keep their original meaning when they enter English. Examples of the latter case are *nice*, which meant "stupid" in Latin but which means "pleasing" in English; *lace*, which meant "noose" in Latin but which means "a patterned cotton fabric" in English; *orchid*, which meant "testicle" in Greek but which is the name of a flower in English. Similarly, *very* and *terrific* have meanings in English that are different from their meanings in Latin.

2.12 What is gender-biased language and how do you avoid it?

Gender-biased (or "sexist") language is language that refers to members of one gender, usually males, when members of both genders should be included. Such language can result in incongruity: "Man is a mammal that suckles his young." Or it can be an insult to half of the human species: "Everyone should do his duty."

Here are six techniques for changing gender-biased into gender-inclusive language.

1 Use common-gender terms.

GENDER-BIASED: *A chairman runs a meeting.*

GENDER-INCLUSIVE: *A chairperson runs a meeting.*

2 In most cases, eliminate the feminine suffixes (endings).

GENDER-BIASED: *Meredith Kinmont is an Australian poetess.*

GENDER-INCLUSIVE: *Meredith Kinmont is an Australian poet.*

With some words, though, the feminine suffix is still standard: *princess, duchess, abbess*. With others (*poet, actor*), the feminine *–ess* suffix is withering away.

> March 25 is the feast day marking the angelic announcement to a young Nazarene Jew that she would give birth to the Son of God. (David van Biema, *Time*, 20 March 2000.)

3 Use masculine and feminine words in tandem.

> The child brings himself or herself to school quite full of history and preoccupations. And the teacher comes with her or his own set of those. (Sara Lawrence Lightfoot, *A World of Ideas*.)
>
> In one day's edition of the *New York Times* there is more information than a single man or woman had to process in the whole of his or her life in the sixteenth century. (Vartan Gregorian, *A World of Ideas*.)
>
> The infalling astronaut would notice nothing especially different as she or he crosses into the black hole. (Paul Davies, *The Last Three Minutes*.)

4 If technique 3 becomes tedious, try turning all the singulars into plurals.

> I believe in the right of individuals to guide their own lives, to think for themselves, to live where they want. (Barbara Tuchman, *A World of Ideas*.)

5 Use a singular word such as *each, everyone, anyone* with a plural pronoun such as *they, them, theirs* ... This practice goes back at least five hundred years, as the following citations show.

> He never forsaketh any creature unless they forsake themselves. (John Fisher, *The Ways of Perfect Religion*, 1535.)
>
> Everybody fell a-laughing, as how could they help it? (Henry Fielding, *Tom Jones*, 1749.)
>
> If a person is born a gloomy temper, they cannot help it. (Earl of Chesterfield, *Letters*, 1759.)
>
> Nobody can deprive us of the Church, if they would. (William Whewell, *Life*, 1835.)
>
> Nobody fancies for a moment that they are reading about anything beyond the pale of ordinary propriety. (Walter Bagehot, *Literary Studies*, 1858.)
>
> Nobody does anything well that they cannot help doing. (John Ruskin, *Crown of Wild Olives*, 1856.)
>
> Paths appear as each individual solves their own problem. (Michael Brooks, *New Scientist*, 24 June 2000.)

6 If you are writing to someone whose name you don't know, use a title in the salutation.

GENDER-BIASED: *Dear Sir*
                   Sorry I was late returning the book.

GENDER-INCLUSIVE: *Dear Librarian*
                   Sorry I was late returning the book.

2.13   When do you write numbers as words, and when as digits?

This is one subject in which practice varies among different writers and different publishers. The system I propose below has two advantages. One is that it is in fairly wide use among recognized writers. The other is that it is a sensible and consistent system.

I divide the subject up into two parts:

1 numbers of people and things

2 numbers with weights and measures.

1 **a** **For numbers of people and things, use words in the following cases.**

If you can express the number in one or two words.

I went on the trip with twenty-five other people, and we visited fourteen places.

At the start of a sentence, regardless of how many words it takes.

A hundred and fifty sheep were in the paddock.

Alternatively, use digits but put them inside the sentence.

There were 150 sheep in the paddock.

For certain commonly used expressions that take more than two words.

I have told you this a hundred and one times.

b For numbers of people and things, use digits in the following cases.

If it takes more than two words to express the number.

There were 250 people at the demonstration.

In a passage that is rich in numbers relating to similar kinds of things.

They have 40 chickens, 100 cows and 26 goats.

2 a For numbers with weights and measures, use words in the following cases.

If you can express the number in one or two words, and if you use words (rather than abbreviations or symbols) for the standard units.

It reached twenty-nine degrees in the shade today.

The car stopped ten centimetres from the edge of the cliff.

I owe you ten dollars.

b For numbers with weights and measures, use digits in the following cases.

If you use a symbol or an abbreviation for the standard unit.

What is 50% of 20 cm?

I owe you $10.

c For numbers with weights and measures, use both words and digits when two numbers come together in the same sentence. In such cases, put the larger number in digits.

I had three 45-metre lengths of pipe.

I had 45 three-metre lengths of pipe.

In mathematics.

2 + 2 = 4.

Following is a sample text showing how a modern author uses words and digits to express numbers.

> For the last five years we have been geared for this year.
>
> We were invited to their formal in Year 10.
>
> A different Australia emerged in the 1950s.
>
> "Welcome to the nineties, Josephine."
>
> "That'll be nine dollars and thirty cents."
>
> She asked me to write a two-thousand word conversation …
>
> "You'll come here every afternoon until four-thirty."
>
> (Melina Marchetta, *Looking for Alibrandi.*)

2.14   What are the right and the wrong ways of using *myself* and other *–self* forms?

The *–self* forms are the pronouns:

myself   yourself   himself   herself   itself   ourselves   yourselves   themselves

1   **When is it right to use the *–self* forms?**

There are two proper uses for these pronouns.

a   One is to emphasize another noun or pronoun in the sentence. This is called the *emphatic use*.

> Had he come himself, I admit I would have gone back to a life of degradation.
>
> I have only just seen it myself.
>
> (Oscar Wilde, *Lady Windermere's Fan.*)

b   The other is to show that the doer (in grammar terms, the subject) and the done-to (the object) of the verb are one and the same person. This is called the *reflexive use*—the action reflects back on the doer of the action.

> Do you think that the wife should not console herself?
>
> Poor Augustus, you know how he repeats himself.
>
> (Oscar Wilde, *Lady Windermere's Fan.*)

In all four example sentences above, each emphatic or reflexive pronoun occurs with a cognate (an associated) pronoun or noun.

he … himself   I … myself   the wife … herself   he … himself

This should always be the case—with one exception: imperative (command) sentences.

> Be *yourself*! (Oscar Wilde, *Lady Windermere's Fan.*)

2   When is it wrong to use the *–self* forms?

It is not quite proper (though some people do use it when they are speaking or writing informally) to use a *–self* form without a cognate noun or pronoun.

My parents and myself went shopping.
[Better: My parents and I went shopping.]

I bought this for Chris and yourself.
[Better: I bought this for Chris and you.]

You can see that the above sentences should have *I* and *you* (instead of *myself* and *yourself*) if you leave out the word (or words) before *and*.

~~My parents and~~ *I went shopping.*

I bought this for ~~Chris and~~ *you.*

The point is that *My parents and …* and *Chris and …* have no effect on how the next pronouns should look. Therefore, the pronouns should be *I* and *you* rather than *myself* and *yourself*.

Apparently cricketers are prone to the wrong use of *–self* forms.

> "Myself and Damien Martyn are there to stabilize things." (Steve Waugh, quoted in *The Canberra Times*, 23 February 2000.) [Better: "I and Damien Martyn …]
>
> "Coach Steve Rixon spent a lot of the last year of his time in charge, with Stephen Fleming, Chris Cairns, myself and other senior players really hammering those lessons home." (Adam Parore, quoted in *Inside Edge*, March 2000.) [Better: "… with Stephen Fleming, Chris Cairns, me and other senior players …]

2.15 When do you use *said,* and when *said that?*

You can please yourself: the two are equally good.

> *They said it was a lovely day.*   *They said that it was a lovely day.*

What goes for *said* also goes for such words as *told, explained, reported* and many more. Here are some textual examples of indirect quotations.

Harold Lasswell said that we should not succumb to democratic dogmatism.

Edward Bernais said the essence of democracy is that we have the freedom to persuade.

The chairman of the board will always tell you that he spends his every waking hour labouring.

Suppose that some journal emerged which reflected the concerns of the special interests.

Or suppose some journal were to focus on the fact that we are in a tiny minority.

You might say it comes naturally.

(Noam Chomsky, A World of Ideas.)

I am afraid I answered rather roughly in the *Partisan Review* controversy.

I am sorry that what I said rankled.

(George Orwell, Collected Essays, Journalism and Letters.)

2.16 When do you use *which* and when do you use *that?*

The question is: do you say *I want the book which …* or *I want the book that …?*

There are two ways to decide: (1) an intuitive way and (2) a grammar way. The former is by far the easier, and we look at that first.

1 The intuitive way

If you are in doubt whether to use *which* or *that,* always try *that* as the default option. If it sounds good, use it; if it doesn't, try *which.*

Try your hand at the following sentences. You can fill five of the blanks with *that*, and four with *which*.

1   *What is the name of the town _____ lies right next to Albury?*

2   *Wodonga, _____ is in Victoria, lies right next to Albury, _____ is in New South Wales.*

3   *I'd like to buy a car _____ hasn't done too many kilometres.*

4   *You can buy mine, _____ has done only 50,000 kilometres.*

5   *Physics is a science _____ creates ten problems for every one it solves.*

6   *A diet is something _____ starves you to death so that you can live a little longer.*

7   *Cradle Mountain, _____ is in central Tasmania, is 1,545 metres high.*

8   *It is a mountain _____ attracts many visitors.*

Here are the answers.

1   *What is the name of the town that lies right next to Albury?*

2   *Wodonga, which is in Victoria, lies right next to Albury, which is in New South Wales.*

3   *I'd like to buy a car that hasn't done too many kilometres.*

4   *You can buy mine, which has done only 50,000 kilometres.*

5   *Physics is a science that creates ten problems for every one it solves.*

6   *A diet is something that starves you to death so that you can live a little longer.*

7   *Cradle Mountain, which is in central Tasmania, is 1,545 metres high.*

8   *It is a mountain that attracts many visitors.*

2   **The grammar way** (You won't need this if you scored well in the quiz above.)

The clause starting with *which* or *that* is called "a relative clause" (also "an adjective clause"). The grammar rule for using *which* and *that* at the head of such a clause is as follows.

a   Use *that* if the clause defines which one or what kind of thing the clause relates to. In sentence 3 above, for example, the sentence (minus the relative clause) reads: "I'd like to buy a car." One could naturally ask, "Which car—or what kind of car—would you like to buy?" And the relative clause answers that question: "A car <u>that</u> hasn't done too many kilometres."

b Use *which* if the clause doesn't define which one or what kind of thing the clause relates to. In sentence 7 above, for example, the sentence (minus the relative clause) reads: "Cradle Mountain is 1,545 metres high." It doesn't make sense to ask, "Which Cradle Mountain—or what kind of Cradle Mountain—are you talking about?" So the relative clause, "which is in central Tasmania", doesn't define the kind of mountain it is. Rather, it adds incidental information about the already identified mountain.

> One of the greatest pleasures that I have in life is by virtue of my financial position. I collect jade, which I think is a very tactile material. (Rene Rivkin, *The Search for Meaning Collection.*)
>
> Housing and agriculture break up the pre-existent natural ecosystem into little patches. As a result, the gene pool becomes isolated, which limits genetic exchange. The population finding is intended to help conservationists understand population dynamics in these hotspots, which cover 12 per cent of Earth's terrestrial surface. John Williams is a population and environment fellow at a Washington-based organization that backs conservation as a strategy for biodiversity. "We think the same factors that encourage biodiversity also encourage people to move into those landscapes." (John Roach, *National Geographic News*, 27 May 2000.)

In informal English—conversations and personal letters, for example—the distinction between *which* and *that* is not so important. It doesn't much matter which of the following you choose to use.

FORMAL: *I want shoes that won't pinch.*

INFORMAL: *I want shoes which won't pinch.*

2.17 When do you use *who, whom* and *whose*?

These three pronouns have two uses: (1) as interrogative pronouns and (2) as relative pronouns.

1   The interrogative pronouns *Who? Whom?* and *Whose?*

a   Use *Who?* in the question if the answer is a subjective pronoun (*he, she, they* ...).

QUESTION	ANSWER
Who spilled the soup?	*They* did.
Who wants more soup?	*They* do.

b   Use *Whom?* in the question if the answer is an objective pronoun (*him, her, them* ...).

QUESTION	ANSWER
Whom did you call?	*I called* him.
Whom is he waiting for?	*He is waiting for* her.

c   Use *Whose?* in the question if the answer is a possessive pronoun (*his, hers, theirs* ...).

QUESTION	ANSWER
Whose is this diamond?	*It's* mine.
Whose is that imitation?	*It's* yours.

> *Who* are Miss Worsley's parents? [Answer: *They* are.]
>
> *Whom* are you talking about? [Answer: I'm talking about *them*.]
>
> *Whose* glove is this? [Answer: It's *hers*.] (Oscar Wilde, *A Woman of No Importance*.)

2   The relative pronouns *who, whom* and *whose*

To determine with certainty which of these pronouns to use, you need to change the relative clause (the clause headed by the relative pronoun) into a free-standing sentence.

a   If the free-standing sentence contains *he, she* or *they*—use *who.*

> He had none of the appearance of a man *who* sailed before the mast. [*He* sailed before the mast.] (Robert Louis Stevenson, *Treasure Island*.)

b If the free-standing sentence contains *him, her* or *them*—use *whom*.

> A man stepped in on whom I had never set my eyes before. [I had never set my eyes on him before.] (Robert Louis Stevenson, *Treasure Island*.)

c If the free-standing sentence contains *his, hers* or *theirs*—use *whose*.

> I am walking beside my father, whose name is Simon Dedalus. [His name is Simon Dedalus.] (James Joyce, *A Portrait of the Artist as a Young Man*.)

Some more texts:

> It was Mr Riach who gave the boy a drink. [He gave the boy a drink.]
>
> I came across a dapper little man whom I saw to be a barber. [I saw him to be a barber.]
>
> My first officer, whom I could ill spare, has got your sword. [I could ill spare him.]
>
> The women, whose voice had risen, turned and was gone. [Her voice had risen.]
>
> This drink restores speech to those who have the dumb palsy. [They have the dumb palsy.]
>
> I had a man under my eyes whose life was forfeit. [His life was forfeit.]
>
> (Robert Louis Stevenson, *Kidnapped*.)

In informal English—conversations and personal letters, for example—the distinction between *who* and *whom* is not so important. It doesn't much matter which of the following you choose to use.

FORMAL: *Whom are you waiting for?*
INFORMAL: *Who are you waiting for?*

FORMAL: *This is the person whom I work with.*
INFORMAL: *This is the person who I work with.*

2.18 When do you use *less*, and when *fewer*?

The difference between *less* and *fewer* is as follows.

a *Less* is the comparative form of *little*; *fewer* is the comparative form of *few*. These words fit the following pattern.

POSITIVE	COMPARATIVE	SUPERLATIVE
big	*bigger*	*biggest*
small	*smaller*	*smallest*
little	*less*	*least*
few	*fewer*	*fewest*

b *Little* and *less* (in the sense of "not much") go with singular nouns; *few* and *fewer* (in the sense of "not many") go with plural nouns.

*There is <u>little</u> **time** left.*
SINGULAR

*There is <u>less</u> **time** left.*
SINGULAR

*There are <u>few</u> **hours** left.*
PLURAL

*There are <u>fewer</u> **hours** left.*
PLURAL

*You have <u>little</u> **money**.*
SINGULAR

*I have <u>less</u> **money**.*
SINGULAR

*You have a <u>few</u> **dollars**.*
PLURAL

*I have <u>fewer</u> **dollars**.*
PLURAL

And some illustrative texts.

One would feel fewer hesitations.

The fewer words he risked, the better.

Being of less account he was given away.

There were fewer men one wanted to meet.

For him alone the less English education he got, the better.

The Sioux Indians would have taught him less mischief.

The less a tourist knows, the fewer mistakes he need make.

They seemed to have even less personal concern.

(Henry Adams, *The Education of Henry Adams*.)

2.19   When do you use *if*, and when *whether*?

If and *whether* are different words with different meanings.

- *If* expresses a condition:

  If you like, I will help you.

- *Whether* introduces an indirect question:

  I will ask whether they are ready.

Some people use *if* informally in the sense of *whether*.

  I will ask if they are ready.

Notice that *if*, in the above sentence, is ambiguous. It could have either of two meanings.

  I will ask whether they are ready.

Or: *In the event that they are ready, I will ask them something.*

Because of the sort of ambiguity illustrated above, it is worth preserving the distinction between *if* and *whether*, at least in formal texts. Most good users of the language do distinguish between *if* and *whether*.

To live your life worrying about whether other people find you attractive—well, you may as well not bother to have lived.

You have people saying, "God is a power whom we must simply take on trust." Whether that's a belief in God or not some people would call that God; others wouldn't.

If you are wealthy, then you have a lot of means of getting people to accept your construction of reality.

If you want to teach people not to commit crimes, you have to do something other than lock them up.

I don't know whether the Trobrianders still live like this.

(Dorothy Rowe, *The Search for Meaning.*)

Do you know whether to laugh or cry?

You would laugh at me if I dealt in duels and ghosts.

If you don't like my preaching, you must lump it.

I do not know whether you have any illusions left.

Democracy will ruin us if we are ill-bred.

Who knows whether we might not have done as he did.

I give you the handbook at full length if you care to read it.

I wonder whether I ought to tell you or not.

(George Bernard Shaw, *Man and Superman.*)

2.20 When do you use *shall*, and when *will*?

1 **The use of *will***

In modern usage, to express the future, you can use *will* for all persons: *I, you, he, she, it, we, you, they—will.*

2 **The uses of *shall***

a As an alternative to *will* you may, if you like, use *shall* with *I* and *we*. Both *shall* and *will* are all right, but *shall* has a slightly old-fashioned air about it.

I will be going soon.   Or: *I shall be going soon.*

We will be going soon.   Or: *We shall be going soon.*

b In questions with *I* or with *we*, use *shall* to express "Would you like ...?" or "Is it your preference that ...?"

Shall we play tennis?

Shall I do the dishes now or shall I leave them for tomorrow?

The above two sentences are not "pure" future: they don't mean "Is this going to happen?" They mean something like:

"Would you like us to play tennis?" and "Would you prefer me to do the dishes now or tomorrow?"

c   There is a limited range of idiomatic expressions in which *shall* still features.

They shall not pass.
We shall not be moved.

This does not have a "pure" future meaning. Rather, it means "I am determined not to let them through"; "We are determined not to be moved."

Texts with *shall* and *will*:

As far as Jordan and Israel are concerned, I hope eventually we will be together ... I certainly hope it will be a comprehensive peace ... When the time comes and there is a need for us to meet, we will meet and we will meet publicly.

(King Hussein, *Presidents & Prime Ministers*, 1994.)

Without economic hope we will not have peace.

(James Wolfensohn, *Presidents & Prime Ministers*, February 1998.)

There are lessons to be learned here, so I shall return to this point.

(Michel Camdessus, *Presidents & Prime Ministers*, October 1998.)

By using genetic information, along with hominid fossils, we shall learn what genetic changes made it possible for the ancestors of modern people to stand upright (about 4 million years ago) and then to speak. As a by-product, we shall be able to trace the migration routes of our human ancestors who emigrated from Africa and came to populate the surface of the earth. A half-century from now, we shall have a rich and authentic history of the human race.

(*Time*, 29 March 1999.)

We will never see King Hussein's like again.

(*The Economist*, 30 April 1999.)

2.21   How do you use acronyms (combinations formed from initial letters)?

Take your pick among the following techniques.

1   **Use familiar acronyms without explanation.**

> In recent years, Professor Hamilton became interested in the origins of HIV, the virus that causes AIDS. (*The Economist*, 24 March 2000.)

2   **Use the full name first, and then use the acronym alone if it appears near the full name.**

> In 1998 a loan team from the Asian Development Bank found the nation in precipitous decline. The ADB recorded the island's "extremely grave" financial plight. (*Time*, 28 February 2000.)

3   **Use the full name first, followed by the acronym in brackets, and then use the acronym.**

> One class of dark objects astronomers are keen on finding are so-called Massive Compact Halo Objects (MACHOs). These are things the size of large planets, but have no parent star to illuminate them. Dr Alcock is one of the leaders of a project that is looking for MACHOs by exploiting a prediction of relativity theory—gravitational lensing. (*The Economist*, 28 January 2000.)

4   **Use the acronym first, followed by the full name in brackets, and then use the acronym.**

> All people in our communities have a stake in the success of APEC (Asia Pacific Economic Cooperation). We particularly welcome the more active participation of women and business in APEC's work this year. (*Presidents & Prime Ministers*, August 1999.)

5   Use both the full name and the acronym in the text without brackets.

> At the heart of the scandal is CRASH, or Community Resources Against Street Hoodlums.
>
> Or: At the heart of the scandal is Community Resources Against Street Hoodlums, or CRASH. (Cathy Booth, *Time*, 28 February 2000.)

6   Leave the acronym unexplained, if you're not sure of the full name but know what it means anyway.

> The veteran KGB officer opened his campaign for the Russian presidency. (Andrew Meier, *Time*, 28 February 2000.)
>
> "KGB" is an initalism for Russian words that mean "State Security Police".

2.22   *None of them is* or *none of them are*—and all the rest

What has worked for solving the problems of usage that we have dealt with so far also works for other problems of usage. First, consult your language intuition; next check what occurs in real texts.

We can apply these methods, for example, to the question of whether it is better to say "None of them is ready" or "None of them are ready." You might intuitively feel that both sound all right. So the next step is to look for instances of *none* and *none of them* in texts. Here's what you will find.

> There was none of the men of the house there within. (Genesis 39:11.)
>
> There is none that I can smile at half so much. (Charles Dickens, *David Copperfield*.)
>
> None has suffered so little from the ravages of time. (Washington Irving, *Alhambra*.)

None was so excited as Anne Shirley. (LM Montgomery, *Anne of Green Gables*.)

There is none like thee among the dancers. (Ezra Pound, "Dance Figure".)

None of them was quick enough to see her go. (Joseph Conrad, *Lord Jim*.)

None of those fields seems to be suffering unduly. (*The Economist*, 2 July 1999.)

None of the rest are so much as spoken of. (Thomas Paine, *The Age of Reason*.)

This is an objection which none of my critics have urged against me. (John Dryden, *All for Love*.)

Barclay's remarks were subdued and abrupt so that none of them were audible to the listeners. (Arthur Conan Doyle, "The Crooked Man".)

So the answer is that both usages exist: *none* and *none of them* go either with singular or with plural verbs.

In general, to improve your grasp of usage, you should keep an eye out for interesting usages in the texts that you read. To illustrate: I picked up an old copy of *Reader's Digest* and, within minutes, I found things I had not previously paid attention to.

"What I mean is, ah, I would like to talk to you about it. Could we go and, ah, have some coffee?" (Charlton Heston.)

As the curtains parted, eager faces crinkled with glee, and "oohs" and "aahs" rang through the auditorium. (Editorial.)

A frazzled mother was dragging her three-year-old son behind her in a department store. The saleswoman behind the counter remarked, "Ahh, a husband-in-training." (Lynne D Aiken.)

A guy will be talking with some other guys about women, and out of the blue he'll say, "Elaine and I, we have, ummm … We have, ahhh … We … We have this thing." And he will sincerely mean it. (Dave Barry.)

(*Reader's Digest*, January 1996.)

Chapter 3

Punctuation and the use of capitals

Punctuation is a difficult matter, and worth a writer's serious attention.

(HW and FG Fowler, *The King's English*.)

3 Punctuation and the use of capitals

3.1 Why is punctuation worth a writer's serious attention?

Good punctuation can save your text from ambiguity. Mostly, though, it helps to pace your writing and make it more readable. Not everybody is good at punctuation. The story goes that the American author Mark Twain sent a manuscript to his publisher with a list of the punctuation marks at the end. "Please," he wrote in an attached note, "distribute these as you will." Mark Twain could get away with it, but only because he was already a famous author. You and I have to get it right.

There are some fifteen punctuation marks, each one with several uses. It is a good idea to become familiar with the more important punctuation marks and with their uses. Here are some ideas to keep in mind as you go through this chapter.

a   If you see a use of any punctuation mark in this chapter that seems to be interesting, look for other examples of it in the books or magazines that you read.

b   Experiment with some of the uses of the punctuation marks in your own writing. This will make your writing not only better but also more interesting to read.

c   In many cases, there are options—choices—in the use of punctuation marks. You can put one in, or leave it out; or you can use one punctuation mark instead of another. Wherever I present options, make your own mind up as to which one to use.

3.2 The three end stops

There are three punctuation marks that you can end sentences with. They are the full stop (.), the exclamation mark (!) and the question mark (?).

1 **Full stops (.)**

a To end statement sentences

I like fruit juice.   *I don't like loafing.*

b But not in the following cases:

INITIALS: *NSW*   *NZ*   *GPO*

CLIPPINGS: *fax* (for *facsimile*)   *Tas* (for *Tasmania*)

CONTRACTIONS: *Mr* (for *Mister*)   *Libs* (for *Liberals*)

ADDRESSES: *Mrs J Whatsit*   *Dr R Whosit*
                   18 Dent St   *40 Broadwood Ave*
                   Lyons ACT 2606   *South Morang Vic 3752*

2 **Exclamation marks (!)**

a To end exclamations and imperatives (commands)

EXCLAMATIONS: *Wow, that's great!*   *What a shame!*

IMPERATIVES: *Stop it!*   *Don't pull!*

Optionally, you can end a longer imperative with a full stop.

IMPERATIVE: *Don't go near the water.*
                   Don't go near the water!

b Optionally, at the end of statement sentences for emphasis

At last they've done the job!   *I didn't enjoy that at all!*
At last they've done the job.   *I didn't enjoy that at all.*

3 **Question marks (?)**

a To end question sentences

What are you doing?   *Won't you tell me?*

b At the end of statement sentences that you intend to be taken as questions

You think I'd believe such a thing?   *You've finished already?*

c You can, of course, express the above as question sentences followed by question marks.

Do you think I'd believe such a thing?   *Have you finished already?*

4 Any of the three end stops (.) (!) (?)

If a question is really a veiled command, you can use any of the three end stops.

A POLITE REQUEST: *Would you mind shutting the door?*

A NEUTRAL REQUEST: *Would you mind shutting the door.*

A SHARP REQUEST: *Would you mind shutting the door!*

3.3 Commas (,)

Commas mark the lightest pauses in sentences. The following are the main uses of commas.

1 Between a series of words (in blue below) except before the word *and*

I have been in Queensland, Tasmania and Victoria.

2 Between a series of phrases except before the word *and*

They were willing to work, eager to help and ready for anything.

3 In the form of address (the "vocative"), to separate the noun or pronoun referring to the person you are addressing

NOUNS: *Pat, what is it that you want?* *What is it, Pat, that you want?*

PRONOUNS: *You, hand me that box!* *Hand me that box, you!*

Notice that the vocative can stand at the beginning, in the middle or at the end of a sentence.

4 To separate noun phrases in apposition—two nouns or phrases that refer to the same person

Bob Hawke, the former prime minister, was born in South Australia.

The noun phrases *Bob Hawke* and *the former prime minister* refer to the same person.

5 Between inverted names

Carnell, Kate *Namatjira, Albert* *Jones, RE*

6 Between repeated words

They were very, very happy.

7 To separate city from state or country names

They live in Perth, Western Australia, and their friends live in Perth, England.

8 To separate an adjunct from the rest of a sentence

An adjunct is a word or a string of words that modify a sentence as a whole—a typical example: "Once upon a time, …" (See chapter 5.10.)

Once upon a time, there was a beautiful swan.

Normally, we eat breakfast at eight o'clock.

Yes, I think I'll go and have a shower.

9 After *for example, that is, namely, ie, eg* and similar terms

I've been to some outback towns in Queensland: for example, Alpha and Winton.

There's something I want to read: namely, Shakespeare's Hamlet.

10 Optionally, to separate off a present participle or a present participle phrase

A present participle is a verb form ending in *–ing*.

PRESENT PARTICIPLE: *Panting, they lifted the rock.*
Panting they lifted the rock.

PRESENT PARTICIPLE PHRASE: *The group, realizing the time, hurried along.*
The group realizing the time hurried along.

11 Optionally, to separate off a past participle or a past participle phrase

A past participle is a verb form typically ending in *–n* (*seen*), *–d* (*noted*) or *–t* (*kept*).

PAST PARTICIPLE: *They proceeded, unseen, towards the bridge.*
They proceeded unseen towards the bridge.

PAST PARTICIPLE PHRASE: *I am playing for a team, unbeaten so far this year.*
I am playing for a team unbeaten so far this year.

12 **Before a question tag**—words tagged onto the end of a statement to turn it into a question

They are here, aren't they?

They aren't late, are they?

13 **To separate sentence segments that share the same preposition**

We travelled in the direction, and to the vicinity, of the bridge.

Both different colour segments share the preposition *of*.

14 **To separate sentence segments that end in different prepositions and that have the same prepositional object**

They flew over, and we sailed under, the bridge.

The segments in blue end in different prepositions (*over* and *under*), but they share the same object (*the bridge*).

15 **Optionally, to separate something that you say as an aside**

They are, to the best of my knowledge, perfectly reliable.

They are—to the best of my knowledge—perfectly reliable.

They are (to the best of my knowledge) perfectly reliable.

16 **To separate a transition word**—a word such as *however, therefore, nevertheless*

Note that a transition word can stand at the beginning, in the middle or at the end of a sentence.

We wrote to them. However, they haven't answered.

We wrote to them; they, however, haven't answered.

We wrote to them. They haven't answered, however.

17 **To avoid ambiguity**—a possible misreading of a sentence

Jack said Jill was very helpful.   [Jack said it of Jill.]

Jack, said Jill, was very helpful.   [Jill said it of Jack.]

18 Between two clauses (sentence parts) connected with a conjunction (bold)

    a   If each clause has a stated subject, the comma is optional.

        She knocked on the door, **but** *nobody answered.*
        She knocked on the door **but** *nobody answered.*

        The first clause has *She* as a subject; the second, *nobody*.

    b   If the second clause does not have a stated subject, omit the comma.

        They arrived at the party **and** *immediately started dancing.*

        The first clause has *They* as a subject; the second clause has no stated subject.

19 For relative clauses (See chapter 2.16b.)

    a   To separate non-defining clauses

        I phoned my mother, who was on an overseas vacation.

    b   But not to separate defining relative clauses

        She is a mother who often goes on overseas vacations.

20 To separate an ordinary one-sentence quotation

    Kim said, "I'm glad it's all over with."
    "I'm glad," Kim said, "it's all over with."
    "I'm glad it's all over with," Kim said.

3.4 Semicolons (;)

Semicolons give a greater separation between clauses than do commas. Often, as you will see below, you can choose between using semicolons and end stops.

1 Optionally, to separate two or more similar clauses that are not joined by a conjunction

    TWO STATEMENTS: *We waited until it was dark; still nobody showed up.*
                                 We waited until it was dark. Still nobody showed up.

TWO QUESTIONS:	*Will you think about what you have done; will you make it good?*
	Will you think about what you have done? Will you make it good?
THREE EXCLAMATIONS:	*What cheek; what daring; what impudence!*
	What cheek! What daring! What impudence!

2 **Optionally, to separate clauses, one of which has a transition word**—that is, a word such as *however, therefore, nevertheless*.

They were late; however, they dawdled.

They were late. However, they dawdled.

3 **To separate sentence parts that contain internal commas**

Some movies I have seen are Paris, Texas; Hello, Dolly; *and* The Good, the Bad and the Ugly.

3.5 Colons (:) and dashes (—)

Horizontal strokes come in three different lengths, each with a different name:

hyphen (-)		(On a PC: the hyphen or the minus sign.)
en dash (–):	as wide as the letter *n*	(On a PC: "Ctrl" and the minus sign.)
em dash (—):	as wide as the letter *m*.	(On a PC: "Ctrl", "Alt" and the minus sign.)

The em dash is also simply called a "dash", and it is this that we are looking at in this section. For the hyphen and the en dash, see section 3.11.

For most purposes the colon and the dash (em dash) are interchangeable. The difference between them is one of tone. The colon is more sober; the dash is more dramatic. Colons and dashes have the following uses.

1 **Between a promise of information and its delivery**

I can guess what has happened: you've passed the test.
I can guess what has happened—you've passed the test.

2 **Between one statement and another that explains it**

They didn't join us in the meal: they'd already eaten.
They didn't join us in the meal—they'd already eaten.

3 **With quotations**

a Before a significant one-sentence quotation

Disraeli said: "Almost everything that is great has been done by youth."
Disraeli said—"Almost everything that is great has been done by youth."

b Before an unintroduced quotation—a quotation without an introductory *She said* or *He remarked*

They had come to the end of the journey: "Here we are at last."
They had come to the end of the journey—"Here we are at last."

c Before a quotation made up of more than one sentence

She said: "It's a lovely day. Let's go for a stroll."
She said—"It's a lovely day. Let's go for a stroll."

4 **Between a statement followed by a question in the same sentence**

I'm dying to ask you this: where have you been?
I'm dying to ask you this—where have you been?

5 **Between a title and a subtitle**

"Education and development: a report for the twenty-first century."
"Education and development—a report for the twenty-first century."

6 **Before bringing together the parts of a subject**

Joan, Gavin, Bowen and Nancy: all these will report to the office.
Joan, Gavin, Bowen and Nancy—all these will report to the office.

7 In a play or a dialogue, to separate the speaker from the speech

FATHER: I think it's time we discussed the facts of life.
CHILD: Sure. What do you want to know?

FATHER—I think it's time we discussed the facts of life.
CHILD—Sure. What do you want to know?

8 Optionally, to show interrupted or hesitant speech

I would like to ask you whether—
Sorry, I haven't time for you now.

I would like to ask you whether ...
Sorry, I haven't time for you now.

Well—er—you see—um—I don't know the answer.
Well ... er ... you see ... um ... I don't know the answer.

9 Optionally, to set off an aside

They are—to the best of my knowledge—perfectly reliable.
They are (to the best of my knowledge) perfectly reliable.
They are, to the best of my knowledge, perfectly reliable.

10 Before a list

We need to take along with us some:
  a.   knives
  b.   forks
  c.   spoons.

We need to take along with us some—
  a.   knives
  b.   forks
  c.   spoons.

3.6   Round brackets ( )

The main uses of round brackets is to enclose explanations and asides.

1 To enclose an explanatory word or words

In the 2000 Olympic Games (Sydney) Cathy Freeman (Australia) won a gold medal in a track event (the 400m race).

2   To enclose one of a pair of terms that express the same thing in different ways

I owe you twenty dollars ($20).
I owe you $20 (twenty dollars).

3   Optionally, to indicate the possible addition of a letter to a word

You may borrow my book(s) any time.
You may borrow my book/s any time.

4   To enclose a textnote

"I am optimistic about the global economy" (Smith 2000:118).

(For "textnotes", see chapter 6.11.)

5   Optionally, to set off an aside

They are (to the best of my knowledge) perfectly reliable.
They are—to the best of my knowledge—perfectly reliable.
They are, to the best of my knowledge, perfectly reliable.

3.7   Square brackets [ ]

Square brackets show that the writer has edited a quoted text by adding to it or by commenting on it.

1   To capitalize a letter that, in the original text, was in lower case

The US declaration of independence states, "[A]ll men are created equal ..."

The original sentence reads: "We hold these truths to be self-evident, that all men are created equal, that they are endowed by their Creator with certain unalienable rights, that among these are life, liberty and the pursuit of happiness."

2   To add a word or words to a text

The US declaration of independence states, "All men [and presumably women too] are created equal ..."

3 To explain a term in a text

Sir John Falstaff complains: "Men of all sorts take pride to gird [mock] at me."

4 To enclose an editorial *sic*—a Latin word meaning "thus"

You use *sic* when you are quoting something with a mistake in it, to show that you know it's a mistake, but that's the way the quotation runs.

A listener wrote to the radio station, "We don't want any more music by Johann Amadeus [sic] Bach."

The name of the composer is Johann Sebastian Bach.

3.8 Apostrophes (')

The two main uses of apostrophes are to show:

a the omission of one or more letters from a word or words (as in *don't* = *do not*)

b the possessive of nouns (as in *the cat's tail* = *the tail of the cat*).

Here is when to use apostrophes—and when not to—in cases where there are omitted letters.

1 To mark the missing letters in a blend (two words blended into one)

Don't [= do not] *tell me we're* [= we are] *late.*

2 To mark the missing letter in an elision (a word with a letter missing at the end)

He was always comin' [= coming] *and goin'* [= going] *like a will-o'* [= of]*-the-wisp.*

3 To mark the letters missing in the middle of some (mainly poetic) words

O'er [= over] *the hills they went at six o'clock* [= of the clock] *in the e'en* [= evening].

4   Nowadays, omit the apostrophes from other abbreviated words.

pram [= perambulator]   *flu* [= influenza]

phone [= telephone]   *bus* [= omnibus].

5   Distinguish between *it's* and *its*.

BLEND: *It's* [= it is] *a lovely day.*

BLEND: *It's* [= it has] *been a lovely day.*

POSSESSIVE: *The dog chased its tail* [= the tail belonging to it].

6   Distinguish between *one's* and *ones*.

POSSESSIVE: *One should do one's duty.*   [= The duty one has]

PLURAL: *You can have two red ones.*   [= Plural of *one*]

7   Distinguish between *others*, *other's* and *others'*.

ORDINARY PLURAL: *He chose some magazines; she chose others.*

SINGULAR POSSESSIVE: *They like each other's friends.*

PLURAL POSSESSIVE: *I care about others' troubles.*

8   Don't use apostrophes with ordinary plurals such as the following.

WORDS: *The Greens played against the Blues.*

NUMBERS: *There are two 9s in "the 1990s".*

LETTERS: *You spell "difficult" with two fs.*

ACRONYMS: *MPs like to be treated as VIPs.*

9   Here is the rule for the use of apostrophes with possessive nouns.

Put the apostrophe immediately after the non-possessive form of
the noun, regardless of whether that puts it before or after the
letter −*s*. One way to determine where to put the apostrophe is to
turn the phrase round (as in the left-hand column below) to see
what the non-possessive noun looks like:

NON-POSSESSIVE NOUN (in blue)	POSSESSIVE NOUN (same word in blue)
the head of the girl	the girl's head
the heads of the boys	the boys' heads
the head of the baby	the baby's head
the heads of the babies	the babies' heads
the head of the child	the child's head
the heads of the children	the children's heads
the head of the man	the man's head
the heads of the women	the women's heads
the head of the sheep	the sheep's head
the heads of the sheep	the sheep's heads

Another way of correctly placing the apostrophe is to count the number of letters in the non-possessive word; then to count the same number of letters in the possessive word and insert the apostrophe.

10 **Apostrophes with possessive proper nouns**—the names of people and places.

a If the name doesn't end with a sibilant (see item 10b below), use the apostrophe as shown in item 9 above.

This is Kim's book and that is Robin's book.

b If the name ends in a sibilant, things get complicated. But first: what is a sibilant?

A sibilant is a hissing sound like "ss" (unvoiced) or a buzzing sound like "zz" (voiced).

i If the name ending in a sibilant consists of one syllable, always add the possessive "s" after the apostrophe.

Dr Moss's friends
St James's Park.

ii If the name consists of more than one syllable and ends in consecutive sibilants, always omit the possessive "s" after the apostrophe.

Jesus' disciples
Moses' laws.

iii If the name is multisyllabic and ends in a sibilant, the addition or omission of the possessive "s" after the apostrophe depends on whether the sibilant is voiced (buzzing) or unvoiced (hissing).

- If it's voiced, omit the possessive "s" after the apostrophe.

  Evans' friend
  Boaz' friend.

- If it's unvoiced, add the possessive "s" after the apostrophe.

  Horace's verse
  Mavis's friend.

The reason for the above rule is that the possessive "s" is voiced. It is hard to pronounce two voiced sibilants in a row, therefore the possessive "s" is omitted after a voiced sibilant, but not omitted after an unvoiced sibilant.

3.9 Ellipses (...) or (. . .)

The main use of ellipses (or, in the singular, an ellipsis) is to show that a word or words are missing from a cited text. There are two ways of writing an ellipsis: spaced (. . .) or unspaced (...). As long as you use either consistently it doesn't matter which you opt for. In the example sentences below I opt for unspaced ones, but spaced ones are just as good.

We now look at the following sentence from which we omit various parts: "In the first four example sentences below, I leave some bits out of this sentence."

1   To indicate that a word or words are left out of a quoted text

a   At the beginning of a quoted text:

  "... I leave some bits out of this sentence."

b   In the middle of a quoted text:

  "In the ... sentences below, I leave some bits out of this sentence."

c At the end of a quoted text:

"In the first four example sentences below, I leave some bits out ... "
"In the first four example sentences below, I leave some bits out.... "

In the last pair of example sentences, the fourth dot—a full stop—is optional.

2 Optionally, to indicate interrupted or hesitant speech

I would like to ask you whether ...
Sorry, I haven't time for you now.

I would like to ask you whether—
Sorry, I haven't time for you now.

Well ... er ... you see ... um ... I don't know the answer.
Well—er—you see—um—I don't know the answer.

3 To hint at incomplete information

Here everything is all right ... And how are things with you?

3.10 Slashes (/)

Slashes separate the elements that come on either side of them.

1 To indicate alternative words

You will need a hammer and/or a drill.

2 Optionally, to indicate the possible addition of a letter to a word

You may borrow any book/s of mine.
You may borrow any book(s) of mine.

3 Optionally, to separate the letters of some initials

They travelled at 80 km/h.
They travelled at 80 kmh.

4 To separate the letters of some abbreviations

c/o (for "care of" or "carried over")   *a/c* (for "account")

5 To separate a unit (or flat) number from a street number in an address

They live at 4/20 Kookaburra Street, Launceston.

6 To show the line breaks in verse that is written out in prose form

The road to wisdom / Is easy to express. / You err and err and err again, / But less and less and less.
(Piet Hein.)

3.11 Hyphens (-) and en dashes (–)

A hyphen is a short stroke (without a space on either side) that joins words or parts of words. In many cases, the use or the omission of the hyphen is not so much rule-bound as it is dependent on usage. If you are not sure whether to use a hyphen for any particular word, look it up in a modern dictionary.

The en dash is a slightly longer stroke than a hyphen. On a PC, you can get an en dash by keying Ctrl and the minus sign. It is all right to use a hyphen instead of an en dash. Following are the uses (and some non-uses) of the hyphen.

1 Hyphenate some prefixes to a following word.

non-Jewish   *pro-Australian*   *re-read*

2 Nowadays most prefixes are amalgamated with the following words.

cooperate   *supermarket*   *nonsense*

3 Adjectives that consist of several words

a Hyphenate them if they stand before the nouns (bold) that they modify.

Fred Williams is a twentieth-century **artist**.

b Don't hyphenate the same words if they stand after the noun (bold).

Fred Williams is an **artist** *who lived in the twentieth century.*

c But ignore the above two rules for some routinely hyphenated or amalgamated words.

It's an *old-fashioned* **dress**.
The **dress** is *old-fashioned*.

They gave it a *thoroughgoing* **inspection**.
The **inspection** was *thoroughgoing*.

4 Many compound words that used to be hyphenated are nowadays (not "now-a-days") often amalgamated.

printout   nightclub   folklore   classroom   spreadsheet   overworked

5 Hyphenate the parts of a word if you want to split the word between two lines.

They did it un-
thinkingly.

6 Hyphenate the tens and the units in numbers written as words.

Forty-five thousand, two hundred and *twenty-seven*.

7 Use a hyphen to join a letter to a word.

T-junction   U-turn   L-shaped   X-ray (or x-ray)

8 A hyphen that doesn't join up to another word is all right—as long as its partner does join up.

I met my brother- *and my* sister-in-law.
[= I met my brother-in-law and my sister-in-law.]

Following are the uses of the en dash—with the hyphen as an alternative.

9 Use the en dash (or hyphen) to indicate a sports score or a number range.

They won 5–3 in the 2001–02 season.
They won 5-3 in the 2001-02 season.

10 Use the en dash (or hyphen) to bind two like words or terms together.

They used the east–west *route on their* Melbourne–Adelaide *trip.*
They used the east-west *route on their* Melbourne-Adelaide *trip.*

3.12 *Italics* or <u>underlining</u>

These are alternative, but equally good, ways of highlighting words in a text. Italics are easy to do on a word processor; underlining, if you are writing by hand. The following are the uses of italics or underlining.

1   To cite the titles of—

    a   literary, artistic and similar works:

        Voss   *Hamlet*   *Mona Lisa*   the *Choral Symphony*
        <u>Voss</u>   <u>Hamlet</u>   <u>Mona Lisa</u>   the <u>Choral Symphony</u>

    b   but not the titles of sacred works such as:

        the Bible   the Koran

2   To cite the names of newspapers, journals or comics

    The Age   *The Bulletin*   *Batman*
    <u>The Age</u>   <u>The Bulletin</u>   <u>Batman</u>

3   To cite the titles of radio and TV shows and movies

    The Saturday Night Show   *Titanic*
    <u>The Saturday Night Show</u>   <u>Titanic</u>

4   To cite the names of particular vehicles

    HMAS Otway   *Air Force One*   *Voyager*
    <u>HMAS Otway</u>   <u>Air Force One</u>   <u>Voyager</u>

5   For emphasis

    I just *don't* believe it: they've eaten *all* the food.
    I just <u>don't</u> believe it: they've eaten <u>all</u> the food.

6   Optionally, to highlight words used as words rather than for their meaning

    I know how to spell *garlic,* and I like garlic in my food too.
    I know how to spell <u>garlic</u>, and I like garlic in my food too.
    I know how to spell "garlic", and I like garlic in my food too.
    I know how to spell 'garlic', and I like garlic in my food too.

7   For foreign words and expressions —

a   if they are still thought of as foreign:

joie de vivre   [French for "the joy of life"]
<u>joie de vivre</u>

b   but not if they have become naturalized into English:

kindergarten   [German for "children's garden"]
QED   [The initials for the Latin words that mean
                            "which was to be demonstrated"]

3.13   Quotation marks (' ') or (" ")

The main use of quotation marks is to enclose quotations from speech
or from writing. You can opt either for single (' ') or for double
quotation marks (" "), as long as you use one or the other consistently.

1   To enclose quotations

My friend rang me and said, "I'll see you next week."
My friend rang me and said, 'I'll see you next week.'

2   To enclose a quotation within a quotation, use one set of quotation marks
on the outside; a different set on the inside.

She said, "He asked me, 'What's the time?'"
She said, 'He asked me, "What's the time?"'

For all the examples from here on, I use double quotation marks as my
primary ones. I omit examples with single quotation marks, simply in
order to save repeating every example.

3   To cite the title of an essay, an article or a chapter

Over the weekend I wrote an essay: "What the student council does".
There was an article called "Budget surprises" in The Bulletin.
I read the chapter "How to paint with ink" in Art Techniques.

4   To indicate the idea of "so called"

When I really needed them, all of my "friends" disappeared.

5 **How to punctuate short quotations**

a With an introductory clause (such as *She said*, *He told me*, *They wrote*), before an ordinary one-sentence quotation, use a comma.

   She said, "I hope the weather clears up."

b With an introductory clause, before a significant one-sentence quotation, use a colon or a dash.

   Caesar said: "I came, I saw, I conquered."
   Caesar said—"I came, I saw, I conquered."

c Without an introductory clause, use a colon or a dash.

   They hadn't given up hope: "We'll find a way."
   They hadn't given up hope—"We'll find a way."

d Before a multi-sentence quotation, use a colon or a dash.

   She said: "It's no use waiting. Let's pack it in."
   She said—"It's no use waiting. Let's pack it in."

6 **The punctuation mark associated with the quoted text comes inside the closing quotation mark.**

This holds true for all cases where the quotation is a complete sentence.

   She said, "It's a fine day." I said, "Is it really?"
Not: *She said, "It's a fine day". I said, "Is it really"?*

7 **The punctuation mark goes outside the closing quotation mark in two cases—**

a if the quotation is a fragmentary one:

   They wrote that I was a "really fine person".

   (In US—but not in British or Australian—publications you will see fragmentary quotations with the punctuation marks inside the closing quotation marks as well.)

b if the introductory clause is a question, and the quotation is a statement:

   Did you hear him say, "Punctuation is fun"?

8 Omit quotation marks from short quotations if you don't really need them.

When they asked me out I said yes, and at the end of the day I said thanks.

9 Use only one end stop after a quotation.

She asked, "Is it time to go?"
Not: *She asked, "Is it time to go?".*

10 How to punctuate a multi-paragraph quotation

a Use opening quotation marks at the beginning of each paragraph; closing quotation marks only at the end of the last paragraph.

> I read a short piece about some early inventions. "The ancient Sumerians, in what is now Iraq, invented writing at least 4000 years ago. They wrote on clay tablets, which they then baked hard.
>
> "The ancient Egyptians, at about the same time, had their own system of writing. We know from wall paintings of that period, that they also played flutes and harps."
>
> (Author's text.)

b Alternatively, omit the quotation marks and set the quotation off from the rest of the text by writing it separately, perhaps in a smaller font or indented from the rest of the text, or both.

> I read a short piece about some early inventions.
>
> > The ancient Sumerians, in what is now Iraq, invented writing at least 4000 years ago. They wrote on clay tablets, which they then baked hard.
> >
> > The ancient Egyptians, at about the same time, had their own system of writing. We know from wall paintings of that period, that they also played flutes and harps.

3.14 CAPITAL (or UPPER-CASE) LETTERS and small (or lower-case) letters

Following are uses of capital letters:

1 **At the beginning of a sentence—after a full stop, a question mark or an exclamation mark**

   Here's a question. Do you know what day this is? It's the end of term. What a relief! Now we can relax.

2 **For the titles of books, movies, music titles and other art works: start all major words with capital letters; minor words, with lower case letters.**

   The minor words are articles (*a, an, the*), conjunctions (*and, but, or* …), prepositions (*in, on, with* …). At the beginning of the titles, these words also start with capital letters.

   One Flew over the Cuckoo's Nest (Book and movie)

   A Tale of Two Cities (Book)

   The Very Best of the Rolling Stones (Music album)

   Wreck of a Transport Ship (Painting)

3 **For headings, headlines and chapter titles**

   a Use minimal capital letters:

   Sock-knitting contest ends in tie (A newspaper headline)
   "Painting with watercolours and acrylic" in How to Draw and Paint (A chapter in a book)

   b also all right for a heading is the use of all-capitals:

   HELP STAMP OUT ATHLETE'S FOOT

   c but old-fashioned is maximal capitals:

   Lack of Concrete Holds Up Bridge

4 **At the start of a quotation**

   a Use a capital letter if the quotation is a full sentence:

   Malcolm Fraser said, "Life wasn't meant to be easy."

b but use a lower-case letter if the quotation is not a full sentence.

What Malcolm Fraser said about life was that it "wasn't meant to be easy".

Notice also the position of the full stops in the last two quotations above.

5 **For initials, use whatever the convention is.**

a All capitals

GPO (General Post Office)   *USA (United States of America)*

b All lower-case letters

radar (radio detection and ranging)   *pm (Latin post meridiem for "afternoon")*

c Mixed capital and lower-case letters

DSc (Doctor of Science)   *Qantas (Queensland and Northern Territory Aerial Services)*

6 **For the titles of official organizations and title-bearers in a prose text**

In the 21st century, these are no longer automatically capitalized. The current spelling convention for these words in a prose text is as follows.

a The words start with capital letters, if and only if, you use the full formal title:

the Department of Defence   *the Minister for Defence*

b The words start with lower-case letters if you use a short, informal title:

the department   *the minister*

In accordance with the above rule, you should use initial lower-case letters for the following titles, even if you precede them with the word *the*.

act (legislative)	coalition government	minister
ambassador	commission	opposition
authority	constitution	parliamentarian
bar (judicial)	corporation	parliamentary
bench (judicial)	court (judicial)	presidential
bill	department	press
board	deputy leader	referendum
branch	director	right wing
budget	embassy	royal
bureau	establishment	royal family
cabinet	federal	secretary (departmental)
cabinet submission	federal government	section (legislative)
centrist	federation	shire
chair	government	shire council
chairman	head of government	state
chairperson	left wing	state government
chairwoman	legislation	state minister
clause (legislative)	legislature	tax office
coalition	local council	university

c There are some exceptions to rule 6b above. The following words conventionally start with capital letters even though they are short and informal.

Aboriginal (Australian)	Liberals
Attorney-General	Nationals
Commonwealth	North (sociopolitical)
Crown	Parliament House
Democrats	Queen
East (political)	Representatives (House of)
Governor-General	Senate
Greens	South (sociopolitical)
High Court	Supreme Court
Independents (political)	West (political)
Labour	

d For the following words, some publications use initial capital letters; others, initial lower-case letters. You can use whichever option you like, as long as you use it consistently.

Governor / governor	Prime Minister / prime minister
House / house (legislative)	Speaker / speaker (of a legislature)
Parliament / parliament	Treasurer / treasurer
Premier / premier	Treasury / treasury
President / president	Whip / whip (of a legislature)

Here are textual examples from *The House of Representatives Weekly Hansard*.

Examples of lower casing as used in *Hansard*

In opposition he has had shadow portfolios in immigration, foreign affairs and science.

This minister has been in the parliament for only two days.

She has given her evidence to the royal commission on WA Inc.

We owe him a debt of gratitude for his corporate role in the government and as a cabinet minister.

He attacks the federal government over environment policies, most of which are governed by state governments.

Examples of capitals as used in *Hansard*

Department of Social Security clients are not given these particulars.

The honourable member for Bonython has mentioned the Child Support Agency.

I thank all the people who work in Parliament House.

This is a matter that is relevant to the Department of Foreign Affairs and Trade.

I raise two matters of privilege concerning the work of the House of Representatives Standing Committee on Environment, Recreation and the Arts.

You will find a similar use of capitals and lower-case letters in all modern publications.

Examples from *The Bulletin*

The budget rewarded pensioners and retirees.

The state and federal governments have encouraged the development of an education marketplace.

The Reserve Bank estimates that there are more than one million small businesses.

The NSW Labour Council set out deliberately to prevent Labour MPs from attending parliament.

If we haven't got a Labour majority we hand parliament over to the Coalition.

The government had estimated that some 2.1 million businesses would sign up for the new Australian Business Numbers.

> Examples from *The Economist*
>
> He reshuffled his government, tossing aside ministers and departments.
>
> This has implications for Labour's second term.
>
> Officials at the Ministry of Agriculture learnt their department was to be merged with environment.
>
> The only job on offer was the post of leader of the House of Commons.
>
> The European Commission's conditions were tough: the commission demanded disposal of all avionics businesses.

e For short, informal titles, use capital letters in the following cases.

- In a salutation: *Dear Librarian*   *Dear Minister*
  (But use lower case in a text: *I spoke to the librarian and wrote a letter to the minister.*)

- If the title is attached
  to a name: *Professor Brown*   *Sergeant Green*
  (But use lower case in a text: *I wrote to the professor about the sergeant.*)

- As a form of address: *How are you, Mum? Come here, Dad.*
  (But use lower case if it is not a form of address: *I get on well with my mum and dad.*)

7 In an email, writing "all-caps" is equivalent to raising your voice.

> Dear Lee
>
> I wish you A HAPPY BIRTHDAY! Hope my present reached you all right.
>
> See you soon.
>
> Tam

8 Another fifteen uses of capital letters

These uses are well known and present few problems.

a People's names: *Kitty, Bernard, Joe*

b Most words derived
from people's names: *an Elizabethan play*
(But not others: *a machiavellian plot*)

c	Place names:	*Australia, Britain, Japan*
d	Most words derived from place names:	*Australian, British, Singaporean*
	(But not others:	*venetian blinds, a china plate*)
e	The names of national and ethnic groups:	*Aboriginal, Maltese, Scots*
f	The names of most cosmic objects:	*the Milky Way, Jupiter, Alpha Centauri*
	(But not others that are in everyday use:	*the sun, the moon, the universe*)
g	The names of gods:	*God, Christ, Allah*
h	The names of religions:	*Christianity, Islam, Buddhism*
i	Words derived from the names of religions:	*Christian, Muslim, Buddhist*
j	The names of festivals and holidays:	*New Year, Ramadan, Melbourne Cup Day*
k	The names of days and months:	*Sunday, Monday, January, February*
	(But not of seasons:	*spring, summer, autumn, winter*)
l	Proprietary and company names:	*Telstra, Optus*
m	The pronoun *I* and the interjection *O*:	*Hear what I have to say, O you people.*
	(But not the interjection *oh*:	*Where, oh where, have they gone?*)
n	Personifications used as a form of address:	*Come heal me, Mother Nature.*
o	Normally, the first letter of each line of a poem:	

I'll write because I'll give
You critics means to live;
For should I not supply
The cause, the effect would die.

(Robert Herrick.)

Words, words, words

**Polonius: What do you
read, my lord?
Hamlet: Words,
words, words.**

(William Shakespeare.)

4.1 A list of the most often misspelt words

Following are the correct spellings of the words, UK and Australian style.

absence	camouflage	deceive
abundance	cantaloupe	defendant
accessible	cemetery	deferred
accidentally	chagrined	definite
acclaim	challenge	dependent
accommodate	changing	descend
accomplish	characteristic	description
accordion	chief	desirable
accumulate	cigarette	despair
achievement	climbed	desperate
acquaintance	collectible	develop
across	colonel	development
address	colossal	diarrhoea
advertisement	column	difference
aggravate	coming	dilemma
alleged	commitment	dining
annual	committee	disappearance
apparent	comparative	disappoint
appearance	competent	disastrous
argument	completely	discipline
atheist	concede	disease
athletics	conceive	dispensable
attendance	condemn	dissatisfied
auxiliary	condescend	dominant
balloon	conscientious	drunkenness
barbecue	consciousness	easily
barbiturate	consistent	ecstasy
bargain	continuous	efficiency
basically	controlled	eighth
beggar	convenient	either
beginning	coolly	eligible
believe	corollary	enemy
biscuit	correlate	entirely
bouillon	correspondence	equipped
boundary	counsellor	equivalent
Britain	courteous	escape
business	courtesy	especially
calendar	criticize (or: criticise)	exaggerate

exceed	hoarse	loneliness	omitted
excellence	hoping	losing	opinion
excellent	humorous	lovely	opponent
exhaust	hypocrisy	luxury	opportunity
existence	hypocrite	magazine	oppression
expense	ideally	maintain	optimism
experience	idiosyncrasy	maintenance	ordinarily
experiment	ignorance	manageable	origin
explanation	imaginary	manoeuvre	outrageous
extremely	immediately	marriage	overrun
exuberance	implement	mathematics	panicky
fallacious	incidentally	medicine	parallel
fallacy	incredible	millennium	parliament
familiar	independence	millionaire	particularly
fascinate	independent	miniature	pavilion
February	indicted	minutes	peaceable
fictitious	indispensable	mischievous	peculiar
finally	inevitable	missile	penetrate
financially	influential	misspelt	perceive
forcibly	information	mortgage	performance
foreign	inoculate	mosquito	permanent
forfeit	insurance	mosquitoes	permissible
formerly	intelligence	murmur	permitted
forty	intercede	muscle	perseverance
fourth	interference	mysterious	physical
fulfil	interpret	narrative	physician
fundamentally	interrupt	naturally	picnicking
gauge	introduce	necessary	piece
generally	irresistible	necessity	pilgrimage
genius	island	neighbour	pitiful
government	jealousy	neutron	planning
governor	jewellery	ninety	pleasant
grievous	judicial	ninth	portray
guarantee	knowledge	noticeable	possess
guerrilla	laboratory	nowadays	possessive
guidance	legitimate	nuisance	potato
haemorrhage	leisure	obedience	potatoes
handkerchief	length	obstacle	practically
happily	lenient	occasion	prairie
harass	licence (noun)	occasionally	preference
height	license (verb)	occurred	preferred
heinous	lieutenant	occurrence	prejudice
heroes	lightning	official	preparation
hesitancy	likelihood	omission	prescription
hindrance	likely	omit	prevalent

primitive	representative	specifically	thorough
privilege	resemblance	specimen	though
probably	reservoir	sponsor	through
procedure	resistance	spontaneous	till
proceed	restaurant	statistics	tomorrow
professor	rheumatism	stopped	tournament
prominent	rhythm	strategy	tourniquet
pronounce	rhythmical	strength	tragedy
pronunciation	roommate	strenuous	transferred
propaganda	sacrifice	stubbornness	truly
psychology	sacrilegious	subordinate	twelfth
publicly	safety	subtle	tyranny
pursue	salary	succeed	unanimous
quandary	satellite	success	undoubtedly
quarantine	scenery	succession	unnecessary
questionnaire	sceptic	sufficient	until
quizzes	sceptical	supersede	usage
realistically	schedule	suppress	usually
realize (or: realise)	secede	surprise	vacuum
really	secretary	surround	valuable
recede	seize	susceptible	vengeance
receipt	separate	suspicious	vigilant
receive	sergeant	syllable	village
recognize (or: recognise)	several	symmetrical	villain
recommend	shining	synonymous	violence
reference	similar	tangible	visible
referred	simile	technical	warrant
relevant	simply	technique	Wednesday
relieving	sincerely	temperature	weird
religious	skiing	tendency	wholly
remembrance	soliloquy	themselves	yacht
reminiscence	sophomore	theories	yield
repetition	souvenir	therefore	zoology

(Reproduced, with permission, from Professor Paul Brians
<http://www.wsu.edu/~brians/errors.html>)

4.2 Words that are often confused

Have you ever wondered whether to use "affect" or "effect" in a sentence;
whether to use "its" or "it's"? The quoted words are called *confusables*, and
this section deals with the following 140 sets of confusables.

accede, exceed
accept, except, expect
access, excess
adapt, adopt
admission, admittance
adverse, averse
advice, advise
affect, effect
affection, affectation
afflict, inflict
aisle, isle
allusion, illusion
already, all ready
altar, alter
alternate, alternative
altogether, all together
ambiguous, ambivalent
among, between
amoral, immoral
angel, angle
ante-, anti-
appraise, apprise
assure, ensure, insure
aural, oral
award, reward
bare, bear
base, basis, bases
bated, baited
bazaar, bizarre
because, since, as
beside, besides
biannual, biennial
breathe, breath
bridal, bridle
can, may
cannon, canon
canvas, canvass
casual, causal
chord, cord
cite, site, sight
coarse, course
collaborate, corroborate
common, mutual
complement, compliment
compose, comprise

comprehensive, comprehensible
confidant, confident
connote, denote
continual, continuous
council, counsel
criterion, criteria
currant, current
dairy, diary
datum, data
debar, disbar
decent, descent, dissent
declaim, disclaim
defuse, diffuse
dependent, dependant
desert, dessert
discover, invent
discreet, discrete
disinterested, uninterested
does, dose
drank, drunk, drunken
economic, economical
eg, ie, etc
elicit, illicit
emigrant, immigrant
enormity, enormousness
envelop, envelope
enviable, envious
equable, equitable
everyday, every day
explicit, implicit
faint, feint
farther, further
faze, phase
ferment, foment
fewer, less
flammable, inflammable
flaunt, flout
forego, forgo
formally, formerly
foul, fowl
gamble, gambol
got, gotten
grisly, grizzly
hanged, hung
hear, here

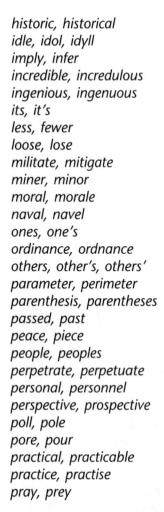

historic, historical	*precede, proceed*
idle, idol, idyll	*prevaricate, procrastinate*
imply, infer	*principal, principle*
incredible, incredulous	*quiet, quite*
ingenious, ingenuous	*raise, rise*
its, it's	*rapt, wrapped*
less, fewer	*real, really*
loose, lose	*run, ran*
militate, mitigate	*stationary, stationery*
miner, minor	*straight, strait*
moral, morale	*substantive, substantial*
naval, navel	*suit, suite*
ones, one's	*than, then*
ordinance, ordnance	*that, which*
others, other's, others'	*there, their, they're*
parameter, perimeter	*thesis, theses*
parenthesis, parentheses	*throne, thrown*
passed, past	*to, too, two*
peace, piece	*vain, vane, vein*
people, peoples	*vicious, viscous*
perpetrate, perpetuate	*wary, weary*
personal, personnel	*waste, waist*
perspective, prospective	*weather, whether*
poll, pole	*wet, whet*
pore, pour	*which, that*
practical, practicable	*who, whom, whose*
practice, practise	*whose, who's*
pray, prey	*your, you're*

In the explanations and examples that follow, only the most common meanings of the words are given.

accede, exceed

- To **accede** is to agree:

  I accede to your request.

- To **exceed** is to go beyond:

  The performance exceeded my expectation.

> The question is whether England shall accede to the independence of America. (Thomas Paine, *The American Crisis*.)
>
> As men labouring to establish an independent constitution of our own, we exceed all others in our hope. (Thomas Paine, *Common Sense*.)

accept, except, expect

- To **accept** is to agree to take an offer:
  I gladly accepted the tickets.

- **Except** means apart from:
  I eat anything except fat meat.

- To **expect** is to regard as likely, to await:
  I expect I will enjoy the play.

> I think that circumstance determined me to accept the invitation.
>
> Nothing was stirring except a brindled grey cat.
>
> As it rains, I hardly expect them.
>
> (Emily Brontë, *Wuthering Heights.*)

access, excess

- An **access** is an approach or entry:
  The key gave me access to the house.

- **Excess** is more than, a surplus:
  She has in excess of a hundred books.

> Dr Forrest's group should detect unauthorized access to a computer network. (*The Economist*, 14 January 2000.)
>
> Corals deal with excess pollutants, and similar irritants by secreting more of the mucous protein that coats their outer tissues. (Douglas H Chadwick, *National Geographic*, January 1999.)

adapt, adopt

- To adapt is to change to suit the conditions:
  Fir trees are adapted to cold climates.

> The only member of our small society, who positively refused to adapt himself to circumstances, was Jip. (Charles Dickens, *David Copperfield.*)

- To **adopt** is—

  a   to take legal charge of a child:
      They adopted baby twins.

b   generally to accept as one's own:

She adopted a new style of swimming.

> Aunt Sally is going to adopt me and civilize me. (Mark Twain, *The Adventures of Huckleberry Finn*.)
>
> The French educational community is returning to the three Rs it has adopted over the past two years. (*Time*, 17 May 1999.)

admission, admittance

- An **admission** is—

a   a confession:

I made an admission of my guilt.

b   an entry requirement:

The admission to the concert was $20.

> Tokyo consumer groups are up in arms over the government's admission. (*Time*, 29 April 1999.)
>
> Enrico Fermi's competition essay for university admission was judged worthy of a doctoral examination. (*Time*, 29 March 1999.)

- **Admittance** is the right of entry:

The ticket gave me admittance to the show.

> Into one house in this neighbourhood they shall never have admittance. (Jane Austen, *Pride and Prejudice*.)

adverse, averse

- **Adverse** is hostile or harmful:

I laboured on under adverse conditions.

- **Averse** is opposed or unwilling:

I am averse to starchy foods.

> Like other defaulters, I like to lay half the blame on ill fortune and adverse circumstances. (Charlotte Brontë, *Jane Eyre*.)
>
> The youth seemed averse to explanation. (Thomas Hardy, *A Pair of Blue Eyes*.)

advice, advise

- **Advice** is a noun:

  You should take good advice.

- **Advise** is a verb:

  I advise you to drive carefully.

> Our advice is, get started as soon as possible. (Marcus Chown,
> *New Scientist*, 8 January 2000.)
>
> The council does little more than advise the cabinet. (*The Economist*,
> 10 March 2000.)

affect, effect—two words with different, though overlapping, meanings as nouns and as verbs: four meanings in all.

a *Af*-fect, as a noun (with the stress on the first syllable), is a term now used only in psychology. It means a feeling or an emotion, especially one that leads to action.

  He has an affect [emotion] *that makes him avoid enclosed spaces.*

  Unless you are a psychologist, you can forget this use of *affect*. As a noun, this word simply does not occur in ordinary speech.

b *Af-fect*, as a verb (with the stress on the second syllable), is to influence or to act on.

  The things we do affect [influence] *other people.*

c *Ef-fect*, as a noun (with the stress on the second syllable), is an influence or a result—a meaning close to that of *affect* as a verb (item b above); hence the confusion.

  Their action had a big effect [influence] *on me.*

d *Ef-fect*, as a verb (with the stress on the second syllable), is to implement or to put into action.

  They effected [implemented] *the plan.*

Some more examples of the use of *affect* and *effect*:

> Their psychic lives are overfull of complexes and <u>affects</u> [emotions].
> NOUN
>
> (*The Weekly Westminster Gazette*, 24 March 1923, cited in *The Oxford English Dictionary*.)
>
> He had been favourably <u>affected</u> [influenced] by my courage.
> VERB
>
> (Robert Louis Stevenson, *Treasure Island*.)
>
> Our merchants complain much about the <u>effects</u> [influences] of high wages.
> NOUN
>
> (Adam Smith, *The Wealth of Nations*.)
>
> If our political ruin is to come, it will be <u>effected</u> [implemented] by ardent
> VERB
>
> reformers.
>
> (George Bernard Shaw, *Man and Superman*.)

affection, affectation

- **Affection** is liking:

  I have an affection for my cousins.

- An **affectation** is phoney behaviour:

  His posh talk is an affectation.

> Frederick the Great, who became king in 1740, craved affection.
> (*The Economist*, 12 April 2000.)
>
> Louis Halle found Rachel Carson quiet, proper and without affectation.
> (Peter Matthiessen, *Time*, 29 March 1999.)

afflict, inflict

- To **afflict** is to make someone suffer:

  Bullies afflict their classmates.

- To **inflict** is to impose:

  They inflicted blows on their enemies.

> Researchers are now looking at plants to learn more about diseases that afflict people. (Trisha Gura, *New Scientist*, 19 February 2000.)
>
> The development of electronic commerce in Europe could come screeching to a complete halt, inflicting a huge cost on the EU's economy. (*The Economist*, 7 May 1999.)

aisle, isle

The two words are pronounced alike but they have different meanings.

- An **aisle** is a passage between rows of seats:
  The bride and groom walked down the aisle.

- **Isle** is short for "island":
  They holidayed on the Isle of Capri.

> We are thinking of restoring the tower and aisle of the church in this parish. (Thomas Hardy, *A Pair of Blue Eyes*.)
>
> My recruits have been all marched off for the depot at the Isle of Wight. (Sir Walter Scott, *Chronicles of the Cannongate*.)

allusion, illusion

- An **allusion** is an indirect reference, a hint:
  The author made an allusion to his suffering.

- An **illusion** is a mistaken idea or a false vision:
  They are under the illusion that they are always right.

> A man of Claggart's accomplishments, who never made allusion to his previous life ashore, opened to the invidious a vague field for unfavourable surmise. (Herman Melville, *Billy Budd*.)
>
> On the whole tour we undergo an optical illusion which often seems to be incredible. (Mark Twain, *A Tramp Abroad*.)

already, all ready

- **Already** is by a certain time:
  It was already getting late.

> There are already a few poor countries that have developed their own broad-based anti-poverty programmes. (*The Economist*, 14 January 2000.)

- **All ready** has two meanings—

  a everybody is ready:

  We are all ready for the exams.

  b completely ready:

  I am all ready for the start of the game.

> Well, if we are all ready, I judge the dinner is. Come, fall to.
>
> I was at the platform and all ready to do the honours.
>
> (Mark Twain, *A Connecticut Yankee in King Arthur's Court.*)

altar, alter

- An **altar** is a table for worship in a church:

  The minister stood before the altar.

- To **alter** is to change:

  They need to alter some of their habits.

> Inside the altar rail stood a strange clergyman. (Thomas Hardy, *A Pair of Blue Eyes.*)
>
> In the 1950s the house, having been substantially altered over the years, was restored and opened as a museum. (*The Economist*, 1 October 1999.)

alternate, alternative

- To **alternate** is to take turns:

  Their relations alternate between love and enmity.

- An **alternative** is another choice:

  You have an alternative to staying—you can leave.

> Oceanic weather patterns may alternate in form and severity. (*National Geographic*, March 1999.)
>
> Ignoring public worries may drive people towards New Age alternatives. (*New Scientist*, 22 April 2000.)

- "Alternately" and "alternatively" are the adverb forms of the above words.

> The lightning came quick and sharp now, and the place was alternately noonday and midnight. (Mark Twain, *A Connecticut Yankee in King Arthur's Court.*)
>
> Biometrics could mean doing away with today's security passes. Alternatively, pocket-sized "smart" cards might soon be able to store all of a person's medical or credit history. (*The Economist*, 7 May 1999.)

altogether, all together

- **Altogether** is entirely, completely:
  It was an altogether marvellous concert.

- **All together** is everybody in unison:
  The class went to a picnic all together.

> Multinational companies could avoid tax on their profits altogether by setting up in business where taxes were lowest. (*The Economist*, 14 February 2000.)
>
> The birds sang all together. (Robert Browning, *Dramatic Lyrics.*)

ambiguous, ambivalent

- **Ambiguous** is having an obscure or a double meaning:
  Their answer was ambiguous.

- **Ambivalent** is having two feelings at the same time:
  I am ambivalent about my relations with them.

> Cubism was hard to read, wilfully ambiguous. (*Time*, 14 June 2000.)
>
> Charlie Chaplin's Tramp is always ambivalent and many-sided. (*Time*, 14 June 1999.)

among, between

- **Among** is for more than two:
  There are exotic places among the restaurants of Sydney.

- **Between** is for two:
  Between you and me, we can finish the job.

> Among the youths, you find an urge for self-expression. (Todd Carrel, *National Geographic*, March 2000.)
>
> Miller says creationists attract people by creating a false choice between creationism and atheism. (Debora MacKenzie, *New Scientist*, 22 April 2000.)

amoral, immoral

- **Amoral** is without morals:

  For animals, killing is amoral.

- **Immoral** is having bad morals:

  For humans, killing is immoral.

> Machiavelli was the first truly modern amoral thinker. (Michele Orecklin, TIME, 1 January 2000.)
>
> Everything you have said today seems to me excessively immoral. (Oscar Wilde, *A Woman of No Importance*.)

angel, angle

- An **angel** (with a soft *g* pronounced like *j*) is a heavenly creature:

  Nurses are like angels.

- An **angle** (with a hard *g*) is the distance between two meeting lines:

  The stick was bent at a sharp angle.

> Where angels might have sat enthroned, devils lurked. (Charles Dickens, *A Christmas Carol*.)
>
> A vortex produces a stable fireball if the air enters at an angle of 66 degrees. (Philip Cohen, *New Scientist*, 22 May 1999.)

ante-, anti-

- **Ante-** is before (the opposite of *post-*):

  The expectant mum went to the antenatal clinic.

- **Anti-** is against (the opposite of *pro-*):

  They went to an anti-war demonstration.

> The study is the ante-room of his bed-chamber. (Arthur Conan Doyle, "Charles Augustus Mulverton".)
>
> Anti-virus software has long played up its medical overtones, with talk of vaccination and inoculation. (*The Economist*, 14 January 2000.)

appraise, apprise

- To **appraise** is to evaluate:

  The lecturers appraised our essays.

- To **apprise** is to inform:

  They apprised us of the results of the exam.

> I would like to have you appraise some jewellery belonging to my young friend here. (Horatio Alger Jr, *Cast Upon the Waters*.)
>
> Has science fully apprised us of the effects on kids of medication designed for an adult brain? (Howard Chua-Eoan, *TIME*, 31 May 1999.)

assure, ensure, insure

- To **assure** is to try to convince:

  They assured us that the job would be finished on time.

- To **ensure** is to make certain:

  They worked hard to ensure their success.

- To **insure** is to pay for compensation against loss:

  I insured my house against flood and fire.

> Alarcón assured me there was no jockeying to succeed Fidel Castro. (John J Putnam, *National Geographic*, June 1999.)
>
> Trade in rare species should be permitted, but only if it can be monitored to ensure it does not endanger the species' survival. (*The Economist*, 21 April 2000.)
>
> I asked him where the ships he insured mostly traded to at present. (Charles Dickens, *Great Expectations*.)

aural, oral

- **Aural** relates to hearing:

  She has good aural understanding of French, but can't speak it.

- **Oral** relates to speaking:

His oral skills are good, but he is not so good at writing.

> Deafness is the result of destructive aural disease. (A Hamilton, cited in *The Oxford English Dictionary*.)
>
> The *Iliad* is the end result of an inspired oral poetic tradition spanning 500 years. (Caroline Alexander, *National Geographic*, December 1999.)

award, reward

- An **award** is a prize, a medal:

He received the essay award.

- A **reward** is prize money:

They got a $1000 reward for finding the missing painting.

> The Beatles had become such a huge British export that they were given a royal award: the Member of the Order of the British Empire. (Kurt Loder, *TIME*, 14 June 1999.)
>
> The parrot learns to say the name and is given the object as a reward. (Irene Pepperberg, *New Scientist*, 15 January 2000.)

bare, bear

- Bare is naked:

They went into the shower bare.

> His eyes and ears are protected, but the rest of his face and head are bare. (Mark Twain, *A Tramp Abroad*.)

- **Bear** has two meanings—
  - **a** a **bear** (noun) is an animal:

    The bear looked after her cub.

  - **b** to **bear** (verb) is to carry:

    They bear heavy loads.

> Matched with them, the bear is civilized, the wolf is mild. (Lord Byron, *Don Juan*.)
>
> In 1906 Alois Alzheimer, a German neurologist, first found the clumps of fibrous protein that are characteristic of the disease that now bears his name. (*The Economist*, 31 March 2000.)

base, basis, bases

- **Base** (verb) is support; **bases** is the third person, singular form of the same verb:

  I base my claim on my calculation; he bases his claim on his.

- A **base** (noun) is a pedestal; **bases** is the plural form of the same noun:

  The statue stood on a base; the statues stood on bases.

- A **basis** (noun) is a foundation; **bases** is the plural of the same noun:

  The house stands on a solid basis; the houses stand on solid bases.

> He bases this claim on a simple computer model. (Marcus Chown, *New Scientist*, 5 February 2000.)
>
> The whole statistical basis of quality engineering was imported from America in the 1950s. (*The Economist*, 10 March 2000.)
>
> They are reluctant even to speculate except on the basis of decades of data. (*The Economist*, 21 April 2000.)

bated, baited

- **Bated** is reduced, referring to breathing:

  I awaited the result with bated breath.

- **Baited** is having a bait or a lure:

  The hook was baited with a shiny fly.

> They grouped themselves about and mumbled in bated voices. (Mark Twain, *A Tramp Abroad*.)
>
> To entrap these birds in their giddy circlings, with hooks baited with flies, is one of the favourite amusements of the ragged sons of Alhambra. (Washington Irving, *Alhambra*.)

bazaar, bizarre

- A **bazaar** is a market:

  I shopped in an oriental bazaar.

- **Bizarre** is weird:

  The actors wore bizarre costumes.

> The Terence Conran Shop is a design bazaar, with everything from $17
> digital watches to $3,550 violet-coloured lounges. (Frank Gibney Jr and
> Belinda Luscombe, *TIME,* 20 March 2000.)
>
> The behaviour of a bizarre substance called "quark matter" is still only
> dimly understood. (*The Economist,* 25 February 2000.)

because, since, as

- All three words have the same meaning—"for the reason that":
  They went home because / since / as it was getting late.

- **Since** has the additional meaning "from that time":
  I have been waiting here since 8.00 o'clock.

- **As** has the additional meaning "like":
  Nobody does it as you do.

> The amateur footballers of Calais have succeeded mainly because the
> country's professional teams are now rather bad. (*The Economist,*
> 28 April 2000.)

> Since all proteins have the same backbone, Dr Dobson and his
> colleagues think they would all form amyloid under the right
> conditions. (*The Economist,* 31 March 2000.)
>
> Since 1960, Cuba and the United States have neither traded nor had
> diplomatic relations with each other. (*The Economist,* 28 April 2000.)

> As most of this work has been North American, it is not surprising that it
> concluded that American business people are more "ethically sensitive"
> than their counterparts elsewhere. (*The Economist,* 28 April 2000.)
>
> The same factors that encourage biodiversity, such as a pleasant climate
> and ample rainfall, also encourage people to move into those
> landscapes. (John Roach, *National Geographic News,* 27 May 2000.)

beside, besides

- **Beside** is next to:
  The wastepaper basket is beside the desk.

- **Besides** is apart from:
  I'm tired of work; besides, it's getting late.

> Hour after hour he would sit beside her. (Emily Brontë, *Wuthering Heights.*)
>
> The prospect of four thousand a year, besides the remaining half of his mother's fortune, warmed his heart. (Jane Austen, *Sense and Sensibility.*)

biannual, biennial

- **Biannual** is twice a year:

  Rice is a biannual crop.

- **Biennial** is every two years:

  The chess olympics are biennial: every even-numbered year.

> Every half year his lawyer transmitted him his biannual rent. (Ouida, cited in *The Oxford English Dictionary.*)
>
> The liberties of the people can be in no danger from biennial elections. (*The Federalist Papers.*)

breathe, breath

- To **breathe** is a verb:

  I like to breathe fresh air.

- A **breath** is a noun:

  I took a breath of fresh air.

> There are not two worlds; there is one world. We breathe the same air. We degrade the same environment. (Michel Camdessus, *Presidents & Prime Ministers*, October 1998.)
>
> Will women take a breath of oxygen? (James Poniewozik, *TIME*, 31 January 2000.)

bridal, bridle

- **Bridal** relates to a bride:

  The groom admired the bridal gown.

> She was a commoner, and had been sent here on her bridal night by Sir Breuse Sance Pite. (Mark Twain, *A Connecticut Yankee in King Arthur's Court.*)

- **Bridle** has two meanings—

  a the headgear of a horse:
  The rider slipped the bridle from the horse's head.

  b to become angry:
  They bridled at the ridiculous suggestion.

> A man in foreign garments stood outside the window, leading by the bridle an ass laden with wood. (Charles Dickens, *A Christmas Carol.*)
>
> "I hazard my dear reputation," replied Mademoiselle, bridling. (Susanna Haswel Rowson, *Charlotte Temple.*)

can, may

- **Can** means be able to:
  I can hop on one foot.

- **May** has two meanings—

  a have permission to:
  You may borrow my book if you promise to return it.

  b will possibly:
  They may or may not come to the party.

> "How can we [are we able to] sign on to something that subordinates democracy to corporate power?" (Ralph Nader, *Time*, 24 April 2000.)
>
> He may [will possibly] fall in love with one of them. (Jane Austen, *Pride and Prejudice.*)
>
> Ladies and gentlemen, may we [have we permission to] present the design economy? (*Time*, 20 March 2000.)

Informally, *can* is often used in the first sense of *may* ("have permission to")—see chapter 2.5.

> You can [have permission to] do as you please. (Louisa May Alcott, *Little Women.*)

The past tense of *may* is *might*—technically—but the two forms are often used interchangeably to express a possibility or a hypothesis.

> Music **may** soothe the troubled breast. It **might** even be the food of love. But how does it cast its spell? (*The Economist*, 18 February 2000.)

cannon, canon

- A **cannon** is a big gun:

The president got a twenty-one cannon salute.

> The whistling of a cannon ball would have frightened me almost to death. (Thomas Paine, *The American Crisis.*)

- A **canon** has three meanings—

a an official list:

Genesis to Revelation make up the canon of the Bible.

b an accepted idea:

They acted according to the canons of good taste.

c a church official:

The canon prepared for the Easter service.

> Andrew the Apostle added nothing to the Canon of Scripture. (J Jackson, cited in *The Oxford English Dictionary.*)
>
> Virginity is peevish, proud, idle, made of self-love, which is the most inhibited sin in the canon. (William Shakespeare, *All's Well That Ends Well.*)
>
> Sir William was promoted to the archdeaconry, and made canon of Aberdeen. (Thomas Bulfinch, *The Age of Chivalry.*)

canvas, canvass

- A **canvas** is a rough cloth material:

The artist started on a new canvas.

> Dressed in a sacky T-shirt, black canvas shoes, and bright green running shorts, Q has no home and no family. (Todd Carrel, *National Geographic*, March 2000.)

- To **canvass** has two meanings—

a to campaign for support:

The politicians canvassed in their electorates.

b to discuss an idea:

They canvassed the pros and cons of marriage.

> The Indian could not abstain from canvassing his scheme.
> (James Fenimore Cooper, *The Deerslayer.*)
>
> This matter has been much canvassed among naturalists.
> (James Boswell, *The Life of Samuel Johnson.*)

casual, causal

- **Casual** is informal, laid-back:

  They wore casual clothes to the beach party.

- **Causal** is about cause and effect:

  There is a causal explanation for hailstorms.

> The most casual slip of the tongue must have a meaning and can be
> used to unriddle the often incomprehensible manoeuvres we call
> thinking. (Peter Gay, *TIME*, 29 March 1999.)
>
> The origin of the cosmos and the causal principles of its history remain
> unexplained. (Phillip E Johnson, *Darwin on Trial.*)

chord, cord

- A **chord** is a group of musical notes sounded together:

  The guitarist played a chord.

- A **cord** is a piece of string:

  The parcel was held together with a cord.

> John Lennon quickly worked out the chords to the Buddy Holly hit
> *That'll Be the Day.* (Kurt Loder, *TIME*, 14 June 1999.)
>
> All through the storm, my instincts were anchored to the continent of
> North America, as though an invisible cord still tied me to its coasts.
> (Charles Lindbergh, *TIME*, 14 June 1999.)

cite, site, sight

- To **cite** is to quote:

  They like to cite Shakespeare.

- A **site** is a place:

  They camped at the caravan site.

- A **sight** is what you see:

The sunset was a wonderful sight.

> We tend to cite those individuals who divide most conveniently into good and evil. (*TIME*, 14 June 1999.)
>
> It is the best child-care site I've seen. (Amy Dickinson, *TIME*, 27 March 2000.)
>
> When ions and electrons smash into Jupiter's atmosphere they create a wonderful sight. (Ben Crystal, *New Scientist*, 8 January 2000.)

coarse, course

- **Coarse** means rough:

Mum doesn't like us to use coarse language.

> His hands were coarse and stiff from close acquaintance with farming tools. (Kate Chopin, *Athenaise*.)

- **Course** has two main meanings—

a a series:

I took a course in computing.
I took a course of vitamins.

b a way:

The river followed a winding course.

> I could go through a course complete in thirteen weeks, and four courses in a year. (Benjamin Franklin, *Autobiography*.)
>
> The little stream ran into the churchyard and ran out again, after a winding course of a few dozen yards. (Wilkie Collins, *The Woman in White*.)

collaborate, corroborate

- To **collaborate** is to work together:

Jack and Jill collaborated in getting a pail of water.

- To **corroborate** is to confirm:

The witnesses corroborated each other's testimony.

> We are **collaborating** to take advantage of all this data. (*New Scientist,* 5 February 2000.)
>
> PET scanning showed Dr Zeki that regions V3 and V5 of the brain are particularly sensitive to movement, an observation **corroborated** by the fact that people who sustain damage to V5 suffer from so-called motion blindness. (*The Economist,* 9 April 2000.)

common, mutual

- **Common** has two meanings—

  a shared between two people or things:

  You and I have a common friend.

  b ordinary or prevalent:

  Daisies are very common in fields.

  > Humans did not evolve from chimpanzees. They share a **common** ancestor. (John Roach, *National Geographic News,* 24 March 2000.)
  >
  > The female is much smaller than the male. This distinction between the sexes is **common** among gorillas today. (Trish Beaver, *National Geographic News,* 27 April 2000.)

- **Mutual** is to or for each other (usually of feelings):

  They shared a mutual love.

  > Maurice Wilkins, a colleague who was also working on DNA, disliked the precociously feminist Rosalind Franklin, and the feeling was **mutual**. (Robert Wright, *TIME,* 29 March 1999.)

complement, compliment

You use both words as verbs and as nouns.

- To **complement** (verb) is to complete or to suit:

  That lamp complements the room.

- A **complement** (noun) is a group:

  The job was done by a complement of workers.

> A wit among the guard had complemented the crown upon his head by putting a reed in his hand for a sceptre. (Lew Wallace, *Ben Hur.*)
>
> The ship put to sea short of her proper complement of men. (Herman Melville, *Billy Budd.*)

- To **compliment** (verb) is to praise:

  I compliment you on your effort.

- A **compliment** (noun) is an expression of praise:

  Thank you for that compliment.

> Mrs Swancourt had complimented her step-daughter. (Thomas Hardy, *A Pair of Blue Eyes.*)
>
> That is the first compliment I have ever had in my life. (LM Montgomery, *Anne of Green Gables.*)

compose, comprise

- To **compose** has two main meanings—

  a to create a piece of music:

  Beethoven composed nine symphonies.

  b to make up or to constitute:

  Air is composed of hydrogen and oxygen.

> Frederick the Great composed music and wrote passable poetry. (*The Economist*, 21 April 2000.)
>
> DNA is composed of chemical "letters" that like to cross-pair between strands. (*The Economist*, 21 January 2000.)

- To **comprise** is to include or consist of:

  A strike was called, comprising workers in all industries.

> English-speaking philosophers devoted their efforts to showing that, even if everything is physical, mental organization can yet comprise its own level of reality. (*The Economist*, 7 May 1999.)

comprehensive, comprehensible

- **Comprehensive** is complete:

  They enjoyed a comprehensive victory.

- **Comprehensible** is understandable:

  She wrote in a comprehensible style.

  > Richard Weindruch has made the most comprehensive attempt to get
  > at the genes that are altered by extreme dieting. (Nell Boyce,
  > *New Scientist*, 25 March 2000.)
  >
  > One side or the other of his nature was perfectly comprehensible, but
  > both sides together were bewildering. (Jack London, *The Sea Wolf.*)

- "Comprehensively" and "comprehensibly" are the adverb forms of
  the above adjectives:

  > Philosophy is something that cannot be defined comprehensively
  > except to such minds and temperaments as are philosophical.
  > (Jack London, *The Iron Heel.*)
  >
  > He undertakes nothing that he cannot carry out clearly and
  > comprehensibly. (*The Saturday Review*, cited in *The Oxford English
  > Dictionary.*)

confidant, confident

- A **confidant** is someone you can trust with your secrets:

  My best friend is also my confidant.

- To be **confident** is to be sure:

  I am confident that we will succeed.

  > Hubble's astronomical triumphs earned him worldwide scientific
  > honours and made him the confidant of Aldous Huxley and a friend to
  > Charlie Chaplin. (Michael D Lemonick, *TIME*, 29 March 1999.)
  >
  > Leonhardt is confident that his optical black holes could provide a new
  > way of tackling the most crucial questions in physics. (Michael Brooks,
  > *New Scientist*, 18 March 2000.)

connote, denote

Connote and **denote** are two words with similar but subtly different
meanings: connoting is suggestive; denoting is definite.

- To **connote** is to imply, to hint at something:

  His behaviour connotes that he has something to hide.

- To **denote** is to point at, to be a sign of, something:
  The dark clouds denote an imminent storm.

> Punishment always connotes guilt. (John Wesley, cited in *The Oxford English Dictionary.*)
>
> Sara was crying! The unconquerable Sara! It seemed to denote something new—some mood she had never known. (Frances Hodgson Burnett, *A Little Princess.*)

continual, continuous

- **Continual** means for a long time, on and off:
  The group had a continual run of hit songs.

- **Continuous** means for a long time, without a break:
  There were three days of continuous rain.

> There were continual desertions from Granada to the fortified camp at Montefrio. (Washington Irving, *Alhambra.*)
>
> Anandakrishnan detected the continuous rumble of micro-earthquakes. (*New Scientist*, 17 April 1999.)

council, counsel

- A **council** is a body of people:
  The UN Security Council couldn't agree on what action to take.

- **Counsel** is advice:
  My counsel to you is to proceed carefully.

> Krebs's report and another, published last week by the US National Research Council, stress the need to improve the testing of GM foods for allergens and toxins. (*New Scientist*, 15 April 2000.)
>
> Enrico Fermi's counsel went unheeded, and the US–Soviet arms race that ensued put the world at mortal risk. (Richard Rhodes, *TIME*, 29 March 1999.)

criterion, criteria

- **Criterion** is singular:
  There is one criterion for truth: that it agrees with the facts.

- **Criteria** is plural:

  Their action met all the legal criteria.

  > Piaget recognized that five-year-old Julia's beliefs, while not correct by an adult **criterion**, are not incorrect either. (Seymour Papert, TIME, 29 March 1999.)
  >
  > The only strands left were those that matched all the **criteria** for the right answer, and therefore represented correct solutions. (*The Economist*, 21 January 2000.)

currant, current

- A **currant** is a raisin:

  There were currants in the pudding.

- A **current** (noun) is a wave-like motion:

  The current carried them out to sea.

- **Current** (adjective) is of the present time:

  I am reading the current issue of a magazine.

  > There on the shelf was a bottle containing some of her three-year-old homemade **currant** wine. (LM Montgomery, *Anne of Avonlea.*)
  >
  > Since the conductivity of the ionosphere is reduced, the **current** has to find an alternative path. (Ben Crystal, *New Scientist*, 8 January 2000.)
  >
  > Calais beat Bordeaux, the **current** league title-holders, by three goals to one. (*The Economist*, 28 April 2000.)

dairy, diary

- A **dairy** is where cows are kept (or milk products):

  I like dairy foods.

- A **diary** is a book you write your daily doings in:

  I wrote it in my diary.

  > Marilla walked off to the **dairy** with pails. (LM Montgomery, *Anne of Green Gables.*)
  >
  > Mr Bennett drew a little **diary** book from his pocket. (Arthur Conan Doyle, "The Creeping Man".)

datum, data

- **Datum** is singular:

  One contrary datum can invalidate a generalization.

- **Data** is plural:

  These data confirm the hypothesis.

> All will grant me this datum that the said person is a man of an ordinary capacity. (Henry Fielding, cited in *The Oxford English Dictionary.*)
>
> The account was made to look scientific by scientific-sounding terminology and misused data. (Debora MacKenzie, *New Scientist*, 22 April 2000.)

debar, disbar

- To **debar** is to block or to refuse admission:

  He was debarred from entering the contest.

- To **disbar** is to ban a barrister from practice:

  The lawyer was disbarred for malpractice.

> Amazenus, which, swelled by rain, seemed to debar a passage. (Thomas Bulfinch, *The Age of Fable.*)
>
> In the event of a barrister being disbarred, the judges may revise and reverse the decrees of the benchers. (*Daily News*, cited in *The Oxford English Dictionary.*)

decent, descent, dissent

- **Decent** is fine and proper:

  Their behaviour towards us is decent.

- A **descent** is a downward movement:

  The descent from the mountain was laborious.

- **Dissent** is disagreement:

  They expressed their dissent at the meeting.

> "Decent people didn't go to juke joints," she says. (Charles E Cobb Jr, *National Geographic*, April 1999.)
>
> A figure, pausing a moment upon the verge of the giddy descent, plunged headlong into the canal. (Edgar Allan Poe, "Assignation".)
>
> It required a degree of courage, excited as he was becoming, even to risk a mute sign of dissent. (Charlotte Brontë, *Jane Eyre*.)

declaim, disclaim

- To **declaim** is to speak impressively:
  They declaimed against the evils of their time.

- To **disclaim** is to deny:
  They disclaimed responsibility for the mistake.

> It is the humour of many heads to extol the days of their forefathers, and declaim against the wickedness of times present. (George Eliot, *Middlemarch*.)
>
> He is no longer a brother of mine—I disclaim kindred with him. (Richard B Sheridan, *The School for Scandal*.)

defuse, diffuse

- To **defuse** is to remove a fuse, to reduce danger:
  The arbiter defused the risk of conflict.

- To **diffuse** is to spread out:
  The gas diffused throughout the chamber.

> The early release of the crew would defuse this crisis. (*The Economist*, cited in *The Oxford English Dictionary*.)
>
> The "new economy" will diffuse with time around those parts of the world that are willing to accept it. (*The Economist*, 21 April 2000.)

dependent, dependant

- **Dependent** means depending or conditioned on:
  Your success is dependent on your effort.

- A **dependant** is a person who depends on another:
  One worker may support several dependants.

> Their line of politics is formed and not dependent.
>
> England has now become America's dependant.
>
> (Thomas Paine, The American Crisis.)

desert, dessert

- **Desert** has three meanings—

  a   with the stress on the first syllable (DE-sert), a waterless place:

    A desert is sparsely populated.

  b   with the stress on the second syllable (de-SERT), to abandon:

    Please don't desert us now.

  c   with the stress on the second syllable (de-SERT), worth or value:

    They got their deserts.

  > Biosphere 2 is a sealed environment covering 1.2 hectares in the Arizona desert. (*New Scientist*, 25 March 2000.)
  >
  > The street was quiet, deserted, and hung with a thin bluish haze. (Willa Cather, *Alexander's Bridge.*)
  >
  > You less know how to value her desert than she to scant her duty. (William Shakespeare, *King Lear.*)

- **Dessert**, with the stress on the second syllable (des-SERT), is the sweets after a meal:

  They had pudding for dessert.

  > The rest of the dinner passed away; the dessert succeeded, the children came in, and were talked to and admired. (Jane Austen, *Emma.*)

discover, invent

- To **discover** is to find what is already there:

  Columbus, they say, discovered America.

- To **invent** is to create something new:

  Guglielmo Marconi invented the radio in 1901.

> Do you think biologists will ever **discover** organisms on earth that have a significantly different genetic code? (*TIME*, 23 March 1999.)
>
> Have you had to **invent** any technologies to do forensics on wildlife? (*TIME*, 22 January 2000.)

discreet, discrete

- **Discreet** is trustworthy and tactful:

  You can trust them with a secret: they are very discreet.

- **Discrete** is separate, individual:

  At the micro-level, things are made of discrete atoms.

> I rely upon you to be **discreet** and to refrain from all gossip. (Arthur Conan Doyle, "Beryl Coronet".)
>
> Their life would be morally **discrete** from the life of other men. (William James, *Varieties of Religious Experience*.)

disinterested, uninterested

- **Disinterested** is unselfish—impartial:

  A judge maintains a disinterested attitude.

- **Uninterested** is having no interest—bored:

  A judge is uninterested in irrelevant matters.

> She loved him with the **disinterested** fervour of a woman's first and early love. (Washington Irving, "The Broken Heart".)
>
> The scene would have been solemn and affecting even to an **uninterested** observer. (Mary Shelley, *Frankenstein*.)

does, dose

- **Does** fits with *do, does* (like *go, goes*).

  Who does he think he is?

- A **dose** is a portion or a dollop:

  He refused his dose of medicine.

> Does that mean Asian governments should sit back and do nothing? (*The Economist*, 11 February 2000.)
>
> For a mild **dose** of reality, return to Putrajaya. (*The Economist*, 11 February 2000.)

drank, drunk, drunken

- **Drank** is the past tense of "drink":

  I drank a glass of milk.

  > Bill Wilson (the founder of Alcoholics Anonymous) **drank** to alleviate his depressions and to celebrate his Wall Street success. (*Time*, 14 June 1999.)

- **Drunk** has three uses—

  a as the past participle of "drink":

  I have drunk a glass of milk.

  b as an adjective for a person:

  After two shots of liquor, I became drunk.

  c as a noun for a person:

  I behaved like a drunk.

  > Before she had **drunk** half the bottle, she found her head pressing against the ceiling. (Lewis Carroll, *Alice's Adventures in Wonderland*.)
  >
  > "If the blues were whisky, I'd stay **drunk** all the time." (Charles E Cobb Jr, in *National Geographic*, April 1999.)
  >
  > He found Dr Robert Smith, a skeptical **drunk**, whose family persuaded him to give Wilson 15 minutes. (*Time*, 14 June 1999.)

- **Drunken** is an adjective for a thing:

  My behaviour was drunken.

  > The public saw them in **drunken** brawls and other feats of extreme behaviour. (*Time*, 14 June 1999.)

economic, economical

- **Economic** is about the economy:

  The economic situation, according to the opposition, is in crisis.

- **Economical** is sparing, avoiding waste:

  This soap is very economical—a little bit of it will wash a lot.

> With the world's population growing by 78 million each year, economic growth is unable to keep up. (*Time*, 2 July 1992.)
>
> Buying certain kinds of things on the Web is convenient and economical. (*The Economist*, 2 July 1999.)

The adverb for both "economic" and "economical" is "economically".

> I know the frightful persecution they can wage on a professor who is economically [from "economic"] dependent on his university. (Jack London, *The Iron Heel.*)
>
> They would tell you that governments could not manage things as economically [from "economical"] as private individuals. (Upton Sinclair, *The Jungle.*)

eg, ie, etc

Two points: first, it is nowadays usual to write "eg, ie, etc" without the full stops; second, I prefer the English equivalents—in quotation marks below.

- **eg** means "for example" (from the Latin, *exempli gratia*):

  There are several spices: eg pepper and cinnamon.

- **ie** means "that is" (from the Latin, *id est*):

  It's three in the morning: ie rather late to be up.

- **etc** means "and so on" or "and others of the same type" (from the Latin, *et cetera*):

  Among my friends are Jack, Jill, Adam, etc.

> This rule is observed in most cases (eg we double the "r" in "preferred"). (Lewis Caroll, *Sylvie and Bruno.*)
>
> At 13 Alan Turing showed a flair for mathematics, even if his papers were criticized for being "dirty", ie, messy. (Paul Gray, *Time*, 29 March 1999.)
>
> How long do you think it will be, before science can bio-engineer the perfect human being? No illnesses, weaknesses, flaws, etc. (*Time*, 23 March 1999.)

elicit, illicit

- To **elicit** is to draw out, to evoke:

  My question elicited an answer.

- **Illicit** is illegal:

  Some drugs are illicit.

> Music does indeed elicit emotions. (*The Economist*, 18 February 2000.)
>
> It is a smugglers' paradise—not just for illicit imports, but for everyday household goods subject to high tariffs or stifling regulation. (*The Economist*, 9 April 1999.)

emigrant, immigrant

- An **emigrant** is a person who leaves a country:

  They became emigrants from their home country.

- An **immigrant** is a person who settles in a new country:

  They became immigrants in a new land.

> It is so far true of England, that the same tyranny that drove the first emigrants from home pursues their descendants still. (Thomas Paine, *Common Sense.*)
>
> Three-quarters of Joan of Arc's troops consisted of foreigners. Her values were those of France, which has always absorbed its immigrants. (*The Economist*, 28 January 2000.)

- The verb of **emigrant** is "emigrate"; the verb of **immigrant** is "immigrate".

> Vladimir Zworykin had emigrated from Russia with a PhD in electrical engineering. (Neil Postman, *TIME*, 29 March 1999.)
>
> When Freud was 81, the Nazis took over Austria and he immigrated to England. (Peter Gay, *TIME*, 29 March 1999.)

enormity, enormousness

- **Enormity** is great wickedness:

  These mass killings were an enormity.

- **Enormousness** is great size:

  The enormousness of the whale impressed me.

> Some method of punishment must be found to bring Anne to a proper realization of the enormity of her offence. (LM Montgomery, *Anne of Avonlea.*)
>
> I have ever found that, when narrating some specific example of a whale's enormousness, people have complimented me upon my facetiousness. (Herman Melville, *Moby Dick.*)

envelop, envelope

- To **envelop** (verb) is to cover or to wrap around:

  Dark clouds envelop the moon.

- An **envelope** (noun) is a cover for a letter:

  I put the note in an envelope.

> He watched the great pale coast envelop her. (DH Lawrence, *Sons and Lovers.*)
>
> He takes up a fat letter in a long blue envelope. (George Bernard Shaw, *Arms and the Man.*)

enviable, envious

- **Enviable** is making people jealous:

  Their soft job is really enviable.

- **Envious** is being jealous:

  We are envious of their soft job.

> He was dressed from head to heel in a cool and enviable snow-white linen. (Mark Twain, *A Tramp Abroad.*)
>
> Had she been envious, she might have hated the woman; but she did not do that. (Thomas Hardy, *The Mayor of Casterbridge.*)

equable, equitable

- **Equable** is calm, even-tempered:

  My mother had an equable nature.

- **Equitable** is fair, just:

  The laws of the land were equitable.

> Because Philip's appetites were satisfied, he became more equable and easier to live with. (W Somerset Maugham, *Of Human Bondage*.)
>
> Our goal must be to promote equitable access to the benefits of development regardless of nationality, race, or gender. (James D Wolfensohn, *Presidents & Prime Ministers*, February 1998.)

everyday, every day

- **Everyday** is an adjective:

  I wore my everyday clothes.

- **Every day** is an adverb phrase:

  I wear them every day, but not on festive occasions.

> Maybe for people with everyday concerns "globalization" is too big a word. (Walter Korn, TIME, 24 April 2000.)
>
> A few thousand new neurons pop up every day in an adult rat. (Alison Motluk, *New Scientist*, 5 February 2000.)

explicit, implicit

- **Explicit** is openly expressed:

  I made an explicit request for milk, but they brought me liquor.

- **Implicit** is hinted at, but not stated openly:

  The implicit idea behind my request was that I didn't want to get drunk.

> Mrs Fairfax either could not, or would not, give me more explicit information of the origin and nature of Mr Rochester's trials. (Charlotte Brontë, *Jane Eyre*.)
>
> The future's tools exist now only as ideas and as possibilities implicit in natural law. (K Eric Drexler, *The Engines of Creation*.)

faint, feint

- **Faint** is weak:

  We felt faint after the long voyage.

- To **feint** is to make a misleading move:

  They feinted on one side and attacked on the other.

> Edwin Hubble studied the faint, hazy blobs of light called nebulae that are visible through even a modest telescope. (Michael D Lemonick, *Time*, 29 March 1999.)
>
> Ben Hur feinted with his right hand. (Lew Wallace, *Ben Hur.*)

farther, further

- **Farther** is a greater distance:

  They travelled farther than we did.

- **Further** is additional or additionally:

  The police conducted further investigations.
  The police investigated the matter further.

> If you travelled much, much farther, to Jupiter's moon Io, you could witness one of the most extraordinary sights in the Solar System. (Ben Crystal, *New Scientist*, 8 January 2000.)
>
> Ignoring public worries may disillusion people further. (*New Scientist*, 22 April 2000.)

faze, phase

- To **faze** is to bother or distract:

  Their negative attitude did not faze me.

- A **phase** is a period of time:

  Some children go through a difficult phase.

> Go on. Minister, don't let 'em faze you. (Edith Wharton, *Summer.*)
>
> If you were alive during a cosmic contraction phase you would see nothing untoward. (Marcus Chown, *New Scientist*, 5 February 2000.)

ferment, foment

- To **ferment** is to brew (as in liquor):

  The yeast made the mixture ferment.

- To **foment** is to provoke:

  The agitators fomented a rebellion.

> Great plans fermented in her busy brain. (Louisa May Alcott, *Little Women*.)
>
> This business was, from the very first, fomented and brought about, by these men. (Charles Dickens, *The Pickwick Papers*.)

fewer, less—see chapter 2.18.

flammable, inflammable

Both words mean "easily set on fire". The prefix "in-" in "inflammable" doesn't mean "not" (as in "indecisive"); it means "into". If you want to say that something won't burst into flames, use "nonflammable".

- Dry paper is **inflammable**; wet paper is nonflammable.

- Dry paper is **flammable**; wet paper is nonflammable.

> Arrows, in great sheaves, were brought and laid upon the floor, together with jars of inflammable oil, and baskets of cotton balls. (Lew Wallace, *Ben Hur*.)
>
> The plastic linings will do little to stop your tent catching fire, because they are highly flammable. (*Which?* May 1970, cited in *The Oxford English Dictionary*.)
>
> It was made of foam and covered with nonflammable tape. (Neil Armstrong and others, *First on the Moon*, cited in *The Oxford English Dictionary*.)

flaunt, flout

- To **flaunt** is to show off:
  They flaunted their medals.

- To **flout** is to defy:
  Criminals flout the law.

> She had a flaunting vulgarity which amused and yet horrified. (W Somerset Maugham, *Of Human Bondage*.)
>
> If you had been a sane, sensible person and had written nice, cheering fatherly letters to your little Judy, then perhaps she wouldn't have flouted you in your old age. (Jean Webster, *Daddy-Long-Legs*.)

forego, forgo

- To **forego** is to go before:

  Officers forego other ranks into battle.

- To **forgo** is to go without:

  In my haste I had to forgo breakfast.

> The cause does always his effects forego. (M Fotherby, cited in *The Oxford English Dictionary*.)
>
> High-tech workers in America, who forgo big salaries to work at a start-up, gain precious experience as well as options. (*The Economist*, 11 February 2000.)

formally, formerly

- **Formally** is in a formal manner:

  I invited them formally to a gala dinner.

- **Formerly** is earlier:

  Formerly, I didn't like them; now I do.

> Mr Tung was formally appointed as Chief Executive of Hong Kong on December 16, 1996. (*Presidents & Prime Ministers*, July–August 1997.)
>
> The most desirable lands still to be acquired are some 50,000 acres (20,250 hectares), formerly part of Kodiak National Wildlife Refuge. (*Time*, 19 April 1999.)

foul, fowl

- **Foul** is bad or unfair:

  The referee declared the goal a foul.

- **Fowl** is poultry:

  A turkey is a kind of fowl.

> Hold your tongue, you foul-mouthed thief! (Emily Brontë, *Wuthering Heights*.)
>
> To be burned to death, even in a dream, was a thing to be avoided by any means, fair or foul. (Mark Twain, *A Connecticut Yankee in King Arthur's Court*.)
>
> There is cold fowl, some pasties, and things of that kind. (Thomas Hardy, *A Pair of Blue Eyes*.)

gamble, gambol

- To **gamble** is to take a risk in the hope of greater gain:
  People go to casinos to gamble.

- To **gambol** is to play or frolic:
  The children gambolled in the park.

> A political gamble will determine the fate of Allegre's reform programme. (*Time*, 17 May 1999.)
>
> Children that gambol and play. (Walt Whitman, *Leaves of Grass.*)

got, gotten—see chapter 2.10.

grisly, grizzly

- **Grisly** is horrifying, disgusting:
  The homicide detective came on a grisly sight.

- A **grizzly** is a kind of bear:
  There are grizzly bears in North America.

> Graham insisted on dancing until 1968, long after her onstage appearances had degenerated into grisly self-caricature. (*Time*, 14 June 1999.)
>
> We now have 600 species in our haemoglobin database, ranging from bald eagles to grizzly bears. (Ken Goddard, *New Scientist*, 22 January 2000.)

hanged, hung

- **Hanged** is for people:
  Some criminals were hanged.

- **Hung** is for things:
  The picture was hung on the wall.

> I was sure a man would be hanged that did such a thing. (Thomas Paine, *The Age of Reason.*)
>
> An ivory quiver hung on her left shoulder. (Thomas Bulfinch, *The Age of Fable.*)

hear, here

- To **hear** is what you do with your ear:

  I hear what you say.

- **Here** is the opposite of there:

  Here today, gone tomorrow.

> People didn't want to tie up their phones to hear music. (*New Scientist*, 25 March 2000.)
>
> There is a general point to make here. (*New Scientist*, 22 April 2000.)

historic, historical

- **Historic** means important, history-making:

  The old enemies made a historic agreement.

- **Historical** means true, not mythical:

  Hamlet may have been a historical figure.

> We must improve fiscal management. This applies to all countries, including those now taking the historic step of adopting the euro. (Michel Camdessus, *Presidents & Prime Ministers*, October 1998.)
>
> The ungentle laws and customs touched upon in this tale are historical, and the episodes which are used to illustrate them are also historical. (Mark Twain, *A Connecticut Yankee in King Arthur's Court.*)

idle, idol, idyll

- **Idle** means lazy or not in use:

  Idle people don't get much done.

- An **idol** is an object of worship or of veneration:

  Some ancients worshipped idols.

- An **idyll** is a poem, usually with a pastoral setting:

  Some poets have written lovely idylls.

> Much of Asia's plentiful high-tech money is sitting idle. (*The Economist*, 11 February 2000.)
>
> The Beatles' elegant lyrics and luminous melodies lifted them forever out of the world of simple teen idols and into the realm of art. (Kurt Loder, *TIME*, 14 June 1999.)
>
> Idylls *of the King*. (Title of a series of poems by Alfred Lord Tennyson.)

imply, infer

Imply and **infer** are two sides of the same coin. Somebody may imply (hint at) something in a statement from which someone else may infer (deduce) what the first person means.

> *Are you implying that I am an idiot?*
> *No, but you can infer that if you like.*

The notion of ice sliding on a sloppy lubricant seems straightforward enough. But what does it imply for the fate of the ice sheet? (*New Scientist*, 17 April 1999.)

Using observations from a satellite, the researchers were able to infer information about the relationship between the pulsar's mass and its radius. (*The Economist*, 25 February 2000.)

The noun forms of **imply** and **infer** are, respectively, "implication" and "inference".

The implication is that the public's mind is not made up on these issues. (*New Scientist*, 22 May 1999.)

A casual phrase revealed that she had all along taken her notes and drawn her inferences. (Edith Wharton, *Ethan Frome*.)

---

incredible, incredulous

- **Incredible** is unbelievable:

  I found their story incredible.

- **Incredulous** is not believing:

  Their story left me incredulous.

They embarked on a life of extremes: there were furs, dogs, yachts, incredible cars, houses, gigantic jewellery. (*Time*, 14 June 2000.)

At the end of *City Lights*, when the heroine at last sees the man who has delivered her from blindness, we watch her romantic dreams die. "You?" she asks, incredulous. "Yes," the Tramp nods. (*Time*, 14 June 2000.)

---

ingenious, ingenuous

- **Ingenious** is very clever:

  The safety pin was an ingenious invention.

- **Ingenuous** is innocent, artless:

Their ingenuous air disarmed my suspicions.

> Earlier, Japan had a reputation for ingenious design but rotten manufacturing. (*The Economist*, 10 March 2000.)
>
> With ingenuous frankness he spoke of what a wicked boy he had been. (Kate Chopin, *Awakening*.)

its, it's

- **Its** is a possessive (like *my, your, his, her, their* ...):

The dog wagged its tail.

> Uganda has had tremendous success with its national Poverty Eradication Action Plan. (*The Economist*, 14 January 2000.)

- **It's** is an abbreviation of *it is* or *it has*:

It's [= it is] a lovely day.
It's [= it has] been a lovely day.

> Scientists say it's [= it is] possible that human cells could some day be used to grow replacement parts. (Jessica Reeves, *TIME*, 4 January 2000.)
>
> It's [= it has] been a steady progression. (Irene Pepperberg, *New Scientist*, 15 January 2000.)

less, fewer—see chapter 2.16.

loose, lose

- **Loose** (pronounced "loos") is the opposite of tight:

This jacket is too loose on me.

- To **lose** (pronounced "looz") is the opposite of to find:

Try not to lose your keys again.

> We all had little suitcases, the kind you have to tie together or they would pop loose. (Charles E Cobb Jr, *National Geographic*, April 1999.)
>
> Let this be a lesson to you never to lose your temper. (Lewis Carroll, *Alice in Wonderland*.)

militate, mitigate

- To **militate** is to act against:

  Your previous bad record militates against you in the present case.

- To **mitigate** is to make milder:

  Your confession will mitigate your punishment in the present case.

> She speedily comprehended all his merits; even that quietness of manner, which militated against all her established ideas of what a young man's address ought to be. (Jane Austen, *Sense and Sensibility.*)
>
> Suramin is extremely toxic to patients in its present form, but if pharmacologists can find ways to mitigate its side effects, they may be able to find other uses for the drug. (*New Scientist*, 19 February 2000.)

miner, minor

- A **miner** is someone who works in a mine:

  Miners extract minerals from the earth.

> For some experts, the cooling of the mesosphere may be the "miner's canary". He believes it is the latest, the most unequivocal signal that the global climate really is changing. (*New Scientist*, 1 May 1999.)

- **Minor** has two meanings—

  a an underage person:

  A minor may not be served alcoholic drinks.

  b the opposite of major:

  I can handle minor irritations.

> The New York Court of Special Sessions, in 1905, declared unconstitutional the law prohibiting minors and women from working in factories after nine o'clock at night. (Jack London, *The Iron Heel.*)
>
> Was it sensible to totally reject the six studies on the grounds of what appear to be minor discrepancies? (*New Scientist*, 15 January 2000.)

moral, morale

- **Moral** is ethical:

  They won't cheat—they are too moral for that.

- **Morale** is good spirits, confidence:

  Winning the game boosted the team's morale.

  > We can continue competing for the moral high ground. Or we can decide to make a real difference. (James D Wolfenson, *Presidents & Prime Ministers*, January–February 1998.)
  >
  > The removal of the doomed to a chamber apart was done in order that the morale of the other patients might not be injuriously affected. (Mark Twain, *Life on the Mississippi*.)

naval, navel

- **Naval** is about the navy:

  She's a naval officer.

- A **navel** is a belly button:

  The baby had a big navel.

  > The US Navy wants to improve on scuba diving efficiency, says Lew Nuckols, of the US Naval Academy in Annapolis. (Catherine Zandonella, *New Scientist*, 26 June 1999.)
  >
  > Delhi is the navel of the world. (Rudyard Kipling, *Kim.*)

ones, one's—see chapter 3.8.

ordinance, ordnance

- An **ordinance** is a decree:

  They were in breach of the ordinance.

- **Ordnance** is cannonry:

  We heard the sound of distant ordnance.

  > Eleanor Roosevelt refused to abide by a segregation ordinance that required her to sit in the white section of the auditorium, apart from her black friends. (Doris Kearns Godwin, *TIME*, 14 June 1999.)
  >
  > All the firearms, except the two pieces of brass ordnance, were set in a rack in the aftermost wall of the round-house. (Robert Louis Stevenson, *Kidnapped.*)

others, other's, others'—see chapter 3.8.

parameter, perimeter

- A **parameter** is a measurable feature or variable:
  Good governments stay within reasonable economic parameters.

- A **perimeter** is a boundary:
  There was a fence round the perimeter of the playing field.

> Constant vigilance must be maintained over all the socioeconomic parameters; yet in each of these countries, there were lapses. (Michel Camdessus, *Presidents & Prime Ministers*, October 1998.)
>
> Soldiers moved onto the airport perimeter. (*The Guardian*, 1974, cited in *The Oxford English Dictionary*.)

parenthesis, parentheses

- **Parenthesis** is singular:
  The new moon is almost as thin as a parenthesis.

- **Parentheses** is plural:
  I have enclosed a word ("parentheses") within parentheses.

> The set of symbols in which statements in formal systems were written generally included standard numerals, plus signs, parentheses and so forth. (Douglas Hofstadter, *Time*, 29 March 1999.)

(See also the entry for "thesis, theses".)

passed, past

- **Passed** is the past form of the verb "pass":
  We passed their house on the way home.

- **Past** is of a former time:
  The present is here and now; the past is gone.

> Louisiana passed laws requiring science classes to give equal time to Morris's "creation science" and evolution. (Debora MacKenzie, *New Scientist*, 22 April 2000.)
>
> A groundbreaking new book declares that something awful has happened to American men over the past few decades. They have become obsessed with their bodies. (John Cloud, *Time*, 24 April 2000.)

peace, piece

- **Peace** is the opposite of war:

  The two countries signed a peace agreement.

- A **piece** is a part, a little bit:

  I helped myself to a piece of cake.

> The European powers had made peace in Vienna in 1815.
> (*The Economist*, 4 February 2000.)
>
> Like a piece of music, the film sweeps you along in its own rhythm and its own time. (Richard Corliss, *TIME*, 13 March 2000.)

people, peoples

- **People** is folks or persons, and it goes with a plural verb:

  Some people have strange habits.

- A **people** is a nation, and it goes with a singular verb:

  A people has a right to its freedom.

- A **people** has a plural form—"peoples":

  The Inuit and the Gipsies are different peoples.

> People don't care about good or bad science, but they do care whether their life means something. (Debora MacKenzie, *New Scientist*, 22 April 2000.)
>
> When we as a people can foist the costs of these initiatives upon other villains, such as the auto and oil companies, we will more likely support such programmes. (*Presidents & Prime Ministers*, May 1999.)
>
> The GIs were going forth on a crusade to save democracy and freedom, to defeat tyrants, to save oppressed peoples. (Colin Powell, *TIME*, 14 June 1999.)

perpetrate, perpetuate

- To **perpetrate** is to commit, to do something bad:

  They perpetrated a crime.

- To **perpetuate** is to make something last for ever:

  Mozart's music will perpetuate his name.

> Having perpetrated this atrocious act of vengeance, he escaped. (Washington Irving, *Alhambra*.)
>
> We were the first to perpetuate events by records kept. (Lew Wallace, *Ben Hur*.)

personal, personnel

- **Personal** is private:

  I took my personal belongings with me.

- **Personnel** is staff:

  The personnel of the company got a bonus.

> The sorry state of Proust's own personal affairs strongly suggests that the novelist was ill-equipped to offer advice to anyone. (*The Economist*, 1 October 1999.)
>
> We are designing new personnel policies that explicitly link staff performance to pay and promotion. (James D Wolfensohn, *Presidents & Prime Ministers*, February 1998.)

perspective, prospective

- A **perspective** is an outlook, a view:

  They like to take a broad perspective on major issues.

- **Prospective** relates to the future:

  They were preparing for their prospective baby.

> By a simple shift of perspective, mathematician Kurt Gödel wrought deep magic. (Douglas Hofstadter, *TIME*, 29 March 1999.)
>
> I think those decisions should always be made by prospective mothers of children; not by governments or religious bodies. (James Watson, *TIME*, 23 March 1999.)

poll, pole

- A **poll** is a political election or a survey of public opinion:

  The opposition party led in the poll.

- A **pole** is a long stick:

  They hoisted the flag on a pole.

- **Pole** is also used of the northernmost and the southernmost parts of our planet.

> Nearly half of all Americans, according to recent polls, think children should be taught both evolution and creationism. (Debora MacKenzie, *New Scientist*, 22 April 2000.)
>
> It was after the manner of a canoeist running rapids and seizing a pole at the sight of a submerged rock. (Upton Sinclair, *Jungle.*)
>
> We can live in a laboratory at the South Pole or in a deep-sea submersible. (Joel Achenbach, *National Geographic*, January 2000.)

pore, pour

- **Pore** has two meanings—

  a a **pore** (noun) is a small hole in the skin:

  Sweat was coming out of their pores.

  b to **pore** (verb) is to study closely:

  They pored over the book.

> The sand choked and blinded him; its fine thin grains entered the very pores of his skin. (Charles Dickens, *The Pickwick Papers.*)
>
> Analysts pore over past weather records to determine what kind of conditions have the highest probability of occurring simultaneously. (*National Geographic*, March 1999.)

- To **pour** has two meanings—

  a to rain heavily:

  It was pouring outside.

  b to dispense a drink:

  They poured themselves a drink.

> The runoff from the floods poured into the coastal Sechura Desert. (*National Geographic*, March 1999.)
>
> He poured the ale out of a jug into a large tumbler. (Charles Dickens, *David Copperfield.*)

practical, practicable

- **Practical** is useful, non-theoretical:

  They have a practical attitude: they work in a practical way.

- **Practicable** is able to be carried out:

  Their plan was too fancy; it wasn't really practicable.

> Frederick the Great wrote on the practical arts of government. (*The Economist*, 21 April 2000.)
>
> Emma hoped to make it practicable for Mr Elton to choose his own subject in the adjoining room. (Jane Austen, *Emma.*)

practice, practise

- In the UK and Australia—

  a **practice** is the spelling of the noun:

  They got a lot of practice in tennis.

  b **practise** is the spelling of the verb:

  They like to practise tennis.

- In the US—

  a **practice** is the spelling of the noun:

  They got a lot of practice in tennis.

  b **practice** is also the spelling of the verb:

  They like to practice tennis.

> Nouns—always "practice".
>
> Competitive pressures force firms to treat their staff in ways that depart from past practice. (*The Economist*, 28 April 2000.)
>
> It was beautiful to hear the lad lay out the science of war, all about musket practice, revolver practice, and not a solitary word of it all could these catfish make head or tail of. (Mark Twain, *A Connecticut Yankee in King Arthur's Court.*)

> Verbs—"practise" in the UK and Australia; "practice" in the US.
>
> Whenever he was by, while we were practising, I felt myself the greenest and most inexperienced of mortals. (Charles Dickens, *David Copperfield*.)
>
> They said she was a witch who practiced her arts by help of a devil in the form of a black cat. (Mark Twain, *A Connecticut Yankee in King Arthur's Court*.)

pray, prey

- To **pray** is to worship or request:
  I pray that all will be well.

- A **prey** is an animal that is hunted:
  The panther killed its prey.

> I can pray this away, I thought. (Howard Chua-Eoan, *Time*, 31 May 1999.)
>
> A hungry nestling will fight physically for the prey. (Joanna Marchant, *New Scientist*, 18 March 2000.)

precede, proceed

- To **precede** is to go before:
  Spring precedes summer.

- To **proceed** is to go ahead:
  They proceeded with their work.

> This fragment has not the least connection with the chapter that precedes it, nor with that which follows it. (Thomas Paine, *The Age of Reason*.)
>
> It was settled that, as soon as the ceremony was over, they should proceed to Longbourn. (Jane Austen, *Pride and Prejudice*.)

prevaricate, procrastinate

- To **prevaricate** is to talk evasively, almost lying:
  I asked them straight out, but they prevaricated.

- To **procrastinate** is to dither and delay:
  They procrastinated, so the opportunity passed.

> This man of God, as he is called, could tell a lie or very strongly
> prevaricate, when he supposed it would answer his purpose.
> (Thomas Paine, *The Age of Reason.*)
>
> Man naturally loves delay,
> And to procrastinate;
> Business put off from day to day
> Is always done too late.
>
> (Lewis Carroll, "Punctuality".)

principal, principle

- **Principal** is—

  a   the head or chief:

  The principal of the school called me to her office.

  b   a capital sum of money:

  They earned good interest on their principal.

  > Frank is the principal investigator on Galileo's plasma science
  > experiments. (*New Scientist*, 8 January 2000.)
  >
  > As soon as I was able, I paid the principal with interest and many
  > thanks. (Benjamin Franklin, *Autobiography.*)

- **Principle** is—

  a   a code of conduct:

  They have strong principles.

  b   a fundamental truth:

  We studied the principles of physics.

  > Shell has rewritten its business principles, created an elaborate
  > mechanism to implement them, and worked harder to improve its
  > relations with NGOs. (*The Economist*, 28 April 2000.)
  >
  > Whether by hubris or folly, some projects seem to be guided by
  > the principle "build it and they will come". (*New Scientist*,
  > 25 March 2000.)

quiet, quite

- **Quiet** is the opposite of loud:

  The birds were all quiet.

- **Quite** is somewhat, rather:

  It was quite a warm day.

> These are quiet songs that whisper sad truths over darkly soothing melodies. (Christopher John Farley, *Time*, 28 February 2000.)
>
> It is clear that quite a lot of people have doubts about free trade. (*The Economist*, 21 April 2000.)

raise, rise

- To **raise** (verb) is to lift something:

  I hope they will raise my salary.

- A **raise** (noun) is an increase:

  I hope I will get a raise soon.

> Companies usually begin by trying to sum up their philosophy in a code. That alone can raise [verb] awkward questions. (*The Economist*, 28 April 2000.)
>
> A gigantic raise [noun] in freight rates would have added materially to the inflation. (WG McAdoo, cited in *The Oxford English Dictionary*.)

- To **rise** (verb) is become higher:

  I hope my salary will rise.

- A **rise** (noun) is an upward move:

  That will see a rise in my salary.

> Kenya's elephant population only began to rise [verb] when the trading ban was enforced. (*The Economist*, 21 April 2000.)
>
> Such an approach would be consistent with the rise [noun] of complexity science within the scientific community generally. (*The Economist*, 10 March 2000.)

rapt, wrapped

- **Wrapped** is putting paper (or some other sheet) around something:

  I wrapped the book up.

- **Rapt** is being happily attentive, absorbed:

  I was rapt in the performance.

  > In rushed Diana, with a shawl wrapped hastily around her head. With rapt face, she gazed afar into the sunset west. Starry eyed and rapt, Anne had not uttered a word. (LM Montgomery, *Anne of Green Gables.*)

real, really

- **Real** is an adjective and goes with a noun or a pronoun:

  This is a real diamond.

- **Really** is an adverb and goes with a verb or an adjective:

  I really want to eat a really good cake.

  > There might be a real opportunity [with a noun] to slow growth rates. (John Roach, *National Geographic News,* 27 May 2000.)
  >
  > Could it really be [with a verb] possible? (*New Scientist,* 22 April 2000.)
  >
  > This is a really exciting [with an adjective] idea. (Michael Brooks, *New Scientist,* 18 March 2000.)
  >
  > (Not: This is a real exciting idea.)

run, ran

- **Run** can be a noun—the act of running or a series:

  I take a short run every morning.

  > Let the players, flush with bonuses from their winning run, dream too. (*The Economist,* 28 April 2000.)

- **Run** can also be a verb—

  a use "run" or "runs" in the present simple tense:

  I run and he runs for fun.

  b use "run" with "have", "has", "had":

  I have run out of breath.

  (Not: *I have ran out of breath.*)

  c use "ran" in the past simple tense:

  Yesterday I ran all the way home.

  (Not: *Yesterday I run all the way home.*)

> When companies operate abroad, they **run** up against all sorts of new moral issues. (*The Economist*, 28 April 2000.)
>
> They have **run** a highly effective cartel. (*The Economist*, 13 April 1999.)
>
> Procter & Gamble, a consumer-goods firm, this week **ran** into trouble. (*The Economist*, 17 March 2000.)

stationary, stationery

- **Stationary** is standing still:
  The bus was stationary.

- **Stationery** is paper, envelopes and the like:
  I'll need new stationery for next year.

> They have remained stationary while the multitudinous other arts have flitted so rapidly by them. (Edgar Allan Poe, "Criticism".)
>
> On these occasions Mr Dick never travelled without a leather writing-desk, containing a supply of stationery. (Charles Dickens, *David Copperfield*.)

straight, strait

- **Straight** is not crooked:
  That stick is straight.

- A **strait** is a part of the sea between two land masses:
  There is a strait between Singapore and Malaysia.

> I came straight in from the terrace. (Oscar Wilde, *A Woman of No Importance*.)
>
> I determined to attempt the passage of that strait. (Washington Irving, *The Art of Book-Making*.)

Somebody who is prim and proper—a bit uptight—is "straitlaced".

> A straitlaced, nonsmoking, nondrinking, hymn-singing churchman like my great-grandfather would have been offended by some words. (*National Geographic*, April 1999.)

substantive, substantial

- **Substantive** relates to a matter; of importance:

  They discussed substantive, not procedural, questions.

- **Substantial** is considerable:

  They made a substantial profit from their dealings.

> Many who knew her, thought it a pity that so substantive and rare a creature should have been absorbed into the life of another. (George Eliot, *Middlemarch*.)
>
> Many doctors and patients have been willing to take that risk because it seemed there were substantial benefits to the heart. (Christine Gorman, *TIME*, 27 March 2000.)

suit, suite

1 **Suit** (pronounced "syoot" or "soot") works as—

a a noun:

  - outer clothing, such as a jacket and trousers:

    I am wearing my new suit.

  - a set from a pack of cards:

    Cards have four suits—hearts, diamonds, spades, clubs.

  - a petition:

    The people presented their suit to the president.

  - (old-fashioned) a courtship:

    He presented his suit to her.

  - a law suit:

    Their suit against the company succeeded.

b a verb:

  - to fit:

    The dates they suggested suit me.

> He is a young man in a neat suit [clothes] of blue serge.
>
> When my suit [courtship] was granted she never said "I am happy: my love is satisfied."
>
> The place doesn't suit [fit] you.
>
> (George Bernard Shaw, *Man and Superman*.)

2   **Suite** (pronounced "sweet") is a noun that means—

- a set of rooms or compartments:
  They occupied the honeymoon suite at the hotel.

- a set of matching furniture:
  They bought a new living-room suite.

- a musical composition based on dance themes:
  Bach wrote six orchestral suites.

- a retinue—a group of followers:
  The prince was accompanied by his suite.

> A door separated each of the compartments; but as there were neither bolts nor locks, the whole suite was practically common ground. (Robert Louis Stevenson, *The New Arabian Nights*.)
>
> If you go before six to the hotel where the Prince lodges, you will make the journey as a member of his suite. (Robert Louis Stevenson, *The New Arabian Nights*.)

than, then

- **Than** is about comparisons:
  Some people are better at maths than others.

- **Then** is about time:
  I finished the job; then I went home.

> If it takes longer than 26 months, the optimal strategy is to delay until you can buy a computer fast enough to do the calculation in precisely 26 months. However, after a year of "goofing about", you should then immediately buy a new computer and put your nose to the grindstone. (Marcus Chown, *New Scientist*, 8 January 2000.)

that, which—see chapter 2.16.

there, their, they're

- **There** is—

  a   about a place:
  I like the beach and went there for a swim.

b   "a dummy subject":

There are some good books for sale.

The real subject (in blue) in the last example sentence is:
Some good books are for sale.

> People compete for sustenance and space with the natural species that are there. (John Roach, *National Geographic News*, 27 May 2000.)
>
> There might be a real opportunity to slow growth rates. (John Roach, *National Geographic News*, 27 May 2000.)

- **Their** is like *your, her, our*—a possessive:
  They took their vacation in May.

> Parents who receive such bedding sets should dress their infant in a warm sleeper and hang the adorable quilt on the wall. (Amy Dickinson, *TIME*, 1 May 2000.)

- **They're** is an abbreviation of *they + are*:
  They're very happy.

> But even if brains can be persuaded to make more neurons, the problem may be getting them where they're needed. (Alison Motluk, *New Scientist*, 5 February 2000.)

thesis, theses

- **Thesis** is singular:
  I wrote a thesis.

- **Theses** is plural:
  I wrote two theses.

> So while I finished my chemistry thesis, I also retrained myself in zoology and psychology. (Irene Pepperberg, *New Scientist*, 15 January 2000.)
>
> The principle on which my selection is made is to give adequate illustration to each of the theses enumerated in my introduction. (George Eliot, *Middlemarch*.)

- Similarly, **hypothesis** is singular and **hypotheses** is plural.

> Creation science did not meet requirements such as starting with a falsifiable hypothesis. (Debora MacKenzie, *New Scientist*, 22 April 2000.)
>
> School standards ask students to analyse hypotheses about the extinction of dinosaurs. (Debora MacKenzie, *New Scientist*, 22 April 2000.)

throne, thrown

- A **throne** is what a ruler sits on or, figuratively, rulership:
The monarch sat on a throne.

- **Thrown** is a form of the verb "to throw"—*throw, threw, thrown*:
I have thrown the rubbish out.

> Videogame consoles could challenge not only PCs but every other claimant to the TV-top throne. (*The Economist*, 21 May 1999.)
>
> The Albanian army dissolved, the police ran away, and their armouries were thrown open. (*The Economist*, 3 April 1999.)

to, too, two

- **To** has two uses—

  a in front of a verb:
  I want to go.

  b the opposite of *from*:
  I went to the market.

> Younger women all over the world want to have later pregnancies and smaller families than their mothers did. (John Roach, in *National Geographic News*, 27 May 2000.)
>
> Those landscapes are close to sea level. (John Roach, in *National Geographic News*, 27 May 2000.)

- **Too** has two uses—

  a to mean *also*:
  Give me an apple and take one too.

  b to mean *excessively*:
  It's too dark to read.

> The Internet has helped people keep in touch in a shorter time frame. The Web breeds a sense of togetherness too. (Walter Korn, TIME, 25 April 2000.)
>
> B2ut both sides are far too proud to admit to any complications in their public loathing of each other. (*The Economist*, 28 April 2000.)

- **Two** is a number:

  I have read two books this month.

> Two fossil hominids were introduced to the modern world on Wednesday. (Trish Beaver, *National Geographic News*, 27 April 2000.)

vain, vane, vein

- **Vain** has two meanings:

  a conceited:

  They are vain about their looks.

  b useless:

  They went on a vain quest for riches.

> Hackett was a vain, wealthy, violent gentleman, who held his blood and family in high esteem. (Mark Twain, "A New Crime Legislation Needed".)
>
> His thoughts teased and exhausted him with vain conjectures. (Washington Irving, *Alhambra*.)

- A **vane** is a pointer that shows the direction of the wind:

  There is a weather-vane on the roof.

> O storm-torn people! Unstable and untrue!
> Aye, indiscreet, and changing as a vane.
>
> (Geoffrey Chaucer, *The Canterbury Tales*.)

- **Vein** has two meanings—

  a a blood vessel:

  Veins take blood to the heart.

  b a mood:

  They were in good vein, so they sang and laughed.

> Topper could growl and never swell the large veins in his forehead. (Charles Dickens, *A Christmas Carol.*)
>
> If it puts him in the vein to leave his poor clerk fifty pounds, that's something. (Charles Dickens, *A Christmas Carol.*)

vicious, viscous

- **Vicious** is savage:

  The villains did some vicious things.

- **Viscous** is sticky, half-fluid:

  Honey and treacle are viscous.

> The GIs were as gentle in victory as they were vicious in battle. (Colin Powell, *TIME*, 14 June 1999.)
>
> Her mouth worked separate and apart from the rest of her. Occasionally it would say, "Pt", like some viscous substance coming to a boil. (Lee Harper, *To Kill a Mockingbird.*)

wary, weary

- **Wary** is cautious, distrustful:

  They are wary when they walk on ice.

- **Weary** is tired:

  They are weary after a hard day's work.

> Anthony is wary of media stories. (*TIME*, 24 May 1999.)
>
> She found herself at last within view of the house, with weary ankles and dirty stockings. (Jane Austen, *Pride and Prejudice.*)

waste, waist

- To **waste** is to use badly:

  I didn't waste any time.

- A **waist** is the narrow part of the body:

  I put my arms round my mum's waist.

> Why would the body waste energy creating them for nothing? (Alison Motluk, *New Scientist*, 5 February 2000.)
>
> The quadroon nurse was looked upon as a huge encumbrance, only good to button up waists and panties and to brush and part hair. (Kate Chopin, *Awakening*.)

weather, whether

- **Weather** is sun or rain:
  We're having lovely weather.

- **Whether** relates to questions:
  I asked them whether they were ready.

> From Atlantic weather charts, Wilson calculated that the smoke would have reached Scotland. (David Roche, *New Scientist*, 11 March 2000.)
>
> A company has to decide whether to sack an employee who is productive but naughty. (*The Economist*, 28 April 2000.)

- And a **wether** is a castrated ram.

> I am a tainted wether of the flock. (William Shakespeare, *The Merchant of Venice*.)

wet, whet

- **Wet** is the opposite of dry:
  I got wet in the rain.

- To **whet** is to sharpen:
  They whetted their knives.

> Their hands are soaking wet. (Joel Stein, *Time*, 17 January 2000.)
>
> A gay and pleasant sound is the whetting of the scythe in the mornings of June. (Ralph Waldo Emerson, *Essays*.)

which, that—see chapter 2.16.

who, whom, whose—see chapter 2.17.

whose, who's

- **Whose** has two uses—

  a   as an interrogative pronoun, meaning "belonging to whom?" or "of whom?"

  b   as a relative pronoun, substituting for *his, her, their* and the like.

> **Whose** fault is that? (Charles Dickens, *David Copperfield*.)
>
> **Whose** turn would that have served? (Charles Dickens, *Oliver Twist*.)

> What of those whose [= their] ruin is due to him? What welcome would you get from the girl whose [= her] lips you tried to soil, from the boy whose [= his] life you have shamed, from the mother whose [= her] dishonour comes from you? (Oscar Wilde, *A Woman of No Importance*.)

- **Who's** is an abbreviation of *who is* or *who has*.

> Who's [= who is] trying to deceive you? (George Bernard Shaw, *Pygmalion*.)
>
> Who's [= who is] off? Who's [= who has] gone? (Washington Irving, *Alhambra*.)

your, you're

- **Your** is belonging to you (like *my, our, his, her* ...):
  Now eat your spinach.

- **You're** is an abbreviation of "you are" (like *I'm* is of "I am"):
  You're the best!

> You're about to get sick of game shows. You had never seen such a smart guy in your neighbourhood as you saw on a quiz show.
> (Joel Stein, *Time*, 17 January 2000.)

Chapter 5

A short grammar of current English

The first step to wisdom, as the Chinese say, is getting things by their right names.

(Edward O Wilson, *Consilience.*)

5
A short grammar of current English

5.1 Simply hard

Yes, grammar is both simple and hard. It is simple in the sense that, to a large extent, you already have an intuitive knowledge of the topic. You know intuitively, for example, that *I an ice cream want* is grammatically wrong; *I want an ice cream* is right. Similarly, *Them going home* is wrong; *They are going home* is right.

There are two things, though, that make grammar hard. One is the weird terminology of grammar—a difficulty compounded by the fact that different grammarians use different names for the same grammar features. The other difficulty is created by the very fact of paying conscious attention to what, in general, is an automatic and subconscious activity: speaking grammatically.

So, if it is true that you already have a feel for grammatical rightness and wrongness, you might ask why you should study the subject at all. There are two answers to this question.

First, the study of grammar brings your use of language up from the unconscious to the conscious level of your mind. This, in turn, allows you to use language more skilfully. It is much the same as with numeracy: you already know how to count, but the study of mathematics improves your skill with numbers.

Second, language is the most characteristic, the most widely used, of human activities. Grammar explains the mechanism by which the sounds and signs of language produce something meaningful. As such, grammar is interesting in its own right.

This chapter is a quick romp through the basic concepts of grammar, as a preliminary to a more thorough study of the subject through further reading. In the bibliography at the end of this book you will find a listing of some useful books through which you can enhance your understanding of this subject.

In this chapter we look at two aspects of grammar:

- morphology, which deals with words and their forms: *eat, ate, eating, eaten* (chapter 5.2–5.12).
- syntax, which deals with strings of words: *What's that you're eating?* (chapter 5.13–5.15).

5.2   Word classes

It's handy when we are dealing with grammar to be able to group words into classes of similar type. This is because the members of such classes tend to have broadly similar characteristics and to function in broadly similar ways. Let's look at this principle with a collection of words.

> *Margaret, smell, ah, attentive, cauliflower, boil, gee, handball, fine, wow, buy, hard-working.*

One way to sort these words into classes is to see which words fit comfortably into the same sentence frames. You might like to try this with the dozen words above. There are three words that will fit, one by one, into each of the following four sentence frames.

> *I like _____.*
>
> *They are _____ people.*
>
> *I _____ potatoes.*
>
> *_____, that's tasty!*

Now let's take another group of words and another four sentence frames.

> *At, she, for, but, quickly, twice, towards, although, it, everybody, because, again.*

> *_____ was a winner.*
>
> *I did it _____ they didn't.*
>
> *They looked _____ me.*
>
> *They swam _____.*

If you've managed to sort these words out, you've learned two things: the eight traditional word classes in English, and one method for deciding which word belongs in which class.

The eight traditional word classes, with examples, are the following.

I like _____.
NOUN

[Margaret, cauliflower, handball]

They are _____ people.
ADJECTIVE

[attentive, fine, hard-working]

I _____ potatoes.
VERB

[smell, boil, buy]

_____, that's tasty!
INTERJECTION

[ah, gee, wow]

_____ was a winner.
PRONOUN

[she, it, everybody]

I did it _____ they didn't.
CONJUNCTION

[but, although, because]

They looked _____ me.
PREPOSITION

[at, for, towards]

They swam _____.
ADVERB

[quickly, twice, again]

Here is an old nursery rhyme that describes the traditional eight.

A noun's the name of anything;
As *school* or *garden*, *hoop* or *swing*.

Adjectives tell the kind of noun;
As *great, small, pretty, white* or *brown*.

Instead of nouns the pronouns stand:
Me and *mine, you* and *yours, she, he*—and

Verbs tell of something being done
You *read, count, sing, laugh, jump* or *run*.

How things are done the adverbs tell;
As *slowly, quickly, not* or *well*.

Conjunctions join the words together;
As men *and* women, wind *or* weather.

The preposition stands before
A noun; as *in* or *through* a door.

The interjection shows surprise
As *Oh*! *How pretty*! *Ah*! *How nice*!

It's not a bad first go at the nursery level—but only a first go.

Modern grammarians have added a ninth word class: determiners. Some have added even more. Determiners are words (such as *a*, *the*, *this*, *my*) that tell you how determinate—how definite—an associated noun is.

Here is a ditty that features all nine word classes.

Speak roughly to your little boy,
VERB   ADV   PREP   DET   ADJ   NOUN

And beat him when he sneezes;
CONJ VERB PRON CONJ   PRON   VERB

He   only does it   to annoy,
PRON ADV VERB PRON   VERB

Because he knows   it   teases.
CONJ   PRON VERB   PRON   VERB

CHORUS
NOUN

"Wow, wow, wow!"
INTERJ INTERJ INTERJ

(Lewis Carroll, *Alice's Adventures in Wonderland.*)

In this section (5.2) we have seen three different ways in which we can decide which word class a word belongs to.

- By defining the word class (the nursery rhyme).
- By seeing how the words fit into a sentence (the eight sentence frames with blanks in them).
- By giving examples of the members of the word classes (the ditty by Lewis Carroll).

There is a fourth way.

- By looking at what suffixes (endings) the words can take.

To illustrate the fourth method: we can tell that *boy* is a noun, because it can take the plural suffix *–s*. So can other nouns: *girl—girls, book—books*. And many verbs can take a past tense suffix *–ed*: *walk—walked, talk—talked*.

Usually we have to use a combination of methods in deciding what class a word belongs to. This is because it is often the way we use a word in a particular sentence that determines its class.

Take, for example, the words *table, like* and *only*. Each of these words can have different functions (belong to different word classes) in different contexts.

The vase was on the <u>table</u>.   *I will <u>table</u> the documents today.*
NOUN   VERB

I <u>like</u> chocolate.   *They are <u>like</u> us.*
VERB   PREP

Kerry is an <u>only</u> child.   *I <u>only</u> have a few minutes.*
ADJECTIVE   ADVERB

In the sections that follow we take a closer look at each of the word classes, including determiners, using the four methods discussed above.

5.3 Nouns

How to identify nouns

a **Definition**

In traditional grammar, a noun is said to be a naming word—a word that gives the name of a person (*Alex*), a thing (*bush*), a place (*Perth*) and so on.

b **Sentence frame**

A noun is any word (other than a pronoun or a determiner) that fits into the blank space in the following sentence frame.

(a)
I am thinking about (an) _____. [Mum, whale, evening, resigning,
(the) NOUN   Sydney Opera House]

The words *a*, *an* and *the* are optional: sometimes they stand before the nouns; sometimes they don't. Any of the words in square brackets above are nouns because they fit into the frame—some with, some without *a*, *an* or *the*. The last example (*Sydney Opera House*) is a noun group (or "a compound noun").

c **Suffixes**

Nouns take the suffix *-s* in the plural.

SINGULAR	PLURAL
apple	*apples*
expectation	*expectations*
sighting	*sightings*

But there are also nouns that you make plural without an *-s*: *mouse—mice, goose—geese, sheep—sheep*.

d **Examples**

In the following text, the nouns are in blue.

> Planning a little international travel this summer? Before you renew your passport and figure out how many rolls of film to buy, there are a few precautions you should take to avoid a side trip to the hospital.
> (Christine Gorman, TIME, 19 June 2000.)

Subclasses of nouns

Following are the subclasses of nouns with sample entries.

NOUN
1 PROPER: Jack, Jill, Manchester, Western Australia (a noun group)
2 COMMON
  a COUNT: tree, table, tambourine, tap, toe, telescope
  b NONCOUNT: water, wool, milk, timber, information, peace

1 **Proper nouns** are nouns that normally start with capital letters— they are the names of individual people (*Robin*) or places (*Perth*) and the like (*Christmas*).

2 **Common nouns** are all the rest. There are two kinds of common nouns.

a **Count nouns** are nouns that you can count and that, consequently, have both singular and plural forms: *one tree, two trees* ... Singular count nouns go with singular verbs (*A tree is* ...); plural count nouns go with plural verbs (*Trees are* ...).

Collective nouns are a special subspecies of common noun. Examples of collective nouns are *team, band, government*. They are singular nouns and you can count them: *one team, two teams* ... In this regard they are just like other count nouns.

Their special feature, though, is that singular collective nouns can go either with singular or with plural verbs (*The team is* ... or *The team are* ...). Which kind of verb you use depends on whether you are considering the collection as a whole (*The team is performing well this season*) or as composed of its individuals (*The team are putting on their uniforms*).

> It brings home how critical population is for these areas of high biodiversity. (John Roach, *National Geographic News*, 27 May 2000.)
>
> Most of the population are living outside. (Richard Galpin, BBC News, 6 June 2000.)

b **Noncount nouns** have two characteristics that distinguish them from count nouns.

i Unlike count nouns, which have both singular and plural forms (*tree—trees*), noncount nouns are usually used only in the singular (*ice*, but not *ices*).

ii Unlike count nouns, which can be preceded by *a* or *an* (*a pear, an apple*), noncount nouns are usually preceded either by nothing at all or by the word *some* or *any* (*salt* or *some salt*, but not *a salt*).

> *Water is a compound of oxygen and hydrogen.*
> Not: *A water is a compound of an oxygen and a hydrogen.*
> Nor: *Waters are compounds of oxygens and hydrogens.*

Nouns that are normally noncount nouns can also, in certain contexts, function as count nouns—that is, they can come with *a* or *an* in the singular, and they can have plurals. For example, *coffee* is usually a noncount noun used in the singular (*Coffee grows in Brazil*). But you can also use *coffee* in the sense of "a cup of coffee" (*Please give us two coffees*).

When such a noun functions in this way, it ceases to be a noncount noun and becomes a count noun.

> The task in the postwar years was to sublimate the old conflicts of blood and steel into comparatively harmless commercial issues, over the trade rules for fruits and cheeses. (*Time*, Winter 1996.)

In the text above, *blood* and *steel* are noncount nouns, as indicated by the absence of *a* in front of these singular words. *Fruits* and *cheeses*, which are usually noncount nouns (*some fruit, some cheese*) are used as count nouns. We can see this from the fact that, in the boxed sentence, they occur in the plural—something that occurs only with count nouns.

Words such as *peace* and *information* function only as noncount nouns: they never occur in the plural. You don't say *peaces* or *informations*. (Even my spellcheck is protesting.)

> The European powers had made peace in Vienna in 1815. (*The Economist*, 4 February 2000.)
>
> American business people are ethically sensitive in matters of confidential information. (*The Economist*, 28 April 2000.)

5.4 Pronouns

How to identify pronouns

a **Definition**

A pronoun is a generalized substitute for a noun. *He* is a substitute for the noun "Adam", *she* for "Eve", *they* for "Adam and Eve".

b **Sentence frame**

A pronoun is any word (other than a noun or a determiner) that fits into the blank spaces in the following sentence frames.

_____ *spoke about* _____.
PRONOUN   PRONOUN

[I, everybody, who, we ... me, us, myself, something]

c   Suffixes

Some pronouns can take an *–m* suffix: *he—him, they—them, who—whom*. Other pronouns feature a *–self* (or *–selves*) suffix: *myself, ourselves*. Otherwise, pronouns are all but free of suffixes.

d   Examples

In the following text the pronouns are in blue.

> "Right now, addicted patients have to ask themselves every day if they should take their medicine or get high," says Colin Brewer of the Stapleford Clinic in London. He thinks antibodies would be a big help to recovering addicts who have trouble sticking with therapy.
> (Philip Cohen, *New Scientist*, 10 June 2000.)

Subclasses of pronouns

Following are the subclasses of pronouns with sample entries.

PRONOUN
1 PERSONAL: I, me, mine, myself, we, us, ours, ourselves
2 INDEFINITE: somebody, anyone, nothing, everybody
3 INTERROGATIVE: Who? Whom? Whose? What? Which?
4 RELATIVE: who, whom, whose, which, that

1   **Personal pronouns** are those that refer to you, to me and to other people: *you, us, them*.

When you flatter people it is just telling them what they think of themselves.

2   **Indefinite pronouns** are those that combine *some–, any–, no–, every–* with *–body, –one, –thing*: *somebody, anyone, nothing*.

I know somebody who lives in a penthouse. It's great for anyone living there to know they have a roof under their feet.

3 **Interrogative pronouns** are those that stand either at or near the beginning of questions. The answers to sentences with interrogative pronouns are other pronouns or nouns.

QUESTION	ANSWER
Who was that?	*That was <u>Gene</u>.* NOUN
<u>With</u> whom are you playing?	*I'm playing with <u>them</u>.* PRONOUN
<u>What</u> do you want?	*I don't want <u>anything</u>.* PRONOUN

4 **Relative pronouns** (also called "adjectival conjunctions") relate to nouns or pronouns mentioned in an earlier clause (sentence part). In the sentence *I returned the money that I owed them*, the relative pronoun *that* relates to the noun *money* mentioned in the clause *I returned the money*.

The main relative pronouns are *who, whom, whose, which, that*. For how and when to use these pronouns see chapter 2.16–17.

5.5 Adjectives

How to identify adjectives

a **Definition**

An **adjective** is a word that modifies—that is, changes or enhances the meaning of—a noun or a pronoun.

b **Sentence frame**

An adjective is any word that fits into the following sentence frame.

They were very _____.
ADJECTIVE

[British, small, friendly, interesting, bored, happy, old-fashioned]

c **Suffixes**

An adjective is any word (other than an adverb) that takes a comparative *–er* or a superlative *–est* suffix: *finer, finest; lovelier,* *loveliest*. Some multisyllabic adjectives take *more* and *most* instead of *–er* and *–est*: *more beautiful, most beautiful*.

d   Examples

In the text below, the adjectives are in blue.

> When Ataturk died, in 1938, the government of the day commissioned a shrine to house his old cars, suits, golfing plus-fours, pyjamas, socks, unsmoked cigarettes, even his nail-clippers. (*The Economist*, 16 June 2000.)

Subclasses of adjectives

Following are the subclasses of adjectives with sample entries. The last example below is an adjective group (or "a compound adjective").

ADJECTIVE
- **1** PROPER: British, Australian, Churchillian
- **2** DESCRIPTIVE: big, small, reasonable, wonderful
- **3** VERBAL:
  - **a** PRESENT PARTICIPLE: interesting, boring, loving, laughing
  - **b** PAST PARTICIPLE: interested, bored, half-eaten

1   **Proper adjectives** derive from proper nouns and, like proper nouns, usually start with capital letters (*Britain* [noun] → *British* [adjective]).

2   **Descriptive** (or "**common**") **adjectives** form the largest group of adjectives. Many originate as adjectives (*big, small*); others derive from members of other word classes with the help of suffixes (*reason* [noun] → *reasonable* [adjective]; *wonder* [noun] → *wonderful* [adjective]).

3   There are two kinds of **verbal adjectives**.

a   **Present participles** (also called "*–ing* forms") always have an *–ing* suffix.

It was an interesting book.

b **Past participles** (also called "–en forms") usually have an –n, –d or –t suffix (*seen, walked, kept*).

> *They had* bored *expressions on their faces.*

Verbal adjectives are so called because they derive from verbs (*interest* [verb] → *interesting* [adjective]; *bore* [verb] → *bored* [adjective]).

Interesting and *bored* are adjectives if and only if you use them adjectivally; that is, to modify a noun or a pronoun: *It was an* interesting *book. Interesting* modifies *book. They had* bored *expressions on their faces. Bored* modifies *expressions.*

Otherwise, *interesting* and *bored* are verbs: *The play was* interesting [verb] *the audience. The play has* bored [verb] *the audience.*

5.6 Determiners

How to identify determiners

There are some words (in blue) that sometimes function adjectivally, modifying nouns (bold), and sometimes pronominally, replacing nouns.

ADJECTIVAL FUNCTION	PRONOMINAL FUNCTION
Hand me that **book**.	*Hand me* that.
You can have both **apples**.	*You can have* both.

In traditional grammar these words were called adjectives or pronouns depending on the function that they performed. Nowadays, they are separated out into a class of their own: determiners.

Why don't we call them adjectives any more?

Because they lack a characteristic feature of adjectives: the comparative suffix –er and the superlative suffix –est.

And why don't we class them among the pronouns?

Because, unlike "normal" pronouns, they can also function adjectivally.

The upshot is that they have been given a small, separate class of their own: the class of determiners. To this class of sometimes–adjectives–

sometimes–pronouns, modern grammarians have also added the articles (*a, an, the*), numbers (*one, first, quarter*) and also possessives (*my, your, Jack's, Jill's*). So it is quite a diverse word class.

a Definition

Determiners are words that indicate how determinate—how definite—something is.

b Sentence frames

Determiners are any words—other than adjectives—that fit into either of the frames below. The last example on each of the two lines below is a determiner group (or "a compound determiner").

I want _____ thing.   [a, the, this, one, their, another, Robin's, half a]
    DETERMINER

I want _____ things. [some, the, these, those, five, Robin's, a lot of]
    DETERMINER

c Suffixes

For possessive determiners, –*'s* and –*s'* are typical suffixes: *the boy's head, the girls' heads*.

d Examples

In the text below, the determiners are in blue.

> At a recent conference on interactive publishing, there was only one thing on the minds of the 300 people present. Could they actually make money on the Net? For most, that means supplementing advertising revenues with subscription revenues. That causes a problem. Most believe that, because they have paid for a PC, a second telephone line and a subscription to a service provider, everything else should be free. (*The Economist*, 14 February 1998.)

Subclasses of determiners

Grammarians divide determiners into three subclasses.

DETERMINER
{
1 PREDETERMINER: double, half, all
2 CENTRAL DETERMINER: a, the, this, either
3 POSTDETERMINER: two, fifth, few

The point of the subclassification is that, if more than one determiner occurs in a sequence of determiners, they occur in the sequence 1–2–3 (and not, for example, 3–2–1). So, for instance, we say:

> *(1) All (2) those (3) four students have passed the exam.*
> Not: *(3) Four (2) those (1) all students have passed the exam.*

Native English speakers intuitively order multiple determiners in their natural sequence. So, unless you are a professional grammarian, this is a subclassification that you can note as something interesting—and then ignore.

5.7   Verbs

How to identify verbs

a   Definition

Verbs, traditionally, are predicating (or "doing") words such as *run*, *jump*, *walk* and *talk*.

b   Sentence frames

A verb is any word that fits into any of the sentence frames below.

1   *We _____.*
     VERB
[walked, talked, played, work, swim, were laughing]

2   *We _____ them.*
     VERB
[like, know, saw, helped, recognized, will bring]

3   *We _____ them something.*
     VERB
[tell, lend, asked, wrote, have sent]

4   *We _____ happy.*
     VERB
[are, feel, seemed, would become]

The last example within each pair of square brackets above is a verb group (or "a compound verb"): that is, several verbs combining to express one meaning.

c   Suffixes

Verbs are words that can take an *–ed* suffix in the past tense (*walked, talked*) or an *–ing* suffix (*walking, talking*).

165

Note, though, that there is a small number of "irregular" verbs that:

- form their past tense without *–ed* (*sit—sat, go—went, put—put,* ...)
- do not take *–ing* (*must, shall, may,* ...).

d Examples

In the text below, the verbs are in blue.

> In Western countries, companies increasingly wonder what constitutes ethical corporate behaviour. Business ethics is suddenly all the rage. Those who think companies have wider responsibilities argue about the best way to pursue them. Ulrich Steger, who teaches environmental management in Lausanne, says that companies cannot possibly hope to pursue a single abstract set of ethical principles. No universal set of ethical principles exists; most are too woolly to be helpful; and the decisions that companies face every day rarely present themselves as ethics versus economics in any case. (*The Economist,* 28 April 2000.)

Subclasses of verbs

There are two subclasses of verbs: a large number of lexical verbs and a small number of auxiliary verbs.

VERB
{
1 LEXICAL: eat, drinking, walks, talked

2 AUXILIARY: am, were, had, will, should
}

1   **Lexical verbs** have meanings.

I finished the job. I ate. I slept.
   LEX   LEX   LEX

2   **Auxiliary verbs** are used in association with lexical verbs to form verb groups. They carry no meaning: their use is purely grammatical.

I have finished the job. I am eating. I will sleep.
   AUX   LEX   AUX   LEX   AUX   LEX

Some of the auxiliaries can function either way: as lexical verbs with meanings or as auxiliary verbs without.

I have [= possess] *a new bicycle.*
   LEX

I have [= 0] *done what I could.*
  AUX   LEX

Verb forms

Take any verb: *eat*, for example. It can occur in a variety of forms: *eat, eats, ate, eating, eaten.* (A very small number of verbs, such as *must*, do not have this characteristic.) The forms of the verb subdivide into two groups—finite and nonfinite—each containing three forms: a–c. and d–f.

REGULAR VERBS

1 FINITE FORMS
- **a** walk   talk   jump
- **b** walks   talks   jumps
- **c** walked   talked   jumped

IRREGULAR VERBS

FINITE FORMS
- **a** eat   write   take
- **b** eats   writes   takes
- **c** ate   wrote   took

REGULAR VERBS

2 NONFINITE FORMS
- **d** to walk   to talk   to jump
- **e** walking   talking   jumping
- **f** walked   talked   jumped

IRREGULAR VERBS

NONFINITE FORMS
- **d** to eat   to write   to take
- **e** eating   writing   taking
- **f** eaten   written   taken

You can see from the above that, among irregular verbs (verbs that don't take an *–ed* suffix), forms c and f differ from each other. Among regular verbs (verbs that do take an *–ed* suffix), forms c and f don't differ from each other. Each of the verb forms a–f has a different function, and we now look at these functions below.

1   The three finite forms—a, b, c

All three finite forms (*eat, eats, ate*) combine with subjects: that is, doers (bold) of the verbs (in blue). To put the same thing in technical terms: finite verbs predicate. The examples below show the grammar names for forms a, b, c.

a	PRESENT:	I eat.	**We** walk.	**Jack and Jill** talk.
b	PRESENT–*s*:	He eats.	**She** walks.	**Someone** talks.
c	PAST:	**We** ate.	**They** walked.	**Everybody** talked.

The past form is also called the "–*ed* form" because most English verbs take an –*ed* suffix in the past tense.

The thing that characterizes all three finite forms is that they change in different circumstances. For example, if you change the subject of the sentence from *They* to *It* in the present, the finite verb changes from *work* to *works* (*They work → It works*). Or if you change the sentence from the present tense to the past tense, the finite verb also changes (*It works → It worked*).

The word "finite" means bound; and the finite verb forms are so called because these forms are liable to change with a change of subject or of tense.

2   The three nonfinite forms—d, e, f

In contrast with the finite forms of verbs, the three nonfinite forms do not change with a change of subject or tense. We can show this, for example, with form e (a verb ending in –*ing*). Whatever change you may make to the subject or to the tense of the sentence, –*ing* remains –*ing*.

CHANGE OF SUBJECT:	*I am working.*	*He is working.*	*They are working.*
CHANGE OF TENSE:	*I was working.*	*I am working.*	*I will be working.*

Each of the nonfinite forms of the verb (d, e, f) has a variety of functions. We look at these below.

d   The infinitive form (also called the "*to* form") characteristically has the word *to* in front of it.

  i   One use of the infinitive form is as the second of two consecutive verbs: **want** *to go*, **like** *to dance*.

> Publicly funded researchers **try** to outpace the commercial upstart, which **plans** to complete its project in June.
> (*New Scientist*, 20 May 2000.)

You can see that the infinitive verbs (in blue) are nonfinite by changing the tense of the above passage. The verbs in blue do not change their form; the finite verbs (bold) do.

> Publicly funded researchers **tried** to outpace the commercial upstart, which **planned** to complete its project in June.

ii Another use of the infinitive form is at the start of a sentence, where it acts as the subject of the sentence. In this use, the infinitive verb form has a noun-like function.

> *To fight aloud is very brave.*
> *To know just how he suffered would be dear.*
> *To hear an oriole sing may be a common thing.*
>
> (Emily Dickinson, *Poems*.)

e The present participle form (also called the "*–ing* form") always has the suffix *–ing*. This is its identity badge: *walking, talking, reading, writing*. The present participle has three major uses.

i As a lexical verb, preceded by a form of the auxiliary verb *be*.

We ought to be going soon.
        AUX   PRES PART

Here is a text with the present participles in blue. The auxiliary verb *be* (in varying forms) is in bold.

> The World Bank and the International Monetary Fund have **been** holding their spring meetings in Washington. Campuses across the country have **been** putting on teach-ins. Churches have **been** holding prayer vigils "in solidarity with the victims of the World Bank". Even more has **been** going on behind the scenes. The Ruckus Society and the Direct Action Network **are** teaching civil disobedience. Who are the protesters, and what **are** they trying to say?
> (*The Economist*, 21 April 2000.)

ii An adjective-like function, as the modifier of a noun (bold).

*That was a <u>thrilling</u> **play**.*   [*Thrilling* modifies the noun *play*.]
PRES PART NOUN

Following is a text with examples. The nouns are in bold; the present participles that modify them are in blue.

> This spring's meeting became the most fascinating **event** on the planet. Overwhelming **majorities** of Americans think that their trade negotiators pay too little attention to working **Americans**. Polls taken earlier this year found most **Americans** expressing some sympathy for the protesters at Seattle. A recent study of polling **data** found that 61% of Americans favour globalization. The United States has never been on the receiving **end** of IMF policies. (*The Economist*, 21 April 2000.)

iii A noun-like function (in blue): for example, as the subject of a verb (bold). When it has a noun-like function, the *–ing* form is called "a gerund" and, like any noun, it can take a plural *–s* suffix.

> Martha's home furnishings **helped** wipe the red ink off the bottom line of the discount department chain K Mart. (Debra MacKenzie, *New Scientist*, 22 April 2000.)
>
> Housing **breaks** up the pre-existent natural ecosystem into little patches. The population finding **is** intended to help conservationists understand population dynamics. (John Roach, *National Geographic News*, 27 May 2000.)
>
> The entire proceedings of the Scopes trial were broadcast on the radio. (Debra MacKenzie, *New Scientist*, 22 April 2000.)

f The past participle form (also called "*–en* form") is recognizable as the verb form used after *have*, *has* or *had*. It usually ends with the suffix *–n* or *–d* or *–t*.

I have
- *–n* suffix: eaten, taken, seen, gone, done, known, given
- *–d* suffix: walked, talked, waited, said, made, paid, hoped
- *–t* suffix: sent, kept, slept, put, sat, crept, dealt, felt, meant

The past participle (underlined) has three major functions.

i As a lexical verb, preceded by a form of the auxiliary verb *be*, forming a passive (see chapter 1.8).

Children ought to be loved.
          AUX   PAST PART

Here are some illustrations from a text. The auxiliaries are in bold; the past participles, in blue.

> The danger **was** unperceived.
> Her father and she **were** left to dine together.
> The want of Miss Taylor would **be** felt every hour of every day.
> The evil **was** much increased by his constitution and habits.
>
> (Jane Austen, *Emma*.)

ii As a lexical verb, preceded by a form of the auxiliary verb *have*, forming a perfect tense.

They have taken a walk.
        AUX   PAST PART

Here are some illustrative sentences. The auxiliaries are in bold; the past participles, in blue.

> Her mother **had** died long ago.
> You must **have** found it very damp and dirty.
> Success **has** blessed me in this instance.
> The letter **had** not added any lasting warmth.
>
> (Jane Austen, *Emma*.)

iii An adjective-like function, as the modifier of a noun.

I have a worn carpet.   [*Worn* modifies the noun *carpet*.]
       PAST PART   NOUN

Here are some illustrative sentences. The nouns are in bold; the past participles, in blue.

> It was a long, well-written **letter**.
> Mr Perry's **name**, I dare say, is not unknown to you.
> This wretched **note** was the finale of Emma's breakfast.
>
> (Jane Austen, *Emma*.)

5.8 Prepositions

How to identify prepositions

a **Definition**

Traditionally, prepositions are "positional" words such as *in, on, over*. The word *preposition* come from "pre-position". This indicates the characteristic of the class: namely, that its members are pre-positioned relative to nouns or pronouns—called "prepositional objects". *Them* in the sentence frame below is such an object.

b **Sentence frame**

A preposition is any word that fits into the sentence frame below. The last example below is a preposition group (or "a compound preposition").

We were doing it _____ *them.*   [for, with, over, through, among,
                PREPOSITION   in front of]

c **Suffixes**

Prepositions are uninflected words: that is, they do not take any suffixes. But some prepositions, derived from verbs, come with an *–ing* suffix.

I have a letter concerning **you.**
It details some of the matters regarding **your past.**

d **Examples**

The prepositions in the text below are in blue; their objects are in bold.

> Music is strange stuff. It is clearly different from **language**. People can, nevertheless, use it to communicate things—especially their emotions. And when allied with **speech** in **song**, it is one of the most powerful means of **communication** that humans have. (*The Economist*, 18 February 2000.)

Subclasses of prepositions

Grammarians, you will be happy to know, do not subclassify prepositions.

5.9 Conjunctions

How to identify conjunctions

a Definition

Conjunctions, in traditional grammar, are joining words. They join a variety of language units.

- ONE WORD   Adam   or   Eve.
  WITH ANOTHER: WORD   CONJ   WORD

- ONE PHRASE   In the garden and under the tree.
  WITH ANOTHER: PHRASE   CONJ   PHRASE

- ONE CLAUSE   I went home, because I felt homesick.
  WITH ANOTHER: CLAUSE   CONJ   CLAUSE

- ONE SENTENCE   It was raining.   So   I took an umbrella along.
  WITH ANOTHER: SENTENCE   CONJ   SENTENCE

b Sentence frame

A conjunction is any word that fits into the sentence frame below. The last example below is a conjunction group (or "a compound conjunction").

We are happy _____ *they are happy.*   [and, so, if, when, because,
           CONJUNCTION   that, as soon as]

c Suffixes

Conjunctions do not take suffixes.

Subclasses of conjunctions

There are two subclasses of conjunctions, one of them with three subdivisions.

1 COORDINATING:	and, but, either, neither, nor, or, so, yet, still	

CONJUNCTION

2 SUBORDINATING

a ADJECTIVAL: who, whom, whose, which, that

b ADVERBIAL: if, when, because, unless, before, after, while

c NOMINAL: who, whom, what, that, why, whether, how

The subclassification of conjunctions is closely bound up with that of clauses:

1   a coordinating conjunction heads a coordinate clause

2   a subordinating conjunction heads a subordinate clause—
    a   an adjectival conjunction heads an adjective clause
    b   an adverbial conjunction heads an adverb clause
    c   a nominal conjunction heads a noun clause.

We deal with these clauses—and with the conjunctions that head them—in section 5.14 below.

A note on terminology

"Adjectival conjunctions" (2a above) are also called "relative pronouns" (see chapters 5.4 and 2.16–17). We deal with this type of conjunction again in section 5.14 below.

5.10   Adverbs

How to identify adverbs

a   Definition

Adverbs are words that modify (that is, change or enhance the meaning of) verbs:

They walked slowly.
    VERB   ADVERB

Adverbs modify not only verbs; they also modify a range of other language units.

- An adverb modifies a verb:

  They <u>did</u> everything <u>well</u>.
      VERB   ADVERB

- An adverb modifies an adjective:

  They are <u>very</u> <u>helpful</u>.
           ADVERB ADJECTIVE

- An adverb modifies a determiner:

  I have read <u>nearly</u> <u>every</u> book on that shelf.
               ADVERB DETERMINER

- An adverb modifies a preposition:

  The lamp was <u>exactly</u> <u>over</u> the table.
               ADVERB   PREPOSITION

- An adverb modifies a conjunction:

  I will help you <u>only</u> <u>if</u> you help me.
               ADVERB CONJUNCTION

- An adverb modifies another adverb:

  They acted <u>extremely</u> <u>carefully</u>.
           ADVERB   ADVERB

- An adverb modifies a sentence:

  <u>Luckily</u>, <u>they arrived on time</u>.
   ADVERB   SENTENCE

An adverb that modifies a sentence is also called "an adjunct". See chapters 2.6 and 3.3 (item 8).

b Sentence frame

An adverb is any word that fits into the following sentence frame.

They did the job _____.
          ADVERB

[well, slowly, yesterday, often, intelligently, together]

Oops! There is one rogue word that slips into the frame: the pronoun *themselves*. But apart from that, all other words that fit into the frame are indeed adverbs.

c Suffixes

- Most adverbs (as do adjectives) take comparative –*er* and superlative –*est* suffixes: *sooner, soonest*. For some multisyllabic adverbs you use *more* and *most* instead of –*er* and –*est*: *more intelligently, most intelligently*.
- Many (certainly not all) adverbs derive from adjectives with the suffix –*ly*: *funny* [adjective], *funnily* [adverb].

d **Examples**

In the text below, the adverbs are underlined; the word or words that they modify are in bold.

She would <u>never</u> **rest** until she had ferreted out the whys and
       ADVERB VERB
wherefores.

<u>Very</u> **green** and **neat** and **precise** was that yard.
ADVERB ADJECTIVE   ADJECTIVE   ADJECTIVE

Oh, I know it <u>nearly</u> **all**.
          ADVERB   DETERMINER

Below them was a pond, looking <u>almost</u> **like** a river, so long and
           ADVERB   PREPOSITION
winding was it.

Mrs Rachel Lynde lived <u>just</u> **where** the Avonlea main road
         ADVERB CONJUNCTION
dipped down into a little hollow.

Here sat Marilla Cuthbert, <u>always</u> **slightly** distrustful of sunshine.
            ADVERB   ADVERB

<u>Accordingly</u>, **after tea Mrs Rachel set out**.
 ADVERB   SENTENCE

(LM Montgomery, *Anne of Avonlea.*)

Subclasses of adverbs

There are three subclasses of adverbs.

ADVERB
1 COMMON ADVERB: We walked **slowly**.
2 INTERROGATIVE ADVERB: **How** do you do?
3 CONJUNCTIVE ADVERB: I think, **therefore** I am. (René Descartes.)

1 **Common adverbs** (underlined) tell you where, when, how or to what extent something occurs. Some grammars subdivide common adverbs into adverbs of "place", "time", "manner", "extent", "frequency" and so on.

All of the underlined words below are common adverbs.

The blooms are here today but, sadly, often gone quite quickly
          PLACE TIME   MANNER FREQUENCY   EXTENT MANNER

by tomorrow.
    TIME

2   **Interrogative adverbs** ask questions about the where, when, how (and so on) of an occurrence. The replies to questions headed by interrogative adverbs are common adverbs, or strings of words that do the same job as common adverbs—phrases or clauses (discussed in sections 5.13–14 below).

QUESTIONS WITH INTERROGATIVE ADVERBS	ANSWERS WITH ADVERBS, ADVERB PHRASES OR ADVERB CLAUSES
Where are you? INT ADV	*I am here.* ADVERB
When did you begin? INT ADV	*I began some time ago.* ADVERB PHRASE
Why do you call it sad? INT ADV	*I call it sad because it makes me feel sad.* ADVERB CLAUSE
How are you getting along? INT ADV	*I am getting along well.* ADVERB

(Lewis Carroll, *Alice's Adventures in Wonderland.*)

3   **Conjunctive adverbs** function partly as adverbs, partly as conjunctions. They are also called "transition words". We have met them before, in the chapter on punctuation. See chapter 3.3 (item 16) and 3.4 (item 2).

There are fewer than a dozen of these words. The main ones are:

however	furthermore	otherwise
nevertheless	moreover	therefore

- The conjunctive function of these words is that they link the sentences in which they occur with the sentences before.
- The adverbial function of these words is that they modify the sentences in which they occur—somewhat like adjuncts. (For "adjuncts", see chapters 2.6 and 3.3.)

> If he wanted the money he wanted it, and it was nobody's business to ask why. He therefore made his demand with the awkwardness of a proud man.
>
> She laughed with him, as if she liked his audacity. Nevertheless he sat still a moment, straining his eyes down the long hill.
> (Edith Wharton, *Ethan Frome.*)

Each of the words *therefore* and *nevertheless* in the examples above has the two roles mentioned in the dot points above. It is because of this dual role—part conjunction, part adverb—that these words are called "conjunctive adverbs".

5.11   Interjections

How to identify interjections

a   **Definition**

Interjections are a ragbag collection of words that express—

- emotions: alas, boo, bravo, hallelujah, oh dear
- social greetings: hello, sorry, bye-bye, good morning
- work or sports calls: timber, objection, checkmate, goal
- animal sounds: bow-wow, miaow, purr, tweet-tweet
- oaths or blasphemies: jeez, blast, damn, gosh, hell
- assent or dissent: yes, no, sure, aye, nay, okay, nope

Often, an interjection is followed by an exclamation mark (!).

b   **Sentence frame**

An interjection is any word—other than a name ("Kerrie") or a command ("Stop!")—that fits into the frame below and that can constitute a sentence on its own. The last example in square brackets below is an interjection group (or "a compound interjection").

_____!   [Whoopee, Check, Gosh, Blast, Good evening]
INTERJECTION

c   **Suffixes**

Interjections do not have suffixes. But many interjections double as members of other word classes. *Morning*, for example, can be a noun (with a plural *–s* in *mornings*); but in the context of a greeting (*Good morning*) it becomes part of an interjection group and takes no suffix.

d   Examples

The interjections in the text below are in blue.

> DAUGHTER: Well, haven't you got a cab?
> FREDDY: There's not one to be had for love or money.
> MOTHER: Oh, Freddy, there must be one. You can't have tried.
> FREDDY: Sorry.
>
> (George Bernard Shaw, *Pygmalion.*)

It is a leading feature of interjections that they can double as words of different word classes.

Hand me the sugar, please.
                    INTERJECTION

I'll do that just to please you.
                    VERB

Congratulations on your win.
        INTERJECTION

I appreciate your congratulations.
                        NOUN

5.12   Words and suffixes

Suffixes often change members of one word class into members of another word class. We have already seen this above, with an adjective changing into an adverb through the addition of the suffix *–ly* (*brave—bravely*). This process is called "word formation". Below is a sampling of suffixes that contribute to word formation.

VERB	ADJECTIVE	ADJECTIVE	NOUN	VERB	NOUN
read	*readable*	*wise*	*wisdom*	*develop*	*development*
extend	*extensive*	*happy*	*happiness*	*solve*	*solution*

ADJECTIVE	ADVERB	ADJECTIVE	VERB	NOUN	ADJECTIVE
quick	*quickly*	*bright*	*brighten*	*friend*	*friendly*
slow	*slowly*	*short*	*shorten*	*beauty*	*beautiful*

NOUN	VERB	NOUN	NOUN	ADJECTIVE	ADJECTIVE
glory	*glorify*	*history*	*historian*	*historic*	*historical*
theory	*theorize*	*material*	*materialism*	*young*	*youngish*

What can you do with this, and with other affixes of this type?

179

You can rewrite anything you have written in such a way as to change words of one class into words of another class. Want more verbs? More adjectives? Fewer nouns? Just convert the class of some of the words in your text into words of other classes through the use of affixes. In the example below, the original text is in the bottom section of the box.

As adults, folks born small are less likely to be <u>managers</u> or <u>professionals</u>
                                                    NOUN   NOUN

in their jobs. Their average <u>earnings</u> are about 10% less those whose <u>weight</u>
                              NOUN   NOUN

was more at birth. On the positive side, the once tiny tots <u>reportedly</u> have
                                                             ADVERB

just as much <u>satisfaction</u> with their adult lives as those who were born big
              NOUN

babies.

- -

As adults, folks born small are less likely to hold <u>managerial</u> or <u>professional</u> jobs.
                                                     ADJECTIVE   ADJECTIVE

On average, they <u>earn</u> about 10% less than those who <u>weighed</u> more at birth.
                  VERB   VERB

On the positive side, the once tiny tots <u>report</u> that they are just as <u>satisfied</u>
                                          VERB   ADJECTIVE

with their adult lives as those who were born big babies.

(Janice M Horowitz, TIME, 14 February 2000.)

It's like playing the same song in different keys.

5.13 Phrases

In this chapter so far, we have been dealing with the grammar of words and of affixes. This part of grammar is called "morphology" (from the Greek for "knowledge of form"). We now turn to the grammar of strings of words: phrases, clauses and sentences. This is called "syntax" (from the Greek for "arranging together").

In this section, we deal with phrases. In the next two (5.14 and 5.15), with clauses and sentences.

What are phrases?

Think of a sentence as a set of modules fitted together into a whole—something like a chain of Leggo blocks. Each module in the sentence is a phrase.

[Good old Jack] [went up the hill rather quickly with his pail].
   NOUN PHRASE   VERB PHRASE

The sentence divides naturally into two:

- a noun phrase (or "subject"):   [Good old Jack]
- a verb phrase (or "predicate"):   [went up the hill rather quickly with his pail].

The head word (the most important word) in the noun phrase is the noun *Jack*; the head word in the verb phrase is the verb *went*. That's why they are called "noun phrase" and "verb phrase".

Nesting within each of the two phrases above are other phrases. What we call them depends on their head words (underlined).

[(Good old)   (Jack)]   [(went)   (up the hill)   (rather quickly)   (with his pail)].
ADJ PHRASE   NOUN PHRASE   VERB PHRASE   PREP PHRASE   ADV PHRASE   PREP PHRASE

NOUN PHRASE (OR "SUBJECT")   VERB PHRASE (OR "PREDICATE")

SENTENCE

So, within the overall noun phrase (*Good old Jack*) we have nesting:

- an adjective phrase (*good old*) headed by the adjectives *good* and *old*
- a noun phrase (*Jack*) headed by the noun *Jack*.

Within the overall verb phrase (*went up the hill rather quickly with his pail*) we have nesting:

- a verb phrase (*went*) headed by the verb *went*
- a preposition phrase (*up the hill*) headed by the preposition *up*
- an adverb phrase (*rather quickly*) headed by the adverb *quickly*
- another preposition phrase (*with his pail*) headed by the preposition *with*.

From the above you can see that a phrase may consist of a single word, or it may consist of a string of words. The essential feature of a phrase (in modern grammar) is that it fits, module-like, into a sentence.

This modular approach to sentences, and to the phrases that make them up, gives us two insights into sentence structure.

a   One is that we can easily take out any phrase (any module) and replace it with another of the same kind. So, for example, we can remove the whole of the noun phrase *Good old Jack* and replace it with another noun phrase, without impairing the essential structure of the sentence.

NOUN PHRASE

[*Good old Jack*]
[*He*   ]
[*My best friend*]   *went up the hill with his pail rather quickly.*
[*That person*   ]
[*Any noun phrase*]

We can also change the verb phrase *went* into:

- *scrambled,*
- *gleefully clambered,*
- any other verb phrase.

b   The other insight is that we can disassemble the phrase modules and put them back together in different sequences. The noun phrase (in blue) will always stay the noun phrase however you reassemble the sentence. In the example below I focus on the various positions that the noun phrase *Good old Jack* can take in a sentence. In all of these positions it remains a noun phrase. The other phrases also remain what they are, no matter where they appear in the sentence.

Good old Jack went up the hill with his pail rather quickly.
Up the hill, rather quickly, went good old Jack with his pail.
Up the hill, rather quickly, with his pail went good old Jack.
With his pail, good old Jack went up the hill rather quickly.
Rather quickly, good old Jack, with his pail, went up the hill.

Subclasses of phrases

There are five kinds of phrases (underlined), each with a headword (in bold) of the same type as the phrase—for example, a noun phrase is headed by a noun.

1   A **noun phrase** is headed by a noun.

> <u>My **neighbour** [NOUN] in the house to the left</u> is a good friend.
> NOUN PHRASE

2   An **adjective phrase** is headed by an adjective.

> That cake is <u>**good** [ADJECTIVE] to eat</u>.
> ADJECTIVE PHRASE

3   A **verb phrase** is headed by a verb.

> They <u>**liked** [VERB] your present very much</u>.
> VERB PHRASE

4   An **adverb phrase** is headed by an adverb.

> They came <u>too **late** [ADVERB] to do any good</u>.
> ADVERB PHRASE

5   A **preposition phrase** is headed by a preposition.

> The lamp swung <u>**above** [PREPOSITION] the table</u>.
> PREPOSITION PHRASE

5.14 Clauses

What is a clause?

A finite clause (often just called "a clause") is a coherent group of words consisting of a subject (expressed by a noun phrase) and a predicate (expressed by a verb phrase), with the predicate featuring a finite verb (bold). (For "finite verb" see section 5.7.) In the example below, the boundary between clauses is marked by a slash.

> *We **came** home* / *and they **greeted** us.*
> SUBJECT PREDICATE   SUBJECT PREDICATE
>   CLAUSE 1   /   CLAUSE 2

In the example sentence above, each clause has an explicit subject (*we* and *they*). But the subject can also be implicit.

$$\underline{We} \quad \underline{\textbf{came}\ home} \ /\ and \quad \cancel{we} \quad \underline{\textbf{had}\ a\ shower}.$$

SUBJECT   PREDICATE   SUBJECT   PREDICATE

      CLAUSE 1   /   CLAUSE 2

Subclasses of clauses

There are three subclasses of clauses, one of them having three subdivisions. The slashes mark the clause boundaries, and the finite verbs are in bold. The featured clauses are underlined.

CLAUSE
- **1** MAIN: I **saw** a book.
- **2** COORDINATE: I **saw** a book / and I **opened** it.
- **3** SUBORDINATE
  - **a** ADJECTIVE: I **saw** a book / that **was** pretty valuable.
  - **b** ADVERB: I **saw** a book / when I **looked** at the shelf.
  - **c** NOUN: I **saw** / what **was** on the shelf.

1   A **main clause** is one that can, in all instances but one (see 3c below), stand alone as an independent sentence. (Other names that grammarians use for main clause are "independent clause", "superordinate clause" or "matrix clause".)

2   A **coordinate clause** is one that is headed by a coordinating conjunction. The sign of a coordinate clause is that, if it has the same subject as the main clause, you can choose to omit the subject in the coordinate clause.

I saw a book / and I opened it. OR: I saw a book / and opened it.

MAIN CLAUSE   COORDINATE CLAUSE   MAIN CLAUSE   COORDINATE CLAUSE

Some typical coordinating conjunctions are:

and	either	neither	either … or	so	still
but	or	nor	neither … nor	yet	than

not only … but also   as well as.

3 A **subordinate clause** is one that relates to another clause in any one of the roles of (a) adjective, (b) adverb or (c) noun. We look at these three subtypes of subordinate clause below.

a A subordinate **adjective clause** is one that is headed by an adjectival conjunction. An adjective clause modifies a noun or a pronoun in its companion clause—in the example below, the noun *book*.

The sign of an adjective clause is that you can always substitute for it the phrase *of a certain kind*, leaving the structure and at least part of the meaning of the sentence intact.

I saw a book / that was pretty valuable.
    MAIN CLAUSE   ADJECTIVE CLAUSE

OR:

I saw a book of a certain kind.
    MAIN CLAUSE   SUBSTITUTE

Some typical adjectival conjunctions are:

who   whom   whose   which   that   when   where.

b A subordinate **adverb clause** is one that is headed by an adverbial conjunction. An adverb clause modifies a verb in its companion clause—in the example below, the verb *saw*.

The sign of an adverb clause is that it can always change position with its companion clause.

I saw a book / when I looked at the shelf.
    MAIN CLAUSE   ADVERB CLAUSE

OR:

When I looked at the shelf / I saw a book.
      ADVERB CLAUSE   MAIN CLAUSE

Some typical adverbial conjunctions are:

after   if   because   when   until   whenever   although
before   as   unless   while   since   wherever   though.

c A subordinate **noun clause** is one that is headed by a nominal conjunction. A noun clause functions as a noun relating to its companion clause—in the example below, as the object (the done-to) of the verb *saw*.

The sign of a noun clause is that you can always substitute for it the pronoun *something* (or *someone*), leaving the structure of the sentence intact.

I saw / *what was on the shelf.* OR: *I saw* / *something.*
MAIN CLAUSE   NOUN CLAUSE   MAIN CLAUSE   SUBSTITUTE

Some typical nominal conjunctions are:

whoever	who	which	when	how	why
whatever	whom	that	where	what	whether.

There is an intimate relationship between conjunctions and clauses:

- coordinate clauses start with coordinating conjunctions

- subordinate clauses start with subordinating conjunctions—

     a   adjective clauses start with adjectival conjunctions
     b   adverb clauses start with adverbial conjunctions
     c   noun clauses start with nominal conjunctions.

A second description of clauses

The topic of clauses and their subclasses is a difficult one. So here is another way of looking at the matter.

CLAUSE

1 MAIN: I saw a book.

2 COORDINATE: I saw a book / and I opened it.

3 SUBORDINATE
     a ADJECTIVE: I saw a book / that was pretty valuable.
     b ADVERB: I saw a book / when I looked at the shelf.
     c NOUN: I saw / what was on the shelf.

1   **Main clause**—an independent or a potentially independent sentence.

Any clause that constitutes (or that could constitute) an independent sentence is a main clause.

Grammar is very interesting.
> MAIN CLAUSE

2 **Coordinate clause**—the clausal expansion of a coordinate word.

I spoke to Jack and Jill.
> WORD

The underlined word is coordinate with (of equal grammatical status to) *Jack*. If we expand *Jill* into a clause, we have a coordinate clause.

I spoke to Jack and I spoke to Jill.
> MAIN CLAUSE   COORDINATE CLAUSE

3 **a** Subordinate **adjective clause**—the clausal expansion of an adjective.

I rewarded conscientious Kim.
> ADJECTIVE

The underlined adjective modifies the noun *Kim*. If we expand the adjective into a clause, we have an adjective clause: a clause that does the same job as *conscientious*.

I rewarded Kim, who is conscientious.
> MAIN CLAUSE   ADJECTIVE CLAUSE

b Subordinate **adverb clause**—the clausal expansion of an adverb.

We arrived home late.
> ADVERB

The underlined adverb modifies the verb *arrived*. If we expand the adverb into a clause, we have an adverb clause: a clause that does the same job as *late*.

We arrived home when it was late.
> MAIN CLAUSE   ADVERB CLAUSE

c Subordinate **noun clause**—the clausal expansion of a noun or a pronoun.

Anybody can borrow my books.
> PRONOUN

The underlined pronoun is the subject of the verb group *can borrow*. If we expand the underlined pronoun into a clause, we have a noun clause: a clause that does the same job as *anybody*.

Whoever likes can borrow my books.
    NOUN CLAUSE   MAIN CLAUSE

What's the point of it all?

Once we have mastered the notions of word, phrase and clause, we can play with language as an organist plays an organ. We can realize a concept as a single note: a word—

I like good food.
    ADJECTIVE

or we can expand it into a chord: a phrase—

I like food good to the taste.
    ADJECTIVE PHRASE

or we can pull out all the stops and give it the full treatment: a clause—

I like food that is good to the taste.
    ADJECTIVE CLAUSE

5.15 Sentences

What is a sentence?

A sentence is a coherent and, in context, a fully independent syntactic unit of language. In speech, a sentence is distinguished by a characteristic intonation pattern (or tune). In writing, a sentence is marked with a capital letter at its beginning and with an end stop (a full stop or a question mark or an exclamation mark) at its end.

A sentence can consist of a single word or of many words; a single clause or of many clauses—as long as it meets the criteria stated above. In the example text below, each sentence ends with an end stop, and slashes mark the clause boundaries. The finite verbs are in bold.

LIZA:	**Will** you drop me altogether / now that the experiment **is** over, Colonel Pickering?	
PICKERING:	Oh, **don't**. You **mustn't** think of it as an experiment. It **shocks** me, somehow.	
LIZA:	Oh, I **am** only a squashed cabbage leaf.	
PICKERING:	No.	
LIZA:	I **owe** so much to you / that I **should** be very unhappy / if you **forgot** me.	
PICKERING:	It **is** very kind of you to say so, Miss Doolittle.	

(George Bernard Shaw, *Pygmalion.*)

Subclasses of sentences

There are three classes of sentence, one of them with three subclasses. The class that a sentence belongs to depends on the number and kind of clauses that it consists of. In the examples below, slashes mark the clause boundaries, and the finite verbs, including compound ones, are in bold.

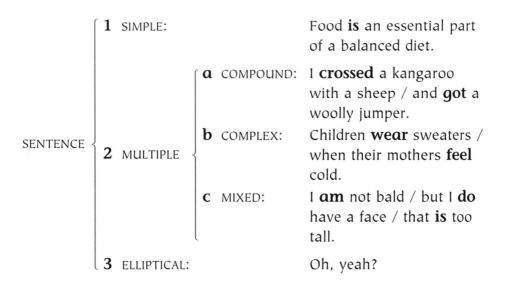

	1 SIMPLE:	Food **is** an essential part of a balanced diet.
	a COMPOUND:	I **crossed** a kangaroo with a sheep / and **got** a woolly jumper.
SENTENCE	**2** MULTIPLE — **b** COMPLEX:	Children **wear** sweaters / when their mothers **feel** cold.
	c MIXED:	I **am** not bald / but I **do** have a face / that **is** too tall.
	3 ELLIPTICAL:	Oh, yeah?

1 A **simple sentence** consists of a single (a main) clause.

*Careful drivers **watch** the car behind the car in front of them.*
MAIN CLAUSE

2   A **multiple sentence** (also called "a clause complex") consists of more than one clause. There are three subclasses of multiple sentences.

a   A **compound sentence** consists of a main clause plus one or more coordinate clauses.

*The fortune-tellers **held** their annual general meeting* /
MAIN CLAUSE

*and **read** the minutes of next year's meeting.*
COORDINATE CLAUSE

b   A **complex sentence** consists of a main clause plus one or more subordinate clauses.

*I **am** changing to a new dentist* /
MAIN CLAUSE

*because the old one **is** getting on my nerves.*
SUBORDINATE (ADVERB) CLAUSE

c   A **mixed sentence** (also called "a compound-complex sentence") consists of a main clause plus one or more coordinate clauses plus one or more subordinate clauses.

*I **do** not care to speak ill of any man* / *but I **believe*** /
MAIN CLAUSE   COORDINATE CLAUSE

*that gentleman **is** an attorney. (Samuel Johnson.)*
SUBORDINATE (NOUN) CLAUSE

3   An **elliptical sentence** is an incomplete sentence: one that has one or more essential elements understood but not explicitly stated—as in the last sentence in the text below.

*I **had** a parrot once* / *that **laid** square eggs.*   MULTIPLE SENTENCE
MAIN CLAUSE   SUBORDINATE (ADJECTIVE) CLAUSE

*ature***Did** it speak?*   SIMPLE SENTENCE
MAIN CLAUSE

*Sometimes—"Ouch!" [It sometimes **said** "Ouch!"]*   ELLIPTICAL SENTENCE
ELLIPTICAL CLAUSE

Essay writing: articles and short stories

Most of us find that writing is full of starts and stops, punctuated by pauses for reflection.

(John Harris, *Introduction to Writing.*)

6

Essay writing: articles and short stories

6.1 Genres of essays

In this chapter we consider the art of writing short prose pieces of, say, 500 to 2,500 words. If such prose pieces are nonfiction, they are usually called "articles" or "essays"; if fiction, "narratives" or "short stories". We can subsume all of these names under the single generic term "essay". *The Oxford English Dictionary* defines "essay" as "a composition of moderate length on any particular subject ..."

The word derives from the French *essai*, "attempt", and it was first used in the above meaning by the sixteenth-century French writer Michel de Montaigne for any piece of prose in which the writer attempts to express personal thoughts, feelings or experiences.

Nowadays, the term "essay" often refers to a written assignment that educators give their students in school or at university. Essays are a means both of training one's skills in language and of organizing one's thoughts. Essays also allow educators to assess their students' skills in these areas.

But the art of essay writing exists beyond the walls of educational institutions. The mass media abound in essays, sometimes so-called, and sometimes going under the names of "feature articles" or "opinion pieces". In this chapter, we look at essay writing in the broad sense, whether it is for school or university assignments or for articles in newspapers or magazines.

In this chapter we consider seven genres, or kinds, of essays or articles.

a Discussion essay or article—looking at the pros and cons of an issue.
b Explanation essay or article—how things work.
c Instruction essay or article—how to do something.
d Report essay or article—factual information on a topic.

e   Recount essay or article—a retelling of a personal experience.

f   Book review—what the writer thinks of a book.

g   Narrative essay or short story.

There are four features that essays have in common across the range of genres. The features are:

1   overall structure
2   paragraph structures
3   cohesive devices
4   language.

First, a general review of point 1 above.

6.2 Overall structure

Essays—like life, like sausages—have a beginning, a middle and an end. For the various genres of essay that we discuss in this chapter these parts have different names.

	BEGINNING	MIDDLE	END
DISCUSSION:	orientation	argument	conclusion
EXPLANATION:	orientation	phenomenon	explanation
INSTRUCTION:	orientation	materials	instruction
REPORT:	orientation	procedure	outcome
RECOUNT:	orientation	events	sequel
BOOK REVIEW:	orientation	description	evaluation
NARRATIVE:	orientation	complication	resolution

Next, we look at all four features—overall structure, paragraph structures, cohesive devices, language—through a sample essay in one genre. Then, in less detail, we look at a sample of each of the other genres. All of the sample essays that follow are miniatures.

6.3   Features of a discussion essay or article

1   A discussion essay, also called "an argument essay", looks at two or more sides of an issue.

In the sample essay below, the texts in square brackets are my comments—not subheadings.

Essay A: Living in Canberra

[Orientation: I introduce the reader to the topic of the essay.]

I've roamed in every continent—except the polar ones—and lived in three. By choice, I've made my present home in Australia. And here, among all the localities in all the states and territories (and I've been to them all) I've made my present home in Canberra.

[Argument: one paragraph discusses the pros of Canberra; another, the cons.]

The place may seem dull to outsiders, but it does have its excitements. There is the excitement of frost on a winter's morning, the view of the hills from my kitchen window, and the splash of colours from a million trees. Who needs the excitement of King's Cross? But Canberra isn't all sweetness and beauty.

The roads do go round and round a bit much, and the city buildings do go up and up a bit much. Some things even go down: for instance, the population in the summer months, when the number of people in Canberra dwindles and, as if by magic, the number in the south coast resorts goes up by the same proportion.

[Conclusion: I reach a conclusion on the balance of the above argument.]

All in all, though, this is as good a place to live in as any in the world— and better than most. Anyway, I guess it is. But I won't know for sure until I've paid at least one visit to the south pole.

(Author's text.)

---

2   Comments on the overall structure of essay A

Essay A begins with an orientation. I set the scene outside Canberra but end the first paragraph in Canberra. It is often advisable not to leap straight into the essay topic but to lead into it. There are several ways of doing this.

- With a question: *Do real people actually live in Canberra?*

- From the outside: *I've roamed in every continent—except the polar ones—and lived in three.*

- With a quotation: *"Canberra is a city without a soul," said Prince Phillip when he visited the place.*

- With something catchy or provocative: *Plastic palace might be a good way to describe Canberra.*

- With a characteristic instance: *I was in the city at 6.00 pm one evening, and the place was deserted.*

- With a definition: *Canberra is the capital of Australia. It lies inland, between the coastal cities of Melbourne and Sydney.*

The middle is an argument of the pros and cons. This is essential to all discussion essays: an attempt to present two (maybe more) sides of a picture. In essay A, I do this by devoting the second paragraph to the advantages of living in Canberra; the third paragraph to the disadvantages. The technical name for such an argument is "a dialectic".

Another way of achieving a dialectic is to look critically at what others have said on a topic before you present your own, fresh views on the topic. This is often the method in scientific writing. Without some sort of dialectic, a non-narrative essay is tedious and one-sided—little more than propaganda.

The end reaches a conclusion on the balance of the pro and con arguments. In the case of essay A, the conclusion is that I like living in Canberra.

The "echo effect" (or "coming full circle"). A good way to give your essay unity is to echo at the end something that you have mentioned at the beginning. I started essay A with: "I've roamed in every continent—except the polar ones ·..." I end the essay with "I won't know for sure until I've paid at least one visit to the south pole." This gives the reader a feeling of: "Ah, I'm back where I started. This must be the end of the essay."

3 Paragraph structures

Beginning, middle and end paragraphs have different structures.

The beginning paragraph starts with a lead-in and ends with a thesis sentence:

- the lead-in sets the scene for the discussion
- the thesis sentence tells the reader what the essay is all about.

The first paragraph of essay A illustrates the structure of a beginning paragraph.

A dialectical paragraph usually begins with a topic sentence and continues with an elaboration of the topic:

- a topic sentence is one that sets the topic for that paragraph
- elaboration sentences expand on the topic sentence—with details and supporting arguments.

The two middle paragraphs of essay A illustrate the structure of a dialectical paragraph. Just for a change, though, one can get out of the routine and put the topic sentence at the end of the paragraph. So, for example, I could rewrite paragraph 3 of essay A as follows (with the topic sentence in bold).

> But the roads do go round and round a bit much, and the city buildings do go up and up a bit much. Some things even go down: for instance, the population in the summer months, when the number of people in Canberra dwindles and, as if by magic, the number in the south coast resorts goes up by the same proportion. **You could think of these as the disadvantages of Canberra.**

The end paragraph finishes with a conclusion and features a lead-out:

- the conclusion is usually in the first sentence
- the lead-out is in the last sentence.

The last paragraph of essay A illustrates this. The lead-out takes the reader beyond Canberra again.

4 Cohesive devices

The paragraphs of an essay can't just be strung out like disconnected railway carriages along a track. They need cohesive—linking—devices that make them pull together. Cohesion between paragraphs takes either of two forms: anaphoric or cataphoric.

- **An anaphor** is a cohesive device in which a reference in a later paragraph refers backward—and therefore links it—to something in an earlier paragraph. In essay A, the second paragraph begins with the words "The place ..." Which place? Obviously, the place mentioned at the end of the previous paragraph. Similarly, the last paragraph begins with the words: "All in all, though, ..." To make sense of these words, we have to refer back to the previous paragraph or paragraphs. Because of this anaphoric pointing back at the beginning of paragraphs 2 and 4, it is obvious that the essay could not have begun at these points.

  Some typical anaphors at the beginning of paragraphs that you will find (and can use) are expressions such as: "Consequently ...", "As we have seen ...", "Another point ..." and the like.

- **A cataphor** is a cohesive device in which a reference at the end of an earlier paragraph refers forward—and therefore links it—to something in a later paragraph. In essay A, the second paragraph ends with the words: "But Canberra isn't all sweetness and beauty." This leads the reader to expect a continuation about the disadvantages of living in Canberra. Because of this cataphoric pointing forward at the end of paragraph 2, it is obvious that the essay cannot end at this point.

  Some typical cataphors at the end of paragraphs that you will find (and can use) are expressions such as: "We now turn to ...", "But that is not all ...", "There are additional factors ..." and the like.

  For most (but not all) paragraphs an anaphoric or a cataphoric cohesive device is desirable.

5 Language

If your essay isn't a pleasure to read, nobody will bother to read it—unless they have to as an assignment or for work. Even then, the reader deserves something better than murky prose. Chapter 1 of this book has a ten-point programme on style. You might like to check the extent to which essay A conforms to the programme.

1   Are the sentences, on average, short?
2   Do the sentence structures vary?

3   Is the language unforced and unadorned?

4   Is the language appropriate for a normal reader?

5   Does the use of capitals reflect modern usage?

6   Does the essay contain first and second person pronouns?

7   Is the text free of passives?

8   Is it reader- and writer-friendly?

9   Does the essay communicate its intended message?

10   Does it sound as though I am writing in my natural voice?

The more yes answers there are to these questions, the better the style.

6.4   Features of an explanation essay or article

An explanation essay tells you how things work. Like other kinds of essays, explanation essays also have a beginning-middle-end structure. The texts in square brackets are my comments—not subheadings.

Essay B: Plugging the hot stuff

[Orientation: the writer establishes the topic—an invention—in a light-hearted tone.]

A lot of inventors obviously get inspiration at bathtime.

[Phenomenon: now we learn what invention the writer is explaining.]

David Newton of Preston has patented a temperature-sensitive plug that empties a bath if the water gets dangerously hot.

[Explanation: how the invention works.]

The plug is made from two halves, with a spiral spring that tries to push them apart. When the plug is cold, a bimetallic latch of aluminium and nickel holds the plug together. But when the water passes a threshold temperature, the latch trips to pop the plug open.

[A second phenomenon and a second explanation.]

And Ronald Harris and Jenny Elphik of Hampshire want to stop baths overflowing. They simply attach the plug to a short chain and air-filled sphere. If the bath gets too full, the chain tightens and pulls the plug out.

(Barry Fox, *New Scientist*, 5 September 1998.)

Comments on essay B

1   Overall structure

A unifying theme—baths—predominates from the first paragraph to the last.

2   Paragraph structures

The paragraphs do not feature topic sentences followed by elaborations. Instead, they get their unity and structure from the progression of the sentences.

3   Cohesive devices

The first paragraph features a cataphor: "A lot of inventors obviously get inspiration at bathtime." The word "obviously" tells me that the writer is going to illustrate the point in what follows. The last two paragraphs of the essay both feature anaphoric cohesives.

4   Language

The essay is in a clear and unfussy prose style, just right for an explanation. As is the case with many essays in this genre, the text is mainly in the present tense.

6.5   Features of an instruction essay or article

An instruction essay tells you how to do or make something. At the least, it should enable the reader to follow the instruction successfully. But, in addition, you can also make it interesting to read. The texts in square brackets are my comments—not subheadings.

Essay C: Making Bedouin bread

[Orientation: a bit of exotic colour and then, in the second paragraph, the thesis sentence.]

The Bedouin of the Sinai Desert dispense with plates. This not only saves them washing dishes in a region where water is scarce; it also leaves them with less to tote along on their nomadic journeys. Instead of plates, the Bedouin make a thin round flat bread. On top of this bread go meat, rice, cheese or whatever it is that they are eating. And this food is rolled up or folded in the bread and eaten along with the bread.

Bedouin bread is very easy to make and—hot and fresh and dripping with butter—makes one of the most appetizing breakfasts or snacks imaginable. Try it for weekend breakfast: the usual desiccated breakfast cereal will never taste the same again.

[Materials: what ingredients and equipment the aspiring bread-maker will need.]

To feed four healthy appetites you will need:

> 30 grams fresh or dried yeast
> 1 teaspoon sugar
> 2 teaspoons salt
> $4^1/_2$ cups plain flour.

You will also need a preheated frying pan—hot, not warm. If you want to do it Bedouin style, try a metal plate on legs over a wood fire. You will also need a wooden board to roll the dough on.

[Instruction: a step-by-step instruction on how to make the bread.]

In a large bowl, mix the sugar and yeast with two tablespoons of warm water. Mix in another two cups of warm water and the salt.

Then, gradually and while stirring, add $4^1/_2$ cups of plain flour. Knead and then divide the dough into eight balls. Roll each ball out thinly, on a heavily floured board, to the size of the frying pan.

Place in a preheated and ungreased frying pan and bake without a lid for four to five minutes on each side.

[A second set of materials and instructions added as a bonus.]

If you want to wash the bread down with Bedouin-style tea, boil up four cups of water in a billy with a sprig of mint. Add tea and sugar, and simmer for a few minutes.

Then enjoy.

(Deborah Stern, *The Canberra Times*, 10 July 1978.)

Comments on essay C

1   Overall structure

The author chooses to start, not by leaping straight into the topic, but by leading in with a catchy preliminary. Likewise, she doesn't close with the end of the recipes but leads out with some reader-friendly words.

2 Paragraph structures

The instruction paragraphs are minimalist: the reader can just prop the piece up on a kitchen shelf and follow the recipe.

3 Cohesive devices

Below, the anaphoric cohesives from the opening words of several paragraphs in the above text are in blue.

You will *also* need a preheated frying pan …
In a large bowl, mix *the sugar* and yeast …
Then, gradually and while stirring …
Place in the preheated and ungreased frying pan …
If you want to wash *the bread* down with Bedouin-style tea …
Then enjoy.

What makes these words anaphoric? The fact that they refer back to something previously mentioned. It would be strange for the piece to have started with a sentence featuring the words in blue.

4 Language

In essay C (as in many instruction essays) the instruction features verbs in the command mode (called the "imperative"). Often in an instruction essay (but not in essay C above), the writer numbers the steps of the instruction.

6.6 Features of a report essay or article

A report essay is one that contains factual information on a topic: any topic that has to do with the physical or social environment—animal species, astronomical bodies, ideas, religion, whatever. A report explains the nature of things but, unlike an explanation, doesn't have to tell the reader how things work. At the least, the writers of report essays need to give factual information on a topic, but they should also try to make the topic generally appealing and relevant to their readers.

Following is an article on the game of chess. The texts in square brackets are my comments—not subheadings.

Essay D: The game of chess

Chess and its history

[Orientation: I introduce the reader to the nature and history of the game.]

Chess is an enjoyable and exciting game. Exciting, because it involves a mental struggle between the players. Enjoyable, because it is full of interesting twists and turns that make each game different from the last.

Nobody knows for sure where or when chess originated. The best guess, according to most scholars, is that it all started as a war game in India. The chess pieces represent the battle order of a sixth-century Indian army—foot soldiers (called pawns), chariots (rooks), cavalry (knights) and elephants (bishops). To these pieces are added a king and a queen. The diagram shows the starting position of a game of chess.

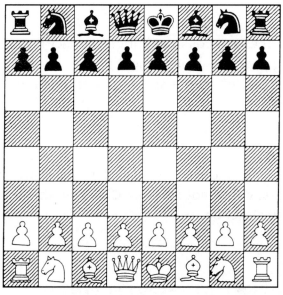

The starting position in a game of chess

The aim of the game

[Procedure: facts and information about the game.]

Each kind of piece has a different kind of move on the chess board. The two contestants, white and black, take turns at moving their pieces. The pieces can threaten and capture the opponent's pieces. The game continues until one side or the other mounts an unstoppable threat against the opponent's king. Such a threat is called "mate", and the side that delivers mate has won. The game can also end in a draw. This occurs, for example, when neither side can mate the other or when the players agree to a draw.

Comments on essay D

1   Overall structure

The essay contains enough information, historical and technical, to tell the readers whether the game is for them. There is an echo effect, from "enjoyable and exciting" in the first paragraph to "excitement and enjoyment" in the last. For a report essay, a diagram or an illustration can be useful. So can subheadings, which act as signposts for the reader.

2   Paragraph structures

All the paragraphs but the last one start with topic sentences followed by elaboration sentences.

3   Cohesive devices

The second paragraph features a cataphor that leads the reader onwards. The next paragraph features an anaphor.

4   Language

As is usual for report essays, the present tense features prominently.

6.7   Features of a recount essay or article

A recount is the telling of a writer's personal experience. It can be confessional, inspirational, sad, funny—but it should have some point of interest for the reader.

The following recount is a 500-word excerpt from a 1,500-word feature article. The texts in square brackets are my comments—not subheadings.

Essay E: Casinos gratefully take your cash in Europe

[Orientation: from libertarianism in matters sexual to matters financial to casinos.]

It was Pièrre Trudeau, the former prime minister of Canada, who coined the fine libertarian slogan: "The state has no business in its citizens' bedrooms." The attitude in Western Europe seems to be that the state also has no business telling its citizens how to spend their money. And that is why citizens who have money burning a hole in their pockets can stroll into a casino and there, in friendly and comfortable surroundings, hand it over to the grateful management. The management, in turn, hands part of its takings over to an equally grateful government.

The aim of casinos is the same everywhere—to give customers the thrill and entertainment of gambling in return for their money. But the style in which this is carried out varies from place to place. On my jaunt through the Continent this year, I observed these variations in [two] cities.

[Events: what I experienced and observed.]

Monte Carlo has a truly palatial casino, housed in a Baroque-style building at the end of a sweeping driveway lined with palm trees. The building contains a whole complex of playing rooms as well as facilities for the performing arts. The rooms are plushly carpeted, and the walls covered with fine oil paintings and gilt reliefs. The croupiers wear formal attire with bow ties.

To this casino come the big spenders, not a few of them betting with big oblong chips worth the equivalent of $1,000 and $10,000 each. But the little spenders are welcome to leave their money behind too. And they do. Every time the little white ball is sent rolling round the roulette wheel for a new round, the little chips come pattering down on the table like rain.

I started play at 11.00 am with ten $5 chips. By 1.00 pm, after seven changes of fortune I was still in possession of my original hoard of chips and decided that this was a good point at which to quit.

In the Netherlands I visited a rather different kind of casino in the harbour town of Amsterdam. The casino resides in a single, small room behind an ordinary shop front. There is only one game offering in the casino—derby poker. Unlike other casino games, the players in derby poker do not compete against the house, but against each other. The house makes its profit by creaming five per cent off the top of every winning pot.

It took me about an hour to figure out that the bank waxes fat on this game at the players' expense and without the slightest risk to itself. So I quit when I was $100 down and still sinking.

[Sequel: what happened after the events recounted.]

The real gamblers would have stayed on to try to recoup their losses. However, having come only in the line of duty, as it were, to look at European casinos for the purpose of writing this article, I strolled out and set off to discover what other entertainments—not all of them government-controlled—Amsterdam had to offer.

(Author's text in *The Canberra Times*, 16 December 1979.)

Comments on essay E

1 Overall structure

The beginning of the first paragraph is way outside the topic of casinos but it quickly leads into the thesis of the essay as a whole. The end of the essay hints lightly at a connection with the beginning, but it is intriguingly ambiguous on the matter.

2 Paragraph structures

Most but not all of the paragraphs feature topic sentences—enough of them to give the readers an idea of what we are dealing with.

3 Cohesive devices

There are a few anaphors and cataphors in the essay. The main cohesion is a conceptual one: the readers know from the second paragraph that the essay deals with casinos in two cities, and the flow of the essay follows from that.

4 Language

A recount essay proceeds much like a short story—except that the events recounted are true. As with a fictional story, a recount follows a series of events to a culmination. There is plenty of scope in a recount essay for the use of the first person, though the writer should make the recount not just an ego trip, but something of wider interest.

6.8   Features of a book review

Writing a book review involves some responsibility. You owe it to the author not to big-note yourself by lightly dismissing something that the author has laboured long and hard to produce. At the same time, you owe it to the reader to give an honest appraisal of the work. You need to strike a fair balance: if the book is good, the reviewer should still point out any weaknesses in the work; if the book is bad, the reviewer should point out its redeeming features.

Writing a book review also involves some knowledge. The reviewer should be familiar with the genre of the book under review and be able to draw comparisons with works of a similar kind. In reviewing non-fiction books, the reviewer should have some expertise—at least some reading background—in the topic of the book. Often this will involve the reviewer in research.

What the readers of book reviews expect and deserve to find in reviews includes the following:

a   bibliographic details in the manner shown in the sample review below

b   setting the scene by saying what kind of book or what topic we are dealing with

c   something about the author and, if relevant, the background of the book

d   what genre the book is in—a novel, a play, a biography or the like—and a comparison with works in a similar genre

e   something about the content of the book and the quality with which the content is presented

f   sample ideas and, perhaps, quotations from the book to give the reader a feel for its style

g   a reasoned evaluation of the book and whether it is or is not worth reading.

Apart from that, you should make the review a pleasure to read by using some or all of the techniques I have dealt with in chapter 1 above.

The texts in square brackets are my comments—not subheadings.

Essay F: Advice on style for the taking—or not

Joe Glaser. *Understanding Style: Practical Ways to Improve Your Writing.*
Oxford: OUP, 1999. 244 pages, paperback. (No published price)

[Orientation: from the general (about style) to the particular (Glaser's book) in one short sentence.]

Style is a pretty wide subject and, to give Glaser his due, he covers a pretty wide range of the subject.

[Description: a concise outline of the contents of the book; some examples of the advice in the book; a critical appraisal of whether the advice is sound.]

The book is in eleven chapters, each with multiple sections. He covers not only good styles for various purposes, but also the avoidance of silly styles such as officialese, discriminatory writing, overwriting, underwriting, and more. There are also twelve rules of thumb for good writing—this constitutes the final chapter.

What are some of these rules?

One of them is: start most sentences with subjects. So, "We travelled interstate last week" rather than "Last week we travelled interstate."

Another is: write mostly in independent clauses. So, "We finished work. We then went home" rather than "When we finished work we went home."

Is this good advice?

I guess it is—but only if you are not much chop at sentence structures. Or, to take Glaser's advice: I guess it is. There is a condition. You are not much chop at sentence structures.

While I'm not too enamoured of the above two writing tips, there is still much that is useful in the book. There is, for example, a good little (three-page) section on figurative language. Glaser deals with personification, apostrophe, hyperbole, understatement, metonymy, synecdoche and paradox. Simile and metaphor also get passing mentions.

But excluded are alliteration, assonance, litotes, onomatopoeia, oxymoron, pun, personification. Another OUP publication (*The Oxford Companion to the English Language*, edited by Tom McArthur) deals with these and at least a dozen more.

Also useful in Glaser's book are the exercises, summaries, glossary and index.

> [Evaluation: damning with faint praise.]
>
> My evaluation? Useful, perhaps, for college and tertiary students or for teachers of the foregoing but—if Professor Glaser will forgive the cliché—try before you buy.
>
> (Author's text in The Australian National Review, February 1999.)

Comments on essay F

1   Overall structure

The above book review adheres to the structure: orientation, description, evaluation. Just for a change, though, you can get out of the routine and start the review with the evaluation.

So, I could have begun the above review as follows.

> [Evaluation: damning with faint praise.]
>
> Glaser's book might be useful for college and tertiary students or for teachers of the foregoing but—if Professor Glaser will forgive the cliché—try before you buy.

And the review would then end where the description leaves off: with the sentence, "Also useful in Glaser's book are the exercises, summaries, glossary and index."

Rules are made for learning and—once learned—for breaking in the interest of variety.

2   Paragraph structures

The last two paragraphs of the description have no topic sentences: more rule-breaking; more variety.

3   Cohesive devices

The opening paragraph ends with a cataphor; the others have anaphors. Another cohesive device that I use to keep the text flowing is a series of questions, to which the reader then anticipates answers.

"What are some of these rules?"
"Is this good advice?"
"My evaluation?"

4 Language

I am evaluating the book from my perspective and sharing it with you, the reader; so I have no hesitation in using first and second person pronouns—*I, you*.

6.9 Features of a narrative essay or short story

Narratives are story-telling texts. A narrative essay is built round a plot—an idea that is developed through the story—and involves such elements as dialogue, description, a sequence of events (not always in chronological order) and, especially, a climax. A narrative essay is perhaps the most difficult genre to control: it has to hold the reader's interest from beginning to end. The texts in square brackets are my comments—not subheadings.

Essay G: The driver who wanted to be a guru

[Orientation: I set the scene for the story.]

Once there was a wise man—I mean a really wise man. People from all over wanted to consult him on important and difficult questions. So he hired a car and a driver and set out on a tour of the towns and the villages of the region. Wherever he stopped, people turned out to honour him with a banquet. After the banquet, they would ask him their questions.

"Tell us, Master, what is the secret of life?"
"How do you remove stains from a synthetic carpet?"
"What can we do to save the world?"
"What is the square of two?"

And he would stroke his beard and listen carefully to the questions and answer them. All this while, his driver would be in the background, without anyone paying him the slightest attention.

[Complication: the characters have to get into a mess, or there would be no story.]

After they had already stopped at several towns, the driver said to the wise man, "Just for once, I'd like to get all the attention. So won't you please let me sit in the back seat of the car while you take the wheel?"

The wise man readily agreed to the driver's suggestion. He put on the driver's uniform, while the driver put on the wise man's clothes. And so they drove into the next town.

There, a big feast was waiting for the wise man. The driver ate it with great gusto and then he rose to field the people's questions.

The mayor got up and asked, "Could you tell us, Sir, please: what came first—the chicken or the egg?"

[Resolution: getting out of the mess, or some other finality, signals the end of the story.]

The driver stroked his chin for a moment, and then he beckoned to his companion to come up and join him. "What easy questions you people ask," said the guest of honour gesturing. "Look here: even my driver can answer that one!"

(Author's text.)

Comments on essay G

1   Overall structure

Some features of non-narrative essays do not apply. Topic sentences, for example, don't necessarily come into narratives—though they can feature in the descriptive paragraphs of narratives too. The main structural thing in a narrative is to keep the story moving along to its climax.

2   Paragraph structures

The first paragraph has the approved topic sentence followed by elaboration sentences. So do the second and third paragraphs of the "complication" section. Otherwise, the story just keeps flowing from event to event.

3   Cohesive devices

The opening paragraph ends with a cataphor. Another one occurs in the last but one paragraph of the middle. Elsewhere, anaphors keep the narrative rolling along.

4   Language

Typical language features of this narrative are:

- dialogue
- descriptions
- a light tone.

6.10   Preparation, writing and editing

Some authors are so naturally gifted, that they can write an essay without preparation or revision and get it right first go. I am not among them, so I take a planned, step-by-step approach to the writing task. You may feel like adopting all or some of the following steps to ensure that the work you present is the best you are capable of.

1   Examine the wording of the essay title for clues on the kind of approach you are expected to take.
2   Research the topic of the essay as thoroughly as you can.
3   Make rough notes on what you have learned from your research.
4   Discuss the essay topic with all and sundry: friends, family members, anyone who will listen.
5   Break the essay up into parts by drafting some subheadings and, perhaps, writing an outline.
6   Write a draft and edit it until it is as good as you can make it.

We now look at each of these steps as they relate to some of the essays presented above.

1   **In a set essay, examine the wording of the title for clues to the kind of approach that you are expected to take.** Some word or words in the essay topic will often give you that information. Here are some typical key words in non-narrative essay topics and the approach that these words will require of you:

"explain"— make the matter clear and easy to understand
"discuss"— examine the topic with arguments for and against
"summarize"—write about the matter in a short and concise way
"compare"— look at two or more things in order to bring out the similarities
"contrast"— look at two or more things in order to bring out the differences.

Often, more than one of these key words will appear in a non-narrative essay topic, and you will then need to combine the relevant approaches in your essay. Among university teachers, the chief complaint about students' essays is that the students haven't actually dealt with the set topic in the way required by the title.

211

2 **Research the topic of the essay as thoroughly as you can.**
This is especially relevant if you are writing a non-narrative essay.
Learn all about the topic from books and from other specialized
sources. Encyclopaedias are a good source of information. So are
other books and journals that you will find in the library or at
home. You can also draw on your personal experience. In writing
essay D, for example ("The game of chess"), I drew on my personal
knowledge as a chess player. I also checked for information in
Hooper and Whyld's *The Oxford Companion to Chess* (Oxford: OUP,
1987).

3 **Make rough notes on what you have learned from your
research.** Order your notes under some subheadings. Here are
some notes I made for essay A ("Living in Canberra").

PROS OF LIVING IN CANBERRA

    the climate
    the scenery
    the trees

CONS OF LIVING IN CANBERRA

    the road system
    lack of a beach

CONCLUSION: *Canberra suits me.*

A pro and con scheme is especially useful—essential, really—in a
discussion essay.

4 **Discuss the essay topic with all and sundry: friends, family
members, anyone who will listen.** The mere act of talking
about the topic—and getting feedback—will help to make your
ideas clearer and give you new ideas. It will also give you words
that you can use later in writing your essay. I tried out essay G
("The driver who wanted to be a guru"), by telling the story to
different people in different ways to see what sort of reactions I
would get.

5 **Plan a division of the essay into parts by drafting up some
subheadings.** This is true both for narrative and for non-narrative
essays. In the latter genre, the essay topic or title might suggest
these parts to you, or your reading and research may suggest a
division of the topic into parts. In essay C ("Making Bedouin
bread"), Deborah Stern wrote out the following headings before she
wrote the essay.

a Bedouin bread—
    introduction
    materials
    instructions
b Bedouin tea.

You should do this even if you don't use the subheadings in the essay itself. The act of preparing subheadings will help to ensure that you give each part of your essay the due weight (often but not always equal weight) that it deserves. Tertiary essays often require treatment in several parts: *Explain this, and account for that* (or the like). The second biggest complaint about students' essays by lecturers is that the students' essays have adequately covered part, but skimped on another part or other parts, of the set topic.

6 **Write a draft and edit it into a final version.** I have done this for all my texts in this chapter. Things I write—even short pieces such as book reviews—often go through three or four drafts. Books go through dozens. The final version is then as good as I can make it.

There are three kinds of editing.

a Content and structure editing (macro-editing) entails two jobs.

- First, a review of all the factual information—names, dates, numbers and so on—that often need checking in reference works.
- Second, a check of the overall structure and sequence of the work. You might need to change the order of presentation, or add or delete material, so as to achieve the right balance of the parts of a multi-part essay.

b Style editing (midi-editing) means looking at paragraph structures, cohesive devices and language features. See the analysis for essay A in section 6.3 above.

c Copy editing (micro-editing) is paying attention to the small-scale features of language: spelling, punctuation, grammar and usage. In copy editing you also need to pay attention to consistency. You can express large numbers, for example, in any of several ways: "2,500,000" or "2 500 000" or "2.5 million" or "2.5m". Any of these is fine, but if you use

"2.5m" for one number, then, for another number, you should use the same option—for instance, "7m".

Finally, beware the knock-on effect. I have often written a paragraph with words such as, "An essay is … It is also …" Then, during the editing I have changed "An essay" into "Essays". But I have sometimes forgotten, later in the text, to change "It is" into "They are"!

6.11 How to write a bibliography and references

Bibliography

For some essays, particularly essays that you write in senior high school or tertiary institutions, you will need to add a list of works that you have quoted or consulted. You arrange this list—the bibliography—alphabetically by author's surname or, in the absence of an author, by the first word of the work (but excluding, for the purpose of sequencing the entries, the words *The*, *An* or *A*).

There are various methods of writing a bibliographic entry, both for the sequence of elements within each entry and for the punctuation. Below, I show a system that is in common use. We look first at book entries.

Bibliography

Chalker, Sylvia and Weiner, Edmund. 1994. *The Oxford Dictionary of English Grammar*. Oxford: Clarendon Press.

Chomsky, Noam. 1997 [1995]. *The Minimalist Program*. Cambridge, Mass: MIT Press.

Cook, VJ. 1988. *Chomsky's Universal Grammar: An Introduction*. Oxford: Blackwell.

Martin, James R. 1984. "Language, Register and Genre" in *Children Writing*. Edited by F Christie. Geelong: Deakin University Press.

Martin, James R; Matthieson, Christian; Painter, Clare. 1997. *Working with Functional Grammar*. London: Edward Arnold.

McArthur, Tom (editor). 1992. *The Oxford Companion to the English Language*. Oxford: Oxford University Press.

Stern, George. 1997a. *The English Tenses and Aspects*. Canberra: Australian National University.

Stern, George. 1997b. *Using Grammar in Your Prose.* Canberra: Australian Government Publishing Service Press.

Style Manual for Authors, Editors and Printers. 1994. Fifth edition. Canberra: Australian Government Publishing Service.

Points to note

a   The sequence is: author/s, year of publication, title (in italic font or underlined), edition details (if any), city of publication, publisher. Note carefully the punctuation between the elements.

b   If, as in the Cook entry, the book has a main title and a subtitle, put a colon between the two.

c   The author's name is given as on the title page: the full name, or surname and initial/s, or a combination.

d   The Chalker entry has two authors: put *and* between the names. The fifth entry has more than two authors: put semicolons between the names.

e   The Chomsky entry was first published in 1995, but I have the 1997 printing. The date of the first printing goes in square brackets.

f   The first Martin entry is a chapter from a book. The title of the chapter is in quotation marks, the title of the book is in italic font or underlined.

g   The McArthur entry has no individual author, so I use the editor's name.

h   The *Style Manual* entry has no author's or editor's name, so it goes in alphabetic sequence for the word *Style*.

i   The two Stern entries were both published in the same year: label one of them "1997a"; the other, "1997b".

Next, we look at journal, magazine and Internet entries.

Bibliography

Benson, JD and Greaves, WS. 1981. "Field of discourse: theory and application". *Applied Linguistics*, vol 2/1, 45–55.

Galèas, Grazia Crocco. 1998. "Scalar Categorization". *The Web Journal of Modern Language Linguistics*, issue 3. http://www.staff.ncl.ac.uk/jon.west/issue03/crocco.htm. (Accessed 5 May 2000.)

Wertheim, Margaret. 1999. "Out of this world". *New Scientist*, vol 161/2172, 38–41.

Points to note

a   The numbers after the titles in the Benson and Wertheim entries are volume and, after the slash, issue numbers followed by page numbers. The Galèas entry, taken from the Internet, has no volume number.

b   For the Wertheim entry, I could have used the date of the issue instead of the volume and issue numbers.

c   For an entry from the Internet (as in the Galèas entry), show the full web address and the date on which you accessed the site.

d   If the entries in the last two boxes above were to form a single bibliography, all twelve entries would be rearranged in a single, alphabetically sequenced list.

References

If you quote from—or credit information to—an author in your writing, you need to show the source from which you have taken the quotation or the information. Of the various options available for doing this, the most modern and, at the same time, the neatest method is to use textnotes (also known as the "Harvard system"). It works as follows.

a   After the quotation (or the information) in your text, write in brackets the author's surname, the year of publication and the page number or numbers. Carefully note the punctuation below.

> According to one view, "English is considered to have two aspects" (Chalker and Weiner, 1994:34–35). But according to another view, English verbs have four aspects (Stern, 1997a:1).

Now you can see why the two publications by George Stern were labelled "1997a" and "1997b" in the bibliography. The reader can find in which of the two books published in 1997 this view is expressed.

b   If you mention the author's name in your text, you omit it from the brackets.

> According to Chalker and Weiner, "English is considered to have two aspects" (1994:34–35). But according to Stern, English verbs have four aspects (1997a:1).

c   If you mention both the author's name and the year of publication of the book in your text, all you need in brackets is the page number.

> According to Chalker and Weiner, writing in 1994, "English is considered to have two aspects" (34–35). But, in *The English Tenses and Aspects*, written in 1997, Stern identifies four (1).

6.12   Enjoying essay writing

This chapter has given you guidelines for a systematic approach to the task of writing essays. In general, you will produce a higher quality essay if you follow these guidelines than if you write spontaneously. At the same time, though, you should not follow these or any other guidelines too slavishly. It is important that you should be your own person and, to some extent at least, write in a way that suits your temperament. That way, the essays you write will reflect your own personality—and you might even enjoy writing them. What's more, the reader might even enjoy reading them!

Here are another two model essays: the first by a journalist; the second by a Nobel Prize Laureate in physics. Both are models of essay-writing excellence; both are worth a first reading for enjoyment and a second reading for a study of what it is that makes them work so well as essays.

Let sleeping flies lie

Do flies sleep? After prodding and tapping fruit flies, measuring their activity with ultrasound and infrared detectors, blasting them with sound waves and monitoring their genes, researchers at the Neurosciences Institute in San Diego have come to a definite conclusion: the flies actually doze off in slumber patterns that are strikingly similar to those of humans.

Writing in the current issue of *Science*, the researchers report that the flies are somnolent mainly at night and active during daylight hours; that elderly flies sleep less and more erratically than younger ones; that fruit flies deprived of sleep must nap longer to recover; that caffeine keeps them awake, and antihistamines make them drowsy.

Perhaps most significant, many of the fly genes that turn off during sleep and on when the insects are active proved to be identical to those that regulate mammalian slumber. That means researchers can use flies to test potential drugs and genetic treatments for aiding sleep and preventing drowsiness, rather than putting humans in danger.

Now that the tiny insect has demonstrated such sophisticated brain function, another question occurs to neurosciences researcher Paul Shaw: "Does the fruit fly dream?"

(Leon Jaroff, *Time*, 20 March 2000.)

Science and morality

I would like to make a little philosophical argument to explain why theoretically I think that science and moral questions are independent.

The common human problem, the big question, always is: "Should I do this?" It is a question of action. "What should I do? Should I do this?" And how can we answer such a question? We can divide it into two parts. We can say, "If I do this what will happen?" That doesn't tell me whether I should do this. We still have another part, which is, "Well, do I want this to happen?"

In other words, the first question—"If I do this what will happen?"—is at least susceptible to scientific investigation; in fact, it is a typical scientific question. It doesn't mean we know what will happen. Far from it. We never now what is going to happen. The science is very rudimentary.

But, at least, if it is in the realm of science we have a method to deal with it. The method is "Try it and see" and accumulate the information and so on. And so the question "If I do it what will happen?" is a typically scientific question. But the question "Do I want this to happen?"—in the ultimate moment—is not. Well, you say, if I do this, I see that everybody is killed and, of course, I don't want that. Well, how do you know you don't want people killed?

You see, at the end you must have some ultimate judgment.

(Richard P Feynman, *The Meaning of It All.*)

Persuasive writing

The main point of writing something for someone else to read (or to hear) is to get your message across clearly and directly.

(George Stern, *Spot On!*)

7
Persuasive writing

7.1 When you need to sell yourself

The time comes when you need to present not only ideas in writing but to present yourself.

Need a job? You will need to show the prospective employer that you are worth hiring. Want to get a book published? If so, you may want to apply for a grant to support yourself financially while you are writing it, and then you will want to persuade a publisher to accept your manuscript and to publish it. Want to get your ideas—or somebody else's ideas—across in a speech? If so, you will need to write the speech in such a way that the listeners don't turn their backs on you. All of these involve the art of persuasive writing, and all of these are dealt with in this chapter.

There are some aspects of persuasive writing that hold across the board. Here are the three main ones.

a   Style

The guidelines that I have given in chapter 1 all hold good. Their application will ensure that the message you want to get across to the reader or the listener gets across clearly, immediately and with the least effort on the part of the person you are addressing.

b   Brevity

An apt illustration of this point is what happened at Gettysburg, Pennsylvania, on 19 November 1863. Two speakers were to address the people who had gathered at Gettysburg for the dedication of a cemetery for the dead of the American Civil War. The first speaker was Edward Everett, a famous orator of the day. He droned on and on. The next speaker was President Lincoln. His speech was over in ten sentences.

Nobody today remembers Everett's speech, but Lincoln's is still seen as a masterpiece of prose. Even

Everett paid tribute to Lincoln. The day after the dedication, he wrote to Lincoln: "I wish that I could flatter myself that I had come as near to the central idea of the occasion in two hours as you did in two minutes."

You will find the full text of Lincoln's speech in section 7.6 below.

c Focus

Even if the style and brevity are there, you will still need to help the reader or listener to navigate through the prose and focus on the main point or points that you wish to convey. There are several ways by which you can achieve focus.

- One of these, relevant to writing, is the use of formatting devices: the use of different fonts, dot-points or alphanumeric subitems such as those that I am using here.

- Another, also relevant to writing, is the use of clear and meaningful headings and subheadings. These act as signposts for the readers and prepare their minds for what they are about to read. Look back at the table of contents to see an example of clear headings and subheadings.

- A third means of achieving focus—one that you can use in writing and in speech—is to use language signposting. Here are some examples of such signposts.

  "There are three matters that I wish to deal with today."
  "I come now to the main point that remains unresolved."
  "The issue at the heart of this is the following."
  "What does this mean for the future?"

  The last of the example sentences above is a question. You can often use questions to keep the prose—and the reader's interest—on track. Look, for example, at the twenty-two section headings in chapter 2: each of them is a question. You will find other questions sprinkled here and there in the text of this book.

So we have looked at a variety of methods of persuasive writing. Keep a look out for the application of these methods in the example texts that follow.

7.2   Job applications: writing a covering letter and a curriculum vitae

The written part of a job application usually involves four parts:

- a covering letter
- a curriculum vitae
- addressing selection criteria
- preparing for an interview.

In this section, we deal with the first two of these; in the next section (7.3), with the last two.

a   The attributes of a successful applicant

As you write the application, bear in mind that your prospective employers are looking for any one or a combination of four attributes. You should therefore—within the bounds of truth— highlight the presence of these factors in yourself. If you are lacking in any one of them, you may be able to make up for that lack with good credentials in some of the others.

Here are the four factors:

- **the right qualifications**—whether the applicant has trained in the area of the job
- **the right experience**—whether the applicant has a proven track-record in the work
- **the right potential**—whether the applicant can make a contribution to the organization
- **the right attributes**—whether the applicant has the personal attributes for the job.

Let's expand a little on the last of these four—your personal attributes. Employers are definitely not looking for people who think that near enough is good enough, or who serve their work hours and then drop everything to rush home, or who look primarily for personal gain and glory. The attributes they are looking for are the ability to produce results, people skills and team work, energy and creativity, initiative and—many employers put this at the top of their list—motivation.

And remember this: don't dwell so much on your past glories—rather, highlight what you can contribute to your prospective employer in the future.

In the government sector, employers look for the same qualities that I have listed above, but government organizations also have guidelines in their hiring practices. The three major factors are: (a) the merit of the appointees, (b) the openness of the selection procedure—which means that the people who do the hiring may have to justify the grounds of their choice of candidates—and (c) cost-effectiveness. Government also has to weigh in the balance, when hiring people for jobs, whether such people are in any of a number of categories of disadvantage and, all other things being equal, to prefer the disadvantaged candidate.

b   The covering letter

Now we are ready to write the covering letter. This is the letter that introduces you to the prospective employers and tells them what position you are applying for.

But beyond that, the letter subliminally conveys important information to the readers. In particular, it tells them whether you are familiar with the modern layout and style of writing correspondence. The letter, and the other documents that you present to your prospective employers, also show them to what extent you have a careful attitude to your work, and how concise and relevant you can be.

We start by looking at a model covering letter. The model illustrates the following features:

- **it is short**—at most, one page
- **it uses the modern method of layout**—left justification and unpunctuated blocks
- **it does not include any self-praise**, such as: "I believe I am most suited for the position"—let the readers deduce that fact from the application rather than state the fact about yourself.

In the model letter that follows, I have incorporated some comments in square brackets about the modern format of a letter.

[Begin with the address block. In modern style, this and the signature block are not punctuated.]

The Recruitment Officer
Personnel and EEO Branch
Department of Education
GPO Box 9000
Sydney NSW 2001

[Next, the salutation. Use the person's name if you know it; otherwise use the person's title.]

Dear Recruitment Officer

[Below the salutation put the position details in a bold, an underlined or all-capital heading.]

POSITION NO 007: SENIOR EDUCATION OFFICER, CLASS 4, CURRICULUM BRANCH

[Next, a few simple paragraphs stating what and why you are writing, and nominating some referees.]

This is my application for appointment to the above position, which was advertised in *The Sydney Trumpet* on 19 March 2003.

Enclosed with this application, please find the following supporting documents:

   a. my curriculum vitae
   b. my response to the selection criteria
   c. transcripts of my academic record.

My referees for the above position are the following.

Dr May Bee	Mr Ivan Hoe
Director of Studies	Principal
Faculty of Education	Cortex High School
Ivy University	Geelong Vic 3220
Seashore Qld 4999	
Phone: 08 1111 0000	Phone: 03 1111 2222
Fax: 08 1111 0001	Fax: 03 1111 2221

I look forward to your notice of interview.

[Last come the complimentary close and the signature block.]

Yours faithfully

Phil Goode

Phil Goode
51 Shade Avenue
Far North NSW 2999

Phone: 02 1111 3333

22 March 2003

c   The curriculum vitae

The term "curriculum vitae" (or "CV") means "course of life". Another name for this part of your job application is "résumé". You can use either heading—or even, if you are courageous, "Course of life". Under the heading you tell the prospective employer those aspects of your life that are relevant to the position. The ideal length for a curriculum vitae is two pages, give or take a page. My own curriculum vitae is one page long.

On the next eleven pages are three model curricula vitae: one by an experienced educationist; another by an experienced engineer; and the third by a school-leaver.

Note the following features of all three models:

- neat, clear and reader-friendly layout of the text
- clear subheadings
- the sequence of the subheadings
- the sequence of the information under each subheading
- short and factual information without self-praise
- less information for the earlier work history; more for the more recent work history
- specific and quantified information about the work history.

There are three other points that you should note. One is that I have used a particular method of formatting—with borders and shading and different styles of font. My aim has been to make the papers easy for the readers to navigate through. But if you have a different preference in formatting, you should by all means feel free to use it.

Another point is that I have sequenced the educational qualifications and the work experience in chronological order. Some people prefer to sequence them in reverse chronological order. You should feel free to adopt whichever method you prefer.

Finally, if you do not have access to a computer, a neat handwritten application will do. After all, the employers will take more interest in the content of your application than in its appearance.

CURRICULUM VITAE: PHIL GOODE

PERSONAL DETAILS

Name: Phil Goode
Place of birth: Wallaby, Queensland
Date of birth: 2 November 1972
Address: 51 Shade Avenue, Far North NSW 2999
Present position: Acting Senior Education Officer
Contacts: Work phone: 02 1111 3333
                       Work fax: 02 1111 4444

EDUCATION AND TRAINING QUALIFICATIONS

1990 **Senior Certificate (Queensland):** English, History, Geography, Mathematics, Economics, French, German, Art.

1993 **BA (Ivy University, Queensland):** Majors: English, Linguistics. Minors: Psychology, German, French.

1998 **Postgraduate Diploma in Education (Ivy University, Brisbane):** History of Education, Education Administration, Language Teaching, Secondary Education, Curriculum Development.

1999 **Postgraduate Diploma in Linguistics (Sandstone University, Sydney):** Linguistic History and Theory, Linguistics and Language Teaching, Syntax and Syntagmatics.

2000 **Certificate in Teaching English as a Second Language (Sandstone University, Sydney).**

2002 **Internet Course (Department of Education, NSW):** Net use and homepaging.

2003 **MA, Ed (Sandstone University, Sydney):** I have completed the course work and am writing the thesis.

PROFESSIONAL AFFILIATIONS

Member of the Secondary Educationists' Association (since 1994).
Member of the Australasian Society of Linguists (since 2000).

PUBLICATIONS

"Teaching grammar: should there be a new start?" *The Victorian Teacher*, June 2002.
"Helping non-English-speaking pupils in Years 9–12". *NSW High School Survey*, 2003.

EMPLOYMENT HISTORY

1990–93   **Part-time assistant bookkeeper while studying at university (Plenty Co, Brisbane).**

1994–95   **High school teacher in English, French and German (NSW Education Department).**

1996–98   **Department Head, Language Department (Cerebellum High School, Sydney).**

- Supervised a staff of twelve teachers.
- Introduced Indonesian studies to school.
- Developed the school language curriculum.
- Oversaw language studies for 450 students.

1998–2000   **Time out for postgraduate studies (Ivy University, Brisbane, and Sandstone University, Sydney) and overseas travel.**

2001   **Acting Deputy Principal (Cortex High School, Geelong).**

- Under the principal's direction, coordinated the work of 60 teachers.
- Oversaw the academic activities of a school population of 700 students.

- Coordinated the school's curriculum development with the Education Department.
- Developed courses for 120 students needing skills in English as a second language.
- Arranged 20 departmental refresher and upgrading courses for the teaching staff.
- Supervised after-hours cultural and sporting activities at the school.
- Liaised with parents and friends organizations.
- Managed student counselling service.

2003–   **Acting Senior Education Officer, Class 4, Curriculum Branch (NSW Education Department).**

Since the beginning of 2003, I have been acting in the advertised position, fulfilling all the duties listed in the duty statement. Apart from these duties, I have also undertaken the following extra tasks.

- Coordinated the training of senior teachers in language departments in the Sydney metropolitan area.

- Surveyed the need for teaching resources in English as a second language. My second report on this matter is due out at the end of next month.

- Chaired an ad hoc committee of 20 departmental staff and principals. The committee is considering the extension of Asian and European languages in additional schools in rural NSW.

Phil Goode

Phil Goode

22 March 2003

CURRICULUM VITAE: ANGIE NEARE

PERSONAL DETAILS

Name: Angie Neare
Place of birth: Venice, Italy
Date of birth: 20 May 1972
Nationality: Australian
Marital status: Single
Address: 8/32 Cockatoo Crescent
                    Perth WA 6000
Contacts: 09-5000 0000 (work) 09-5000 0001 (switch)
                    09-5000 0002 (fax)   09-5000 0003 (home)
                    a.neare@workplace.gov.au

EDUCATION QUALIFICATIONS

1993 **Bachelor of Science** (Westside University, Perth).
      Majors: Pure and Applied Mathematics.

1998 **Graduate Diploma in Applied Computing** (University College
      of Upper Fremantle).
      Majors: Relational Database, Computer Graphics, C/C++.

2003 **Graduate Diploma in Electrical-Electronic Engineering**,
      two-thirds complete (Australian College of Engineering,
      Fremantle).
      Majors: Digital Communications, Image Processing, Digital
      Video Communications.

OTHER COURSES

1994 **Postgraduate Mathematics** (University of Venice, Italy).
1995 **Second Year Mathematical Statistics** (Westside University,
      Perth).

1996 **Electronics Engineering, Stage 2** (Westralian College of Technology, Perth).

2000 **System Managers Course** (Digital Systems Company, Fremantle).

2002 **Network Managers Course** (Digital Systems Company, Fremantle).

2002 **Leadership, Management, Communications Course** (Rosella Management Centre, Perth).

PROFESSIONAL AFFILIATIONS

2000 **Australasian Society of Mathematicians.**
2003 **Australasian Society of Engineers.**

EMPLOYMENT HISTORY

1995–96 **Research Assistant—Programmer** (Eucalypt Hospital, Perth).

Duties: scientific-mathematical programming for a package to analyse DNA gene sequences.

1996 **Electronics Supervisor—Technician** (Numlock Data Systems Corp, Perth).

Duties: factory QA of Automatic Teller Machines; repair LittleSmart mini-computers, word processors, printers, modems, power-supplies.

1996–97 **Software Engineer** (Integers Instrumentation Corp, Perth).

Duties:
• write programs for job control reconciliation (Ratfor/FMS/DCL)
• progress payment control system (Fortran/FMS/DCL)
• cheque system (COBOL/Datatrieve/DCL)

- plant and vehicle allocation system (COBOL/Datatrieve/DCL)
- cable management system (Fortran/FMS/Datatrieve/DCL)
- system programming of VAX/VMS.

1997–98 **Billing Programmer** (Integers Instrumentation Corp, Perth).

Duties:
- modification to billing programs
- managed $1m monthly billing and invoice program
- HISAM interface to billing database
- technical support for MIS implementation
- system interface to new billing system.

1999 **VAX Project Analyst** (Numlock Data Systems Corp, Perth).

Duties: writing CAI/CBT (computer-based instruction and training) on the VAX.

2000 **Education Instructor** (Numlock Data Systems Corp, Perth).

Duties: train students in system management and Numlock COBOL on the VS-operating system.

2000–01 **Computer Engineer, Class 2** (Smart Defence and Aeronautics Company, Perth).

Duties:
- software engineer on over-the-horizon radar
- maintenance of radar software for transmitter and receiver site
- hardware maintenance, working with hardware engineers and technicians at the radar site
- management of VAX cluster

- writing new programs as required (Oracle/Pascal/Fortran/DCL)
- wrote the tender for the $80,000 Oracle database.

2001–02 **Computer Facilities Manager** (Westside University, Perth).

Duties:
- oversee the running of IBM, Apple, Ultrix and DECNET computer networks
- supervise three computer staff
- prepare the yearly budget of $100,000 for the computer centre
- advise quarterly on strategic matters on computing-networking both within the faculty and for the registrar's and vice-chancellor's offices
- project manage the half-yearly implementation of computer hardware-software networks
- advise lecturers and tutors on IT related matters.

2003– **Senior Engineer** (Hemispheric Institute for Remote Sensing, Perth).

Duties:
- write requests for tender, factory acceptance test procedures (up to $3m), on-site acceptance test procedures, carry out quality assurance ISO-9001/2
- synthetic aperture radar specialist, project engineer for procuring ($60,000 a year), commissioning and maintaining new generation SAR processor (Unix)
- carry out validation and calibration procedures for SAR satellites European Space Agency and Space Development Agency, Japan
- project manage the specification and automation of file storage and processing requirements for optical and SAR satellite data in the order of petabytes, tendered $3–5m

- commission and maintain the SAR designed by Inter-Aerospace Australia (VAX/VMS)
- write monthly project status reports and executive summaries
- train three operators each year, write training notes and user manuals
- represent the Hemispheric Institute for Remote Sensing at three international and national conferences, including Committee of Earth Orbiting Satellites and ESA conferences
- chair fortnightly engineering operations and maintenance meetings.

TEACHING EXPERIENCE

1992–96 **Welfare teacher in Mathematics, Physics and Chemistry to Year 12 students** (Perth).

1997 **Assistant Housemaster**, 120 boarders (Knowledge College, Fremantle).

1998 **Full-time Year 12 coach in Mathematics, Physics and Chemistry** (self-employed).

1999 **Part-time Physics teacher** for twenty students (Wisdom High School, Perth).

2000 **Part-time Mathematics teacher** for twenty students (East Wisdom Technical College, Perth).

2001–03 **Computing tutor** for sixty students (Westside University, Perth).

Angie Neare

Angie Neare

2 April 2003

CURRICULUM VITAE: EMMA SKOLLER

Personal details

Name: Emma Skoller
Place of birth: Canberra ACT
Date of birth: 10 October 1986
Address: 16 Bullock Street, Koala ACT 2699
Contacts: Home phone: 06 1111 2222
                    Work phone: 06 1111 5555
                    Facsimile: 06 1111 5556
                    Email: emma.skoller@switchon.com.au

Education and training qualifications

2001   **Young Achievers' Programme** (Young Achievers' Pacific, Melbourne).

Won award for promotions and marketing.

2002   **Small Business Enterprise** (Koala Business College, Canberra).

Topped the year for this course.

2003   **Year 12 Certificate** (ACT)

Year 11	Year 12
Mathematics (Tertiary)	Mathematics (Tertiary)
English (Tertiary)	English (Tertiary)
Indonesian (Tertiary)	Indonesian (Tertiary)
Legal Studies (Tertiary)	Business Management 1
Accounting (Tertiary)	(Tertiary)
Small Business Enterprise	Business Management 2
(Employment)	(Tertiary)
	Information Management
	(Employment).

2002 **Type Quick Course** (Koala Business College, Canberra).
Correspondence and Report Writing (Koala Business College, Canberra).

2003 **Certificate in Business Computer Skills** (Koala Business College, Canberra).
English Usage and Punctuation (Koala Business College, Canberra).
First Aid Course (St Andrew's Ambulance)—I hold a current first aid certificate.
Driver's course—I hold a CA class driver's licence.

Employment history

2002 **Waitress and cashier** (Everest Indian Restaurant, Canberra).

- While studying in Year 11, I worked part-time for eight hours a week at this restaurant.
- I worked as part of a team with the restaurant's staff of twelve.
- As cashier, I handled over $10,000 a week.

2003 **Clerk and cashier** (Skoller Printing Enterprises Pty Ltd, Canberra).

- In Year 12, I assisted part-time in my parents' business.
- I introduced a $50,000 computer accounting system into the business.
- Together with two other employees, I handled the invoicing and receipting for $25,000 a week.

Computer skills

Through training and experience, I have become familiar with both Macintosh and IBM operating systems, and a variety of applications used within those environments:

- Windows 2002
- Spreadsheets
- Mac Publisher
- DOS
- Entire Connection
- Internet Ops
- A1 Homepage Systems
- Hotshot.

Work–related skills

From both my part-time positions, I have gained the following work-related skills and qualities:

- willingness to learn
- very good customer focus
- ability to work effectively in a team
- willingness to take on a variety of tasks
- confidence in the use of computer systems
- responsibility with company money
- knowledge of accounting systems
- small business practice
- knowledge of first aid
- driver's licence.

Emma Skoller

Emma Skoller

12 April 2003

Effectively addressing selection criteria

In many job advertisements, the prospective employer states the criteria that the organization will use to make its choice among the applicants. The applicants then have to address the criteria in their applications. Before we consider how to address the criteria, let us look at some sample criteria.

- Appreciation of occupational health and safety (OH&S), equal employment opportunity (EEO), industrial democracy (ID) and sexual harassment (SH) principles.
- Demonstrated ability to use a variety of word processing systems.
- Extensive experience in organizational and administrative activities.
- Sound knowledge of the organization's operations and policy.
- Well-developed liaison skills.
- Extensive supervisory experience.
- Proven money management skills.
- Ability to lead or to work in a team.
- Well-developed interpersonal skills.
- Ability to work under minimal supervision.
- High quality oral and written communication skills.
- Willingness to travel interstate and overseas.
- Demonstrated initiative and flexibility.
- Sound promotional and marketing skills.
- Ability to conduct formal meetings.
- Well-developed negotiation skills.
- Ability to work to deadlines.

In responding to the criteria, I suggest you use the following strategies.

a   Write one to four complete responses to a page.
b   In addressing a criterion, refer to your qualifications (if any) in the relevant field.
c   In addressing a criterion, refer to your experience (if any) in the relevant field.
d   In referring to your qualifications and experience, give specific and quantified information.

e   In referring to your experience, you may also introduce relevant non-work-related activities.

f   Be honest: if you have little or no experience, or no formal qualification in a given field, say so.

On the next eight pages are some sample responses by the experienced Phil Goode and Angie Neare, and by the school-leaver, Emma Skoller. Note that the responses to the selection criteria are very specific and, where possible, incorporate quantities such as money sums and numbers of people.

RESPONSE TO SELECTION CRITERIA: PHIL GOODE

APPRECIATION OF OCCUPATIONAL HEALTH AND SAFETY, EQUAL EMPLOYMENT OPPORTUNITY, INDUSTRIAL DEMOCRACY AND SEXUAL HARASSMENT PRINCIPLES

OCCUPATIONAL HEALTH AND SAFETY (OH&S)

In my year as acting deputy principal at Cortex High School in Geelong, OH&S was my direct responsibility. As part of this responsibility, I ensured that the appropriate authorities carried out fire and structural safety checks twice a year. I also appointed and supervised twelve trained staff and twenty students to act as safety and first aid resource personnel. At weekly staff meetings, and at periodic parents and friends meetings, I encouraged discussion of OH&S issues and dealt with any matters brought to my attention.

EQUAL EMPLOYMENT OPPORTUNITY (EEO)

For six years I was involved in hiring teachers and ancillary staff at two high schools: one in Sydney and one in Geelong. As a member of selection panels, my decisions were closely guided by EEO principles and, as chairperson of such panels in 2003, I made all panel members aware of these principles. The record of selections made during this period shows that I implemented EEO principles.

INDUSTRIAL DEMOCRACY (ID)

My referee's report (attached) highlights the cooperative manner in which I conducted my duties as acting deputy principal in Cortex High School, Geelong. I invite reference to my former colleagues and supervisors at any of my workplaces. All of them will testify to my devotion to industrial democracy.

SEXUAL HARASSMENT (SH)

As department head and as acting deputy principal, I dealt with several allegations of sexual harassment, one of them subsequently confirmed. My school record will show that the offence was referred to the state police. I dealt with other matters involving sexual harassment through my work as coordinator of student counselling for 700 students at Cortex High School, Geelong. The school records show that I successfully managed all the cases brought to my attention, mainly through preventive measures.

HIGH QUALITY ORAL AND WRITTEN COMMUNICATION SKILLS

FORMAL QUALIFICATIONS

My academic training has given me ample skill in oral and written communication. In particular, please note:

- the English major in my BA degree
- the Postgraduate Diploma in Linguistics.

WORK-RELATED EXPERIENCE

I have practised communication skills throughout my working life. Relevant are:

- five years as a teacher and department head in Sydney and in Geelong
- two publications in professional journals and two published departmental surveys
- chairing meetings of up to sixty staff and an even higher number of parents and friends
- my work in student counselling, where I communicated monthly with some hundreds of students.

OTHER RELEVANT EXPERIENCE

- I am currently working on my master's thesis.
- I write reviews of educational books for *The Sydney Trumpet*.
- I exercise oral communication skills as an active member in four community clubs.

ABILITY TO CONDUCT FORMAL MEETINGS

I have gained extensive experience and ability in this field since 1998, both through my work and through my non-work-related activities.

WORK-RELATED ACTIVITIES

- As department head at Cerebellum High School, Sydney, I convened and chaired monthly meetings of the twelve staff. I conducted these meetings in a formal manner, with an agenda and minutes.
- As acting deputy principal of Cortex High School, Geelong, I chaired similar meetings in a similar manner, this time with a staff of sixty.
- In my present acting position, Senior Education Officer, Class 4, I am the chairperson of an ad hoc committee that is considering the extension of Asian and European languages to additional schools in NSW. The committee meets twice a year.

NON-WORK-RELATED ACTIVITIES

- I am the secretary of the Far North Chess Club and serve as minutes secretary of that organization.
- I am the president of the Far North Bushwalking Club and regularly convene and run meetings of the members and committees of that organization.

RESPONSE TO SELECTION CRITERIA: ANGIE NEARE

Tertiary qualifications in a computing field are highly desirable

- Bachelor of Science (Westside University, Perth), 1993
- Graduate Diploma in Applied Computing (University College of Upper Fremantle), 1998
- Graduate Diploma in Electrical-Electronic Engineering (Australian College of Engineering, Fremantle), two thirds complete.

Extensive knowledge of business applications, development and support

- In 1997–98, at Integers Instrumentation Corp, Perth, I was the billing programmer for the Asia-Pacific region ensuring timely production of invoices. My duties included maintaining and upgrading the billing system.
- In 2001–02, at Westside University, Perth, in the Faculty of Business and Computing, I was on the evaluation team for the suitability of accounting software in the accounting department.
- My current position at the Hemispheric Institute for Remote Sensing (HIRS) requires that I have a good understanding of the business applications of satellite data used by industry for applications such as satellite imaging, telecommunications for transmission coverage, and demographic studies.

Demonstrated project-management ability, together with good analytic, planning, organizational and budgeting skills

As the manager of the computer facilities at Westside University, Perth, 2001–02, I was responsible for a number of projects, including:

- cabling and wiring of new buildings
- installation of the fibre-optic cable between the computer centre and the registrar's office

- hardware and software upgrade to the computer facilities every eighteen months, involving the management of an annual budget of $120,000 for equipment upgrade
- implementing and supervising the help desk for students and lecturers
- running a $100,000 annual budget for the computer centre
- implementing an assignment login system using barcodes to replace a manual system.

At the Hemispheric Institute for Remote Sensing (HIRS), since early 2003:

- I have been the project engineer for the specification, tendering, budgeting and commissioning of the SAR processor
- my current project is the specification of the storage facilities for HIRS satellite data which is in the order of petabytes and which is critical to HIRS business.

Excellent written and oral communication and negotiation skills

I have demonstrated skills in the above fields as follows:

- writing regular project status reports and executive summaries for managers and engineers
- daily communication, both informal and formal, via email, phone and fax internally and externally with other ground stations, satellite operators, customers and contractors to HIRS
- writing the proposal, RFQ, contract to government information technology contract standards in consultation with the Government Solicitor, and writing the factory acceptance test and on-site acceptance test for the processor
- negotiating on behalf of HIRS at the Committee of Earth Orbiting Satellites—a multinational committee with many of the members having English as their second language
- chairing the Engineering Operations and Support meetings for which I prepared the agenda and minutes
- writing both technical and executive summaries for interstate and overseas trips
- writing articles on SAR for the HIRS quarterly newsletter

- writing book reviews for *The Journal of the Australasian Society of Engineers*
- writing project reports and assignments as part of the engineering award towards a graduate diploma
- I explain difficult concepts, particularly related to SAR processing, to those with little or no engineering or mathematical background in simple and understandable terms.

Understanding of and commitment to corporate EEO, OH&S and cultural diversity policies

Corporate EEO policy

During my work at Westside University, my duties included hiring and promoting staff. In association with other officers in the same duties, I studied and practised EEO principles. These principles were entrenched at the university and no one who failed to abide by them could have continued in these duties. Reference to university staff will confirm this.

OH&S policy

As a practising engineer, OH&S is always at the forefront of my consciousness. My membership of the Australasian Society of Engineers requires demonstrated knowledge and implementation of OH&S principles and practices. Since I began practising as an engineer in 2000, I have not been involved in any industrial mishaps of any kind. I attribute this to my own and my colleagues' awareness of OH&S.

Cultural diversity policy

I am particularly sensitive to this as I am an overseas-born Australian citizen. Apart from English, I speak two other languages—Italian and French. At all my workplaces there was a diversity of cultures and ethnicities. This is particularly true of my work as an engineer, a profession that is especially cosmopolitan. I have worked harmoniously with people of Australian, European, Asian, Latin American and African backgrounds.

RESPONSE TO SELECTION CRITERIA: EMMA SKOLLER

Demonstrated ability to use a variety of word processing systems

- **Educational qualifications**

  I have passed two courses in which computer skills featured prominently:

  2002 Type Quick Course (Koala Business College, Canberra)
  2003 Certificate in Business Computer Skills (Koala Business College, Canberra).

- **Work-related experience**

  In 2002 I oversaw the installation and the running of a $50,000 computer accounting system in my parents' business. During the same year, working part-time, I became experienced in the daily operation of the system. Through extensive use of various systems during my school and post-school work, I have become familiar with the following software applications and operating environments.

Windows 2002	Entire Connection
Spreadsheets	Internet Ops
Mac Publisher	A1 Homepage Systems
DOS	Hotshot.

- **Other relevant experience**

  I informally tutor my younger brother and sister, both still at school, in the use of word processing systems.

Proven money management skills

- **Educational qualifications**

   The following subjects that I took in my last two years at school are relevant.

   Year 11
   Accounting (Tertiary)
   Small Business Enterprise
      (Employment)

   Year 12
   Business Management 1
      (Tertiary)
   Business Management 2
      (Tertiary).

- **Work-related experience**

   In 2002 I worked part-time as a waitress-cashier at the Everest Indian Restaurant in Canberra. As a cashier, I handled over $10,000 a week, and I saw to the receipting, bookkeeping and banking of this money.

   The following year, also working part-time, I assisted in the invoicing and receipting of some $25,000 per week in my parents' business, Skoller Printing Enterprises Pty Ltd.

   In both part-time positions I worked with minimal supervision and enjoyed the full confidence of the proprietors.

If your written application appeals to prospective employers, they will short-list you for an interview. Now the real work begins! My recommendation is that you prepare thoroughly for the interview—as thoroughly as you would for an important examination. The preparation can pay off both in terms of the confidence (not overconfidence, please) that you display at the interview and also in the general impression of knowledge and ability that you convey. Here is what you should do in preparing for an interview.

1   **Study the target organization.** You can do this from the organization's brochures, publicity material, annual reports and, if it is a government organization, through its published budget papers.

2   **List some questions that you anticipate the panel will ask.** You should list (a) questions that relate to the specific job and (b) questions of a general nature. Here are some example questions for which you can prepare. You can also list additional questions that you think might come up at the interview.

   a   *Examples of job-related questions*

      What do you know about how our organization operates?
      What do you know about the structure of our organization?
      What qualifications do you have that relate directly to the job?
      How do you see your role in the organization a few years down the track?
      What do you see as the main direction in which the organization is moving?
      What do you think are the priorities of the organization?
      What experience have you had in similar kinds of work?
      Why do you want to work for this organization?
      What can you contribute to the organization?
      Why do you think you can handle this job?

   b   *Examples of general questions*

      Tell us something about yourself.
      Why do you want to change jobs?
      What do you think your main skills are?

What weaknesses do you think you have?
Have you had any achievements in your last job?
How have you handled any disagreements with your colleagues?
Have you had any failures in your last job?
Tell us about your supervisory skills.
How do you relate to your supervisors?
How well do you work in a team?

3   **Prepare written notes of your answers to the anticipated questions.** Base the answers on the documents you have gathered about the organization and on your own knowledge.

4   **Rehearse the questions and answers in a play-acting situation.** Drive your family and friends mad by making them play the part of the panel while you play the part of the applicant. Go over the questions and the answers half a dozen times before the interview—with and without your written notes—until you are ready to answer fluently.

5   **Prepare a good question to ask the panel.** Often the panel members will end an interview by inviting you to ask them any questions that you may have. Be bold and ask a question! But be sure to make it one that shows your interest in the organization.

6   **Bring along a portfolio of your best work.** When the panel asks you how good your writing skills are, for example, or your accounting skills, instead of only talking about your skills you can bring out your portfolio and show how good your work is by displaying examples of it.

7.4   Writing a book proposal

When to write a book proposal, and how to go about it

Have you part-written a novel or are you an expert at something—fishing, cooking, skiing, grammar, rock climbing, stamps, canaries, genetics? Do you feel a book welling up inside you? Do you have an urge to get a book published? If the answers to these questions are yes, then you are ready to write a proposal for submission to a publisher.

Well, almost ready.

First, you should have a hefty part, at least half, of your book written in draft. This will enable you, not only to dazzle the publisher with tales of your ability, but also to show the publisher the quality of your work.

The second step is to select a publisher. Many publishers specialize in certain fields: education, sport, politics, biography, war, philosophy, whatever. There are reference books available in libraries or through authors' associations that will tell you in what fields various publishers accept manuscripts. Focus on the specific publishers you think your material might interest.

Should you approach one publisher or several?

In the interests of not pinning all your hopes on one source of publishing salvation, I suggest several: say, two or three. If you get rejections or no replies from these, approach another two or three. Eventually, you may strike it lucky.

Bear in mind two facts of the publishing world. One is that many publishers don't actually want unsolicited manuscripts: they have their suite of authors who write commissioned works. The other is that publishers are inundated with unsolicited manuscripts. So, unless yours is tailored to the publisher's requirements and has something special to offer, your bid is likely to fail. A kindly publisher, in rejecting your work, may suggest another more suitable publisher for your work.

Following is a sample book proposal for a nonfiction book. The same techniques apply to works of fiction as well.

Book proposal: *English Grammar in Use* by Ava Penn

OUTLINE BOOK INFORMATION

Book title:	*English Grammar in Use*
Word count:	50,000 words, adjustable to your requirements
Estimated date of completion:	31 December 2003

OUTLINE AUTHOR INFORMATION

Author's name: Ms Ava Penn

Home address: PO Box 100, Wattle Patch ACT 2600
Phone: 02 6200 0000
Email: ava.penn@hotshot.com.au

Work address: Wattle Patch High School, Circle Drive, Wattle Patch ACT 2600

Qualifications, professional affiliations and employment

- BA, BA Hons, MA, Diploma in Education.
- Member of: Australian Grammar Association and the ANZ Writers' Guild.
- High school teacher since 2000; head of English department since 2002.

Other works by the same author

English for High Schools. 1997. Sydney: Smudge Press.
Teachers' Manual for Teachers of English in High Schools. 1998. Sydney: Smudge Press.
Effective Punctuation: How to Use the Fifteen Stops. 1999. London: Staines and Sons.
"Renewing Grammar in the Classroom". 1999. *Australian Teachers' Journal.* Vol 14. No 2.
"Review of Jill Wood's *Philosophy of Language*". 2000. *Australian Teachers' Journal.* Vol 15. No 1.
Teaching Grammar in the Twenty-First Century. 2002. Sydney: Smudge Press.

"Accepting Language Change". 2003. *Australian Teachers' Journal*. Vol 17. No 2.

DESCRIPTION OF THE BOOK

English Grammar in Use has an introduction, bibliography, index and the following eight chapters.

1. AN OUTLINE OF ENGLISH MORPHOLOGY. The word classes; affixes; word derivation.
2. AN OUTLINE OF ENGLISH SYNTAX. Phrases, clauses, sentences.
3. AN OUTLINE OF DISCOURSE ANALYSIS. Genre, register, modality, cohesion.
4. PUNCTUATION. The uses of the fifteen stops and of capital and lower-case letters.
5. GRAMMAR APPLICATIONS 1. Word order, phrase and clause combinations.
6. GRAMMAR APPLICATIONS 2. Uses of the subjunctive and of conditionals.
7. THE ENGLISH TENSES AND ASPECTS. The four tenses, each with four aspects.
8. PROBLEMS OF USAGE. The *who-whom* and the *which-that* problems, split infinitives and other problems.

SPECIAL FEATURES

The book has two features that I believe other books of the kind lack.

- **One feature is the wide range of reinforcing activities that go with each section of each chapter.** Other standard high-school grammars have relatively sparing and unvarying activities. My book has lavish and varied activities at every turn. A key with model answers is provided at the end of the book.

- **The other feature is the real-life texts that I use to illustrate the technical points.** I have obtained the permission of copyright holders to use real-life texts to illustrate the points of grammar. Among the sources cited are the following.

Current magazines	Modern authors	
The Economist	George Orwell	Richard Leakey
National Geographic	Jean Aitchison	Francis Crick
New Scientist	Richard Dawkins	Jared Diamond
TIME	Patricia Shaw	Celia Millward

Classics

I also have permission to access copyright material from The Internet Library. This gives me access to UK and US authors such as:

Charles Dickens	HG Wells	Mary Shelley
Thomas Paine	Thomas Hardy	Lewis Carroll
Jack London	John Steinbeck	DH Lawrence
Joseph Conrad	Jane Austen	James Joyce
George Eliot	Jonathan Swift	Oscar Wilde
Daniel Defoe	William James	GB Shaw
Emily Brontë	TS Eliot	

PRINCIPAL MARKET/S

Years 10–12 and universities.

COMPETITION

Following are the titles of three standard texts—none of which has the two features mentioned above.

Fyushon, Con. 1999. *Grammar for Senior High Schools*. Sydney: Honey Publishing Co.
Marve, L. 2001. *How to Do Things with Words*. Perth: Slingshot Press.
Weerd, J and Weerd, K. 2002. *Grammar Made Easy*. Melbourne: Yakka Press.

SAMPLE PAGES

Enclosed please find drafts of the introduction and of chapters 1 and 5.

Features of a successful book proposal

The features illustrated above include the following.

- **Conciseness:** the whole proposal fits onto two pages. Publishers just don't have the time or the will to read through ten pages of self-congratulatory puff. So, keep it short and keep it to the point.
- **Factuality:** the proposal tells publishers what they want to know—author details, the length of the book, the potential markets, possible competitors and so on.
- **Clear format:** headings, subheading, bullet points—everything set out so that the reader can easily navigate through the proposal and easily take the information in.
- **Sample pages:** you should include one or more chapters of your work for the publisher to assess.

7.5   Writing a grant application

Finding a grant body and doing the paperwork

Do you have a book nearly finished? Have you got a contract with a publisher, or are you negotiating a contract?

If you can answer yes to these questions, you are ready to apply for a grant from a government or from a university body to support your work. Grants are also available for dance groups, painters, poets in residence, and other creatively productive members of society.

The first step in applying for a grant is to find out which body you should approach for a grant in your particular field. You can do this by checking with the relevant federal or state government bodies or with university administrations.

The next step is to get application forms from these bodies. Some forms require you to fill in specified details in boxes; others allow you to submit a free-form application.

Take my case. To help get this book published, I applied to the Australian National University Publications Committee. The committee sent me a two-page paper headed, "Subsidy to Assist Commercial Publication" with the following subheadings:

- criteria
- procedures
- conditions of grant
- closing date.

The paper told me that I should submit a free-form application. On the next three pages is the application that I submitted—with some small changes of names and other incidental details.

THE AUSTRALIAN NATIONAL UNIVERSITY

Centre for Continuing Education

Canberra ACT 0200   Phone: 02 6249 2892
Fax: 02 6279 8066   Email: george.stern@uni.edu.au

The Chairperson
ANU Publications Committee
The Chancellery
ANU Campus

Request for subsidy to assist commercial publication of: *Writing in English*

Please consider the following request for a publication subsidy. Following is relevant information on the work.

1. **Details of the proposed publication and its current status**

Title:	*Writing in English.*
Author:	Dr George Stern.
Author involvement:	I am the sole person involved in writing the book.
Negotiating Publisher:	Mr Art Quill, Knowledge Publishing, PO Box 1000, Riverside Vic 3101.
Stage of writing:	The 60,000-word text is complete in first draft.
Intended market:	Senior secondary and tertiary students and general readers.
Projected date of publication:	2003.

2. **Description of the work**

   The work is in eight chapters as follows.

1.   **Style: writing in your natural voice**
     10 sections: dealing with such aspects of style as sentence length and structures, choice of vocabulary and how to integrate the techniques into a whole.

2.   **Good usage: the split infinitive and all that**
     22 sections: split infinitives, ending sentences with prepositions, gender-inclusive language, writing numbers as words or as digits, the etymological fallacy, and how to solve any problem of usage.

3.   **Punctuation and the use of capitals**
     14 sections: dealing with the punctuation marks and the modern use of capital letters.

4.   **Words, words, words**
     2 sections: (a) often misspelt words; (b) often confused words—eg "imply"/ "infer".

5.   **A short grammar of current English**
     15 sections: on morphology and syntax.

6.   **Writing essays and narratives**
     12 sections: dealing with techniques for writing various genres of essays. Also referencing and bibliography writing.

7.   **Persuasive writing**
     6 sections: job application writing, addressing selection criteria, book proposals, speech writing.

8.   **Writing business correspondence**
     4 sections on modern format of correspondence, logical sequence of ideas, appropriate language.

3.   **Features of the work**

The work has two special features.

 - The range of topics dealt with—please see part 2 above.
 - The fact that it is text-based. Model texts throughout the book come from classical and modern literature and from such magazines as *The Economist*, *Time*, *New Scientist*, *National Geographic*.

4. Financial details

Royalties: Royalties will be paid at the usual commercial rate.

Other author payment: None.

No of copies to be published: 5,000–10,000 initially.

Expected published price: $25–$30 with subsidy; more without subsidy.

Distribution: Education and general bookshops.

Other proposed sources of finance: None.

5. Subsidy details

Sum being sought: $5,000.

Calculation: The sum is calculated—
  a. to make publication more attractive
  b. to lower the cost of publication, making the book more affordable.

6. Other details

- **Author-publisher agreement:** attached please find a copy of the book contract.
- **Referees:**
  Mr John Dash (Director of the ANU Centre for Continuing Education), phone: 02 6255 2222.
  Dr Karen Nolan (Dean, Faculty of English, University of Southlands), phone: 03 9444 1111.
- **Declaration:** I have no personal involvement with any of the suppliers concerned with the production and distribution of the work, nor any interest other than that revealed in this letter.

Dr George Stern
Centre for Continuing Education
The Australian National University

10 February 2002

Features of a successful application

I recommend that you adopt all or some of the following features, incorporated in the above model.

- **Keep it short:** the panel that reviews your application will have dozens, maybe hundreds, of applications to consider. It is not good strategy to overwhelm the panel with a massive text from which they have to painfully extract the main points.
- **Use a reader-friendly format:** clear and meaningful subheadings, bullet points, numbering, font features (such as bolding) and the like. This will make it easy for the panel to navigate through your text.
- **Get written references** to support your application. These can come from expert readers or from prospective publishers.

The above model grant application must have had some merit—it was successful.

7.6   Speech writing

a   The preliminaries

There are two preliminaries to writing a speech.

- First, you need to know exactly what it is that you want to convey to the audience.
- Second, you need to know who your audience is. The way you convey your central idea or ideas will differ if you are talking to a primary school assembly or to war veterans. See chapter 1.5 on appropriateness.

b   The structure

Having made your decision on the above two matters, you get down to writing the speech. We look now at the four parts of a speech:

i   the lead-in
ii   the focus
iii the body of the speech
iv   the lead-out.

As an example I take the text of an address that President Abraham Lincoln delivered in November 1863 at the dedication of the Civil War cemetery at Gettysburg in Pennsylvania, USA. The texts in square brackets are my comments—not subheadings.

Abraham Lincoln. 1863. The Gettysburg Address.

[LEAD-IN: HISTORICAL BACKGROUND.]

1   Four score and seven years ago, our fathers brought forth on this continent a new nation, conceived in liberty and dedicated to the proposition that all men are created equal.

2   Now we are engaged in a great civil war, testing whether that nation—or any nation so conceived and so dedicated—can long endure.

3   We are met on a great battlefield of that war.

[FOCUS: WHAT THIS SPEECH IS ABOUT.]

4   We have come to dedicate a portion of that field as a final resting place for those who here gave their lives that that nation might live.

[BODY OF THE SPEECH: THE IDEAS THAT LINCOLN WANTS TO CONVEY TO THE AUDIENCE.]

5   It is altogether fitting and proper that we should do this.

6   But, in a larger sense, we cannot dedicate, we cannot consecrate, we cannot hallow this ground.

7   The brave men, living and dead, who struggled here, have consecrated it far above our poor power to add or detract.

8   The world will little note nor long remember what we say here, but it can never forget what they did here.

9   It is for us the living, rather, to be dedicated here to the unfinished work which they who fought here have thus far so nobly advanced.

[LEAD-OUT: LOOKING TO THE FUTURE.]

10   It is rather for us to be here dedicated to the great task remaining before us, that from these honoured dead we take increased devotion to that cause for which they gave the last full measure of devotion, that we here highly resolve that these dead shall not have died in vain; that this nation, under God, shall have a new birth of freedom and that government of the people, by the people, for the people, shall not perish from the earth.

i **The lead-in.** Lincoln chose, in his speech, to refer to the historical background of the occasion. Of course, other lead-ins are also possible.

- *A joke or a quip.* I once attended a conference in which physicians and other professionals discussed death. The keynote speaker started out as follows: "Ladies and gentlemen, the medical profession is the only profession with a hundred per cent failure rate."
- *A local reference.* If you are delivering a speech in Singapore, you can start by mentioning the modernity of the place or the diligence of the people.
- *A personal anecdote that sets the scene for your central idea.* The sample speech by Vaclav Havel (see the next box below) does this very effectively.

ii **The focus.** After a brief lead-in, you need to make explicit what the speech as a whole is about. This helps the audience to focus mentally on the subject of the speech.

iii **The body of the speech.** This usually takes up the major portion of the speech. In it, you discuss the ideas that you want to convey.

iv **The lead-out.** Instead of an abrupt finish, Lincoln's speech (and Havel's in the next box below) ends by looking to the future. This forward-looking is the most common lead-out in speeches. But you may choose to end as you started, say, with a quip or with a local reference.

Vaclav Havel. 1995. Excerpts from the commencement address at Harvard University.

[LEAD-IN: A PERSONAL ANECDOTE.]

1 One evening, not long ago, I was sitting in an outdoor restaurant by the water. They were playing the same rock music they play in restaurants in most Czech restaurants. I saw familiar advertisements. I was surrounded by young people who behaved as casually as their contemporaries in Prague. Only their complexion and their facial features were different—for I was in Singapore.

[FOCUS: GLOBAL CIVILIZATION.]

2   I sat there thinking about this and I realized an almost banal truth: that we now live in a single global civilization.

[BODY OF THE SPEECH: THE NATURE OF GLOBAL CIVILIZATION.]

3   The identity of this civilization does not lie merely in similar forms of dress, or similar drinks, or in the constant buzz of the same commercial music. It lies in something deeper: thanks to the modern idea of constant progress and to the rapid evolution of science, our planet has for the first time in the long history of the human race been covered by a single civilization—one that is essentially technological. The world is now enmeshed in webs of telecommunications networks consisting of millions of tiny threads or capillaries that not only transmit information of all kinds at lightning speed, but also convey integrated models of social, political and economic behaviour.

4   More than that, the capillaries that have so radically integrated this civilization also convey information about certain modes of human co-existence like democracy, respect for human rights, the rule of law. Such information flows around the world and, in varying degrees, takes root in different places. In theory, at least, this global civilization can also make our life on this earth easier and open up to us hitherto unexplored horizons in our knowledge of ourselves and of the world we live in.

[SECOND FOCUS: DISSATISFACTION.]

5   And yet there is something not quite right about it.

[SECOND BODY: CRITIQUE OF GLOBAL CIVILIZATION.]

6   Many of the great problems we face today, as far as I understand them, have their origin in the fact that this global civilization, though in evidence everywhere, is no more than a thin veneer over human awareness. Humanity has evolved over long millennia in all manner of civilizations and cultures that, in very diverse ways, have shaped our habits of mind, our relationship to the world, our models of behaviour and the values we accept. The new, single epidermis of world civilization merely covers or conceals the variety of cultures, of peoples, of religious worlds and historically formed attitudes.

7   And thus, while the world as a whole increasingly accepts the new habits of global civilization, another contradictory process is taking place: ancient traditions are reviving, different religions

and cultures are awakening to new ways of being, seeking new room to exist, and struggling with growing fervour to realize what is unique to them and what makes them different from others. Ultimately they seek to give their individuality a political expression.

[THIRD FOCUS: THE IMPLICATIONS.]

8   What follows from all of this?

[THIRD BODY: HAVEL'S CREDO.]

9   It is my belief that this state of affairs contains a clear challenge not only to the Euro-American world but to our present-day civilization as a whole. It is a challenge to this civilization to start understanding itself as a multicultural and multipolar civilization, whose meaning lies not in undermining the individuality of different spheres of culture and civilization but in allowing them to be more completely themselves. This will only be possible, even conceivable, if we all accept a basic code of mutual co-existence, a kind of common minimum, that will enable us to go on living side by side.

[FOURTH FOCUS: IS THERE A SOLUTION?]

10   But is humanity capable of such an undertaking? Is it not a hopelessly utopian idea?

[FOURTH BODY: ADDRESSES THE NEW FOCUS.]

11   I don't know. But I have not lost hope. I have not lost hope because I am persuaded again and again that lying dormant in the deepest roots of most, if not all, cultures there is an essential similarity, something that could be made—if the will to do so existed—a genuinely unifying starting point for that new code of human co-existence that would be firmly anchored in the great diversity of human traditions.

12   Don't we find somewhere in the foundations of most religions and cultures common elements such as a respect for what transcends us, whether we mean the mystery of being, or a moral order, certain imperatives that come to us from heaven or from nature or from our own hearts; respect for our neighbours, for our families, respect for human dignity and for nature? Isn't the common, ancient origin of our diverse spiritualities the thing that can genuinely bring people of different cultures together?

13 Naturally, I am not suggesting that modern people be compelled to worship ancient deities and accept rituals they have long since abandoned. I am suggesting something quite different: we must come to understand the deep mutual connection or kinship between the various forms of our spirituality. We must recollect our original spiritual and moral substance, which grew out of the same essential experience of humanity.

14 I believe that this is the only way to achieve a genuine renewal of our sense of responsibility for ourselves and for the world. And at the same time, it is the only way to achieve a deeper understanding among cultures that will enable them to work together in a truly ecumenical way to create a new order for the world.

15 I have been given to see Singapore and countless other exotic places. I have been given to understand how small this world is and how it torments itself with countless things it need not torment itself with—if people could find within themselves a little more courage, a little more hope, a little more responsibility, a little more mutual understanding and love …

16 Thank you for your attention.

President Bill Clinton. 1998. Excerpts from the State of the Union Address.

1 Mr Speaker, Mr Vice President, members of the 105th Congress, my fellow Americans:

2 For 209 years it has been the President's duty to report to you on the state of the Union. Because of the hard work and high purpose of the American people, these are good times for America. We have more than 14 million new jobs; the lowest unemployment in 24 years; the lowest core inflation in 30 years; incomes are rising; and we have the highest home-ownership in history. And the welfare rolls are at their lowest levels in 27 years. Our leadership in the world is unrivalled.

3 Ladies and gentlemen, the state of our Union is strong.

4 A strong nation rests on the rock of responsibility. A society rooted in responsibility must first promote the value of work, not welfare. We can be proud that after decades of finger-pointing and failure, together we ended the old welfare system. And we're now replacing welfare cheques with pay cheques. Last year, I challenged our nation to move 2 million more Americans off welfare by the year 2000. I'm pleased to report we have also met that goal, two full years ahead of schedule.

5 This is a grand achievement, the sum of many acts of individual courage, persistence and hope. For 13 years, Elaine Kinslow of Indianapolis, Indiana, was on and off welfare. Today, she's a dispatcher with a van company. She's saved enough money to move her family into a good neighbourhood. Elaine Kinslow and all those like her are the real heroes of the welfare revolution. There are millions like her all across America. And I'm happy she could join the First Lady tonight. Elaine, we're very proud of you. Please stand up.

6 Child care is the next frontier we must face to enable people to succeed at home and at work. I think this is such a big issue with me because of my own personal experience. I have often wondered how my mother, when she was a young widow, would have been able to go away to school and get an education and come back and support me if my grandparents hadn't been able to take care of me. How many other families have never had that same opportunity? The truth is, we don't know the answer to that question. But we do know what the answer should be: not a single American family should ever have to choose between the job they need and the child they love.

7 Nearly 200 years ago, a tattered flag, its broad stripes and bright stars still gleaming through the smoke of a fierce battle, moved Francis Scott Key to scribble a few words on the back of an envelope—the words that became our national anthem. Today, that Star Spangled Banner, along with the Declaration of

Independence, the Constitution and the Bill of Rights, are on display just a short walk from here. They are America's treasures for the ages.

8   I ask all Americans to support our project to restore all our treasures so that the generations of the twenty-first century can see for themselves the images and the words that are the old and continuing glory of America; an America that has continued to rise through every age, against every challenge, of people of great works and greater possibilities, who have always, always found the wisdom and strength to come together as one nation—to widen the circle of opportunity, to deepen the meaning of our freedom, to form that "more perfect union". Let that be our gift to the twenty-first century.

9   God bless you, and God bless the United States.

c   Persuasive techniques

For speeches, I recommend the following strategies.

- First and foremost, the speech should be honest and forthright. If relevant, this may mean acknowledging the downside of what you are presenting as well as the upside; or acknowledging ignorance. See Lincoln, paragraph 6; Havel, paragraph 11; Clinton, paragraph 6.

- Generalities numb the mind. As far as possible, use real-life examples to enliven what you are presenting. See Lincoln, paragraph 4; Havel, paragraph 1; Clinton, paragraph 5.

- Use the first person (*I, me, my, we, our* ...) and the second person (*you, your, yours*) to indicate that it's me (the speaker) communicating intimately with you (the audience)—and not some disembodied message from on high. All three speeches embody this technique.

- Use language that sounds spoken—not written. After all, it's a speech, and not a written document, that you are presenting. Lincoln's address is an exception to this rule. But Lincoln can be allowed this exception: he makes up for his literary tone with the brevity of the speech. Besides, he was speaking on a solemn occasion. See Havel's and Clinton's speeches: both are in natural, spoken language.

d   Language techniques

You need to ensure that the speech hangs together. Among the ways to give your speech cohesion are the following.

i   **Unity of ideas**—a particular focus for the speech as a whole.

- Lincoln focuses on the reason for the sacrifice the soldiers made.
- Havel develops a theme in stages: from technological to spiritual globalism.
- Clinton's theme is how to get from the good to the better.

ii   **Repetition**—to hammer home key points.

- Lincoln hammers home:

  *a new nation (1), that nation (2), that nation (4), this nation (10);
  we cannot dedicate, we cannot consecrate, we cannot hallow (6);
  the people, the people, the people (10).*

- Havel keeps returning to:

  *global civilization (2), global civilization (4), global civilization (6),
      global civilization (7);
  civilizations and cultures (6), religions and cultures (7), culture
      and civilization (9);
  I have not lost hope, I have not lost hope (11);
  a little more, a little more, a little more, a little more (15);
  respect, respect (12).*

- Clinton's theme words are:

  *a strong nation (4), our nation (4), our national anthem (7), as
      one nation (8);
  the rock of responsibility (4), rooted in responsibility (4);
  people of great works and greater possibilities (8); people ... who
      have always, always found the wisdom;
  treasures (7), treasures (8).*

iii   **Synonymy**—making similar points by using expressions with related meanings.

- Lincoln uses:

  *fitting, proper (5);
  long remember, never forget (8);
  gave their lives (4), gave the last full measure of devotion (10),
      died (10);
  the unfinished work (9), the great task remaining before us (10).*

- Havel uses:

  threads, capillaries (3);
  constant progress, rapid evolution (3);
  manner of civilizations, models of behaviour (6);
  variety of cultures (6), different from others (7);
  mutual connection, kinship (13);
  mutual co-existence, living side by side (9);
  mutual understanding, love (15).

- Clinton uses:

  hard work, high purpose (2);
  finger-pointing, failure (4);
  every challenge, great works, greater possibilities (8).

iv **Antonymy**—making similar points by using expressions of contrasting meanings.

- Lincoln uses:

  living, dead (7);
  add, detract (7);
  remember, forget (8).

- Havel uses:

  technological (3), religious (6);
  essential similarity, great diversity (11);
  heaven, nature (12);
  modern people, ancient deities (13);
  torment, hope (15).

- Clinton uses:

  lowest core inflation, highest home-ownership (2);
  value of work, welfare (4);
  welfare cheques, pay cheques (4);
  the job they need, the child they love (6);
  tattered flag, treasures (7).

v **Collocation**—using words that naturally go with each other to reinforce a concept.

- Lincoln collocates:

  civil war (2), battlefield (3), they who fought (9);
  a final resting place, gave their lives (4);
  unfinished work (9), increased devotion (10).

- Havel collocates:

  young people, rock music, familiar advertisements (1);
  history, civilization, progress, evolution (3);
  religions, cultures, mystery of being, human dignity (12).

- Clinton collocates:

  14 million new jobs, lowest unemployment, incomes rising,
  welfare rolls at their lowest (2);
  a grand achievement, courage, persistence, hope (5).

The above instances of synonymy, antonymy and collocation are only samplings. A close look at the text will reveal more. These, and the unity of ideas that runs through each of the three speeches, are techniques that all good speech-writers use and that you can also build into your own speech writing.

Writing business correspondence

She'll wish there was more, and that's the great art of letter writing.

(Charles Dickens, *The Pickwick Papers*.)

8

Writing business correspondence

8.1 Business correspondence and the corporate image

The correspondence that comes out of private or public sector offices is the public face that an organization presents to its clients and to other organizations. Since both public and private bodies want to present the best possible face to other bodies and to people with whom they deal, it is important for a person who engages in office correspondence to ensure that the correspondence is of a high quality.

You achieve this high quality by attending to the following three aspects of correspondence:

- the layout (or formatting) of the correspondence
- the logical sequence of ideas
- reader-friendly language.

The following three sections of this chapter deal with each of these aspects in turn.

8.2 Layout (or formatting) of correspondence

The sample letter below illustrates the following general features of the layout of correspondence.

- The letter is on office letterhead.
- All lines are left justified—though you indent to the right if you use dot points.
- There is good spacing between the parts of the letter.

The parts of a letter

These, starting from the top, are as follows.

a A reference number or a file
   number— SJ/567

b An unpunctuated address block, with as many of the following
   details as are relevant:

   - name— Mr B Kynde
   - title— Assistant Manager
   - organization— Wheels Transport
     Company
   - address— GPO Box 2000
     Perth WA 6001

c An unpunctuated salutation:

   - by name, if you know it— Dear Mr Kynde
   - by title, if you do not know
     the name but do know the title— Dear Assistant Manager
   - by some other title if the addressee
     does not already have a title— Dear Subscriber

The lattermost is to get away from the old-fashioned "Dear Sir/
Madam" formula.

d Optionally, a subject heading— MEETING OF THE ROAD
   SAFETY BUREAU

e Then follows the text— see the sample letter
   below.

f An unpunctuated complimentary close:

   - if you have used a name in the
     salutation, use— Yours sincerely
   - if you have used a title in the
     salutation, use— Yours faithfully

g Your signature— *Anne Other*

h **The signature block**, with as many of the following details as are relevant:

• your name—	Ms Anne Other
• your title—	Convenor
• optionally your direct telephone— and/or email address—	Direct line: 08 1234 5678 anne.other@safety.gov.au
• the date—	11 May 2003
• a list of enclosures (or "attachments"), if there are any—	Enclosure: your airline ticket.

On the next two pages you will find two examples of business letters that illustrate the aspects of modern layout that I have presented in parts 1 and 2 above.

N A T I O N A L   R O A D   S A F E T Y   B U R E A U

GPO Box 1000 Adelaide SA 5001   Phone: 08 1234 5678   Fax: 08 8765 4321

SJ/567

Mr B Kynde
Assistant Manager
Wheels Transport Company
GPO Box 2000
Perth WA 6001

Dear Mr Kynde

TENTH MEETING OF THE ROAD SAFETY COMMITTEE

I invite you or your delegate to attend the above meeting.

This is a follow-up meeting to the two meetings that we had earlier this year in Sydney and in Melbourne. The details of the next meeting are as follows.

Time: 10.00 am to 4.00 pm
Date: 15 July 2003
Venue: The Gabfest Room
         Conference Centre
         2 Somewhere Street
         Adelaide SA 5000

What we hope to do at this meeting is to discuss ways of implementing the decisions that we reached at the two earlier meetings.

I have booked an open airline ticket for a representative of your company, and you will find it enclosed with this letter.

I have not yet drawn up an agenda, but I will let you have one in plenty of time before the meeting. Please let me know whether you are coming to the meeting or sending a delegate in your place.

Yours sincerely

Anne Other

Ms Anne Other
Convenor

Direct line: 08 1234 5678

11 May 2003

Enclosure: your airline ticket.

Example letter 2

THE DEPARTMENT OF THIS AND THAT

GPO Box 3000 Canberra ACT 2601   Telephone 02 6000 000   Fax: 02 6000 0001

99/432

Ms A Surname
Assistant Secretary
Environment Protection Branch
Department of Something Else
GPO Box 5000
Canberra ACT 2601

Dear Ms Surname

Departmental comments on the environmental impact of the Doyle Plains development project

Many thanks for your letter of 10 June 2003 asking for my department's comments on the above project.

We received the project plans a fortnight ago. Since then, two field officers have been looking at the plans and at the project site. The field officers tell me that they need the following additional information:

a.   a geological survey map for area A
b.   blueprints for stage 2 of the project
c.   a timetable for the stages of the project.

Could you please let me have the items I have listed by the end of June? I then expect to be able to forward my department's comments to you by the end of July.

Yours sincerely

Sue Donim

Sue Donim
Evaluation Officer
Environmental Evaluation Branch

Direct line: 02 6000 002

14 June 2003

8.3 Logical sequence of ideas

It will help the reader of your correspondence if you sequence the information it contains in a logical way.

I suggest that each letter you write should contain the following:

a   an opening paragraph that states in brief and general terms your reason for writing
b   a middle paragraph or paragraphs that contain substantive information, background or elaboration of your opening paragraph
c   a closing paragraph or paragraphs that state what follow-up action you or your reader may need to undertake.

The two example letters on the preceding two pages illustrate the above logical sequence.

a   The reason for writing

> **Example letter 1**
>
> I invite you or your delegate to attend the above meeting.

> **Example letter 2**
>
> Many thanks for your letter of 10 June 2003 asking for my department's comments on the above project.

b   The substantive information, background or elaboration of the above

> **Example letter 1**
>
> This is a follow-up meeting to the two meetings that we had earlier this year in Sydney and in Melbourne. The details of the next meeting are as follows.
>
> Time: 10.00 am to 4.00 pm
> Date: 15 July 2003
> Venue: The Gabfest Room
>   Conference Centre
>   2 Somewhere Street
>   Adelaide SA 5000

What we hope to do at this meeting is to discuss ways of implementing the decisions that we reached at the two earlier meetings.

I have booked an open airline ticket for a representative of your company, and you will find it enclosed with this letter.

Example letter 2

We received the project plans a fortnight ago. Since then, two field officers have been looking at the plans and at the project site. The field officers tell me that they need the following additional information:

a. a geological survey map for area A
b. blueprints for stage 2 of the project
c. a timetable for the stages of the project.

---

c   **The follow-up action for the sender and for the recipient**

Example letter 1

I have not yet drawn up an agenda, but I will let you have one in plenty of time before the meeting. Please let me know whether you are coming to the meeting or sending a delegate in your place.

Example letter 2

Could you please let me have the items I have listed by the end of June? I then expect to be able to forward my department's comments to you by the end of July.

8.4   Plain English and reader-friendly language

Why should anyone use plain English and reader-friendly language?

Most public and private sector businesses have embraced this kind of language as their standard. They do this because correspondence that avoids an artificial, elevated language:

a   makes it easier for people to understand what we write and how to act on it
b   creates a friendlier relationship between the office and its clients
c   improves the organization's corporate image.

For government agencies there is the additional reason that it is official policy. In 1978, US President Jimmy Carter issued an executive order requiring government agencies to write in plain language. The UK followed suit a few years later. In a 1993 document under the title "Social Justice Strategy", Australian Prime Minister Paul Keating stated the policy as follows:

> The government is committed to greater use of plain English in legislation. Laws that are simpler to understand and administer will reduce unnecessary conflict and expensive litigation.

Chapter 1 deals in detail with how you can make your writing plain and reader-friendly. The ten-point programme contained in that chapter relates to letters as well. The particular strategy that I advise you to adopt is as follows:

a   while you are writing the draft letter, focus on two points—short sentences and "Dear Mum" language

b   then edit and revise the draft, checking in particular the following five style matters.

   i   Keep your sentences to an average length of one-and-a-half printed lines—some fifteen words. But vary the sentence lengths and structures. (See chapter 1.2–1.3.)

   ii   Use the "Dear Mum" principle. Write in a way that is normal, everyday, decent, respectful. Use this style of language for any person you are writing to—whether it is the minister or Bloggs in the bush. They are both of equal status as human beings.

   iii   Use capitals only where modern spelling requires them. Start full formal titles with capital letters (*the Department of Whatever*); short informal ones with lower-case letters (*the department*). But remember that there are some exceptions to this rule (*Crown, Labour, Liberals, Commonwealth* ...). (See chapter 1.6.)

   iv   Use first person (*I, me, my, we, us, our* ...) and second person (*you, your, yours*), particularly in correspondence. This will make your writing more personal and, therefore, more reader-friendly. (See chapter 1.7.)

> **v** With some rare exceptions, change the passive into the active. Do it in three steps:
>
> - identify the passive: a form of *be* + a past participle verb (a verb that ends in *–n, –d,* or *–t*)
> - after the verb, add *by* + an agent, but omit this step if the passive already has an agent
> - switch the sequence target–action–agent to agent–action–target. (See chapter 1.8.)

The two sample letters above illustrate these five principles of plain English. Here is another sample letter (minus the address and signature blocks) that does the same.

Dear Librarian

This is to ask whether you could lend my department a copy of Charles Stuart's *Dutch Explorers of the South Pacific.* Melbourne: Mermaid Publishing Co, 2001.

I need the book fairly urgently but only for a few days. I wonder, too, whether you have any other standard texts on the same topic.

Please ring me up, if you can, to let me know whether Stuart's book is available on loan. I can then arrange to have a courier pick it up.

Yours faithfully

My final advice on correspondence writing?

It is that you first do a draft and then check:

a the layout (or format)
b the logical sequence of ideas
c the language.

Each of my own letters goes through at least three drafts and checks before I am satisfied that it is good enough.

If you take the same trouble with yours, the reader will thank you for writing in an accessible way. The manager will thank you—maybe even promote you—for giving the firm a good corporate image. Best of all, you will enjoy a sense of job satisfaction for a job well done.

Appendix

From officialese to plain English

In chapter 1.4 we discussed the need for writers to use plain English ("Dear Mum" style), rather than high-flown language ("Yes, Minister" style), even in official papers. The former is much easier on the reader. In nearly every case, it also saves a lot of syllables. Plain English, therefore, gives the reader less to read for the same amount of information.

In the left column below, I have compiled a list of nearly two hundred terms that one often sees in official papers. I recommend switching to the terms in the right column.

You needn't worry that getting rid of the items in the left column will impoverish the language. This, for two reasons: first, none of the items in the left column has any literary merit; second, there are some 500,000 entires in The Oxford English Dictionary, *and the non-use of 200 of them will hardly matter.*

OFFICIAL ("YES, MINISTER") LANGUAGE	PLAIN ("DEAR MUM") LANGUAGE
able to	can
above-mentioned	mentioned above
accordingly	so / therefore
additional	more
additionally	and
adjacent to	next to / near
advice has been received that	my officers have told me that
advise you that / of	let you know
aforementioned	mentioned before / mentioned above
all things considered	so / therefore
alter / alteration	change
amongst	among
anticipate	expect
approximately	roughly / about
as a (result) consequence of	because of
as noted previously	as I have said above *(Or leave it out.)*
as soon as practicable	as soon as possible
as you would appreciate	you will understand
as you would be aware	as you know *(Or leave it out.)*
ascertain	find out / check
assist / assistance	help
at an early opportunity	soon
at this point in time	now / at present
at your earliest convenience	as soon as possible
attached hereto	attached please find
be applicable	applies
be in accordance with	accords with

by virtue of	under / because of
capable of	can
commence	start / begin
commencement	start / beginning
completion	end / finish
comprise	make up
concerning	about / for / in / ...
concur	agree
concurrence	agreement
consequent	later
consequently	so / therefore
considerable amount of	a lot of / many / much
contiguous to	next to / near
conversely	but / on the other hand
currently	now / at present
dated	of
dispatch	send
due to	because of
eg	for example / for instance
emanating from	coming from
embark on	start
endeavour	try
ensure	make sure
et al	and others
etc / et cetera	and so on
experienced delays	there were delays / had delays
extremely	very
facilitate	enable / make possible
failed to	did not
falls within the responsibility of Bloggs	Bloggs is responsible for
familiarize you with	make you familiar with
for the duration of	during
for the purpose of	to / for
for your consideration	for your decision / for your information
forthwith	immediately
forward	send
further developments	more developments / new developments
a further meeting	another meeting
further to my letter concerning	I am writing again about
furthermore	and / also
hence	so / therefore
henceforth	from now on
hereby / herewith	here / please find
hereunder	below
however	but
I acknowledge receipt of	thank you for
I am advised that	my department tells me that
I am directed to advise you that	(the minister) has asked me to tell you that
I am grateful for	thank you for
I appreciate that	I understand that / I know that

I appreciate your	thank you for your
I can confirm that	(Leave it out.)
I consider that	I think that / I believe that
I refer to your letter dated	thank you for your letter of
I regret the delay / the delay is regretted	I am sorry for the delay
I trust this addresses your concerns	I hope this answers your points (questions)
I will be pleased to	I will be happy to
I wish to advise that	(Leave it out.)
I would appreciate it if	please / would you please / could you please
I would be grateful if	please / would you please / could you please
ie	that is
if so-and-so transpires	if so-and-so happens
in a timely manner	as soon as possible
in accordance with section 12 of the Act	under section 12 of the act
in conjunction with	with / together with
in consideration of	for / because of
in excess of	more than
in keeping with	under
in order to	to
in relation to	about / for / in / ...
in respect of / to	about / for / in / ...
in situ	in place
in spite of the fact that	though / although
in terms of	in
in the course of	during
in the event of	if
in the majority of cases	in most cases
in the vicinity of	near
in this regard	(Leave it out.)
in this respect	(Leave it out.)
in toto	in total / altogether / all up
in view of the fact that	because
inform you of / inform you that	let you know
inter alia	among other things / among others
in applicable	applies
is dependent on / upon	depends on
is located in	is in
it appears to be the case that	it seems that
it is considered that	I think that / I believe that
it is incumbent on you	you should / you must / you need to
it is my considered view that	I think that / I believe that
it should be noted that	(Leave it out.)
locate	find / put / place
location	place
majority of	most
manner	way
Messrs A and B	Mr A and Mr B
negligible amount of	a little / a few

notify you / me	let you / me know
notwithstanding	despite / although
obtain	get
occurred	happened / took place
owing to	because of
paradigm	model
per annum	a year
per se	as such
pertains to	is about
please be advised that	*(Leave it out.)*
please do not hesitate to contact me / Bloggs	please contact (get in touch with) me / Bloggs
predominantly	mainly / mostly
previous	last / latest / earlier
previously	earlier
prior to	before
pro tem	for the time being
proceeded to (walk / drive)	walked / drove / started to walk / started to drive
provide you with further information	give you (let you have) more information
provided / providing	if
purchase	buy
pursuant to clause 12 of the Act	under clause 12 of the act
rectify	fix / correct / repair
regarding	about / for / in / …
relating to	about / for / in / …
rendered	made
reply	answer
request	ask
require	need
requirement	need
respond / response	answer
retain	keep
reveal	show / tell
review the matter	look at the matter again
should it be necessary	if necessary
Should you require further information, please do not hestitate to contact Bloggs	If you need more information, please get in touch with Bloggs *(Or leave it out.)*
should you wish to	if you want to / if you like
significant amount of	a lot of / much / many
status quo	as is / the existing state
subsequent to	after
subsequently	later
substantial amount of	a lot of / much / many
tacit understanding	informal / unstated understanding
take the matter up with Bloggs	contact Bloggs about the matter
the delay is regretted	I am sorry for the delay
thereby	because of this / so
thus	so / therefore
transmit	send

transpire	happen
unable to	cannot
undertake to do so-and-so	will (must) do so-and-so
upon	on
utilize	use
verify	check / confirm
via	through / by way of
viz	namely
where (in the sense of "if")	if
whereas	because
whilst	while
with a view to	to
with due regard for (something)	taking (something) into account
with immediate effect	straight away / immediately
with reference to	about / for / in / ...
with regard to	about / for / in / ...
with respect to	about / for / in / ...
you may care to	you might like to
you will be required to	you should / you must / you need to
your letter of the 20th instant	your letter of 20 May 200X

Acknowledgements

World Library Inc (Irvine, CA, 1994) has kindly permitted the use of quotations from Library of the Future, Compact Disc, of their editions of the following works.

Henry Adams, *The Education of Henry Adams*

Louisa May Alcott, *Little Women*

Horatio Alger Jr, *Cast upon the Waters*

Jane Austen, *Emma*

Jane Austen, *Northanger Abbey*

Jane Austen, *Pride and Prejudice*

Jane Austen, *Sense and Sensibility*

The Bible, Authorized Version

James Boswell, *The Life of Samuel Johnson*

Charlotte Brontë, *Jane Eyre*

Emily Brontë, *Wuthering Heights*

Robert Browning, *Dramatic Lyrics*

Thomas Bulfinch, *The Age of Chivalry*

Thomas Bulfinch, *The Age of Fable*

Frances Hodgson Burnett, *A Little Princess*

Lord Byron, *Don Juan*

Lewis Carroll, *Alice's Adventures in Wonderland*

Lewis Carroll, "Punctuality"

Lewis Carroll, *Sylvie and Bruno*

Lewis Carroll, *Through the Looking-Glass*

Willa Cather, *Alexander's Bridge*

Geoffrey Chaucer, *The Canterbury Tales*

Kate Chopin, "Athenaise"

Kate Chopin, *The Awakening*

Wilkie Collins, *The Moonstone*

Wilkie Collins, *The Woman in White*

Joseph Conrad, *Lord Jim*

James Fenimore Cooper, *The Deerslayer*

Stephen Crane, "The Blue Hotel"

Stephen Crane, *The Red Badge of Courage*

Charles Darwin, *The Origin of Species*

Charles Dickens, *David Copperfield*

Charles Dickens, *A Christmas Carol*

Charles Dickens, *Great Expectations*

Charles Dickens, *Oliver Twist*

Charles Dickens, *The Pickwick Papers*

Charles Dickens, *A Tale of Two Cities*

Emily Dickinson, *Poems*

Sir Arthur Conan Doyle, "Beryl Coronet"

Sir Arthur Conan Doyle, "Black Peter"

Sir Arthur Conan Doyle, "The Blanched Soldier"

Sir Arthur Conan Doyle, "Charles Augustus Malverton"

Sir Arthur Conan Doyle, "The Creeping Man"

Sir Arthur Conan Doyle, "The Crooked Man"

K Eric Drexler, *The Engines of Creation*

John Dryden, *All for Love*

George Eliot, *Middlemarch*

Ralph Waldo Emerson, *Essays*

The Federalist Papers

Henry Fielding, *Tom Jones*

Benjamin Franklin, *Autobiography*

Thomas Hardy, *The Mayor of Casterbridge*

Thomas Hardy, *A Pair of Blue Eyes*

Lee Harper, *To Kill a Mockingbird*

Thomas Hobbes, *Leviathan*

Washington Irving, *Alhambra*

Washington Irving, "The Art of Book-Making"

Washington Irving, "The Broken Heart"

Henry James, *Daisy Miller*

Phillip E Johnson, *Darwin on Trial*

James Joyce, *Portrait of the Artist as a Young Man*

Rudyard Kipling, *Kim*

DH Lawrence, *Sons and Lovers*

John Locke, *An Essay Concerning Human Understanding*

Jack London, *The Call of the Wild*

Jack London, *The Iron Heel*

Jack London, *The Sea Wolf*

W Somerset Maugham, *Of Human Bondage*

Herman Melville, *Billy Budd*

Herman Melville, *Moby Dick*

LM Montgomery, *Anne of Avonlea*

LM Montgomery, *Anne of Green Gables*

Thomas Paine, *The Age of Reason*

Thomas Paine, *The American Crisis*

Thomas Paine, *Common Sense*

Edgar Allan Poe, "Assignation"

Edgar Allan Poe, "Bon Bon"

Edgar Allan Poe, "Criticism"

Alexander Pope, *An Essay on Criticism*

Ezra Pound, "Dance Figure"

Susanna Haswell Rowson, *Charlotte Temple*

Sir Walter Scott, *Chronicles of the Cannongate*

William Shakespeare, *All's Well That Ends Well*
William Shakespeare, *Hamlet*
William Shakespeare, *King Henry IV* (Part 1)
William Shakespeare, *King Henry VI*
William Shakespeare, *King Lear*
William Shakespeare, *Macbeth*
William Shakespeare, *The Merchant of Venice*
William Shakespeare, "Sonnet 16"
William Shakespeare, *Venus and Adonis*
George Bernard Shaw, *Arms and the Man*
George Bernard Shaw, *Man and Superman*
George Bernard Shaw, *Pygmalion*
Mary Shelley, *Frankenstein*
Richard Sheridan, *The School for Scandal*
Upton Sinclair, *The Jungle*
Adam Smith, *The Wealth of Nations*
Robert Louis Stevenson, *El Dorado*
Robert Louis Stevenson, *Kidnapped*

Robert Louis Stevenson, *The New Arabian Nights*
Robert Louis Stevenson, *Treasure Island*
Jonathan Swift, *Gulliver's Travels*
Mark Twain, *The Adventures of Huckleberry Finn*
Mark Twain, *A Connecticut Yankee in King Arthur's Court*
Mark Twain, *Life on the Mississippi*
Mark Twain, "A New Crime Legislation Needed"
Mark Twain, *A Tramp Abroad*
Lew Wallace, *Ben Hur*
Jean Webster, *Daddy-Long-Legs*
Edith Wharton, *Ethan Frome*
Edith Wharton, *Summer*
Walt Whitman, *Leaves of Grass*
Oscar Wilde, *Lady Windermere's Fan*
Oscar Wilde, *A Woman of No Importance*

I gratefully acknowledge the generosity and kindness of the authors, publishers and copyright holders who have allowed me to use citations from the following works:

Paul Davies. 1994. *The Last Three Minutes: Conjectures about the Ultimate Fate of the Universe*. London: Weidenfeld and Nicolson.
Richard P Feynman. 1998. *The Meaning of It All*. London: Penguin.
Bob Hawkins and Ralph Lattimore. 1995. *Science Understanding and Awareness: How Australia Ranks in International Surveys*. Canberra: Australian Government Publishing Service.
Caroline Jones. 1992. *The Search for Meaning: Conversations with Caroline Jones*. Sydney: The Australian Broadcasting Corporation and Collins Dove.
Caroline Jones. 1995. *The Search for Meaning Collection*. Sydney: The Australian Broadcasting Corporation and Harper Collins.
Melina Marchetta. 1992. *Looking for Alibrandi*. Melbourne: Penguin Australia.
Bill Moyers. 1989. *Bill Moyers: A World of Ideas*. Edited by Betty Sue Flowers. New York: Doubleday. (Copyright 1989 by Public Affairs Television Inc. Used by permission of Doubleday, a division of Bantam Doubleday Dell Publishing Group Inc.)
George Orwell. 1968. *Collected Essays, Journalism and Letters*. In four volumes, edited by Sonia Orwell and Ian Angus. Harmondsworth: Penguin.
GW Turner. 1986 [1973]. *Stylistics*. Harmondsworth: Penguin.

The publishers of the following periodicals have kindly made texts from their publications available for citation.

The ABC Cricket Book. Sydney: The Australian Broadcasting Corporation.
The Economist. London: The Economist Newspaper Limited.

National Geographic. Washington: National Geographic Society.
New Scientist. London: New Science Publications.
Presidents & Prime Ministers. Glen Ellyn, IL: EQES.
TIME. New York: Time Inc.

From the citations in the 1992 compact disc edition of The Oxford English Dictionary
I have quoted from the following:

Neil Armstrong	M Fotherby	*The Saturday Review*
William Bagehot	*The Guardian*	Mary Shelley
The Earl of Chesterfield	A Hamilton	Alfred Lord Tennyson
The Daily News	J Jackson	*The Weekly Westminster Gazette*
The Economist	WG McAdoo	John Wesley
Henry Fielding	Ouida	William Whewell
John Fisher	John Ruskin	*Which?*

Additional texts come from the following:

Bill Clinton, "State of the Union Address, 1998"
Lord Denning, *Lloyd's Bank Ltd v Bundy*
Vaclav Havel, "Commencement Address at Harvard University, 1995"
Robert Herrick, "On Blindness"
Robert Herrick, "To His Critics"
Abraham Lincoln, "The Gettysburg Address"
John Milton, "Of Reformation in England"
John Milton, "On His Blindness"
Deborah Stern, "Making Bedouin Bread"

For a critical note (chapter 2.3) I have quoted from the following:

Edward Down. 1991. *Mastering Grammar.* Melbourne: Longman Cheshire.

I have quoted brief texts from the following additional sources:

Winston Churchill (chapter 2.4), attributed.
US Declaration of Independence (chapter 3.7).
René Descartes (chapter 5.10), *The Discourse on Method.*
Richard Galpin (chapter 5.10), BBC News.
Piet Hein (chapter 3.10), attributed.
Charlton Heston, Lynne D Aiken (chapter 2.22), *Reader's Digest.*
Steve Waugh, Adam Parore (chapter 2.14), *The Canberra Times.*

The quotations at the beginnings of the chapters come from the following sources:

Chapter 1	GW Turner. 1986 [1973]. *Stylistics.* Harmondsworth: Penguin.
Chapter 2	Noam Chomsky. 1972. *Language and Mind.* Enlarged edition. San Diego: Harcourt Brace Jovanovich.
Chapter 3	HW and FG Fowler. 1931. *The King's English.* Third edition. Oxford: The Clarendon Press.
Chapter 4	William Shakespeare. 1603. *Hamlet.*
Chapter 5	Edward O Wilson. 1998. *Consilience: The Unity of Knowledge.* London: Little, Brown and Company.
Chapter 6	John Harris. 1993. *Introducing Writing.* London: Penguin.

Chapter 7   George Stern. 1995. *Spot On! Correspondence and Report Writing with Guidelines on Plain English.* Canberra: Australian Government Publishing Service.

Chapter 8   Charles Dickens. 1836. *The Pickwick Papers.*

It remains for me to acknowledge my debt to several people who have helped and inspired me in one way or another:

- Wayne Beswick, Misty Cook and Debby Gairns carefully trawled through drafts of this book and picked out many errors and infelicities. Any that remain are purely my own. Coralie Walker, a good friend and skilled operator, did me an essential service by preparing my disks for the publisher.
- The Australian National University came good with a vital grant at the vital moment. My thanks go to the members of the ANU Publications Committee.
- Last, but far from least, my thanks to Chris Carter, Janine Dodson and their colleagues at R.I.C. Publications and to Mew Yew Hwa of Learners Publishing for their expertise and patience.

Bibliography

Aitchison, Jean. 1997. *The Language Web: The Power and Problem of Words*. Cambridge: Cambridge University Press.

Aitchison, Jean. 1998 [1991]. *Language Change: Progress or Decay*. Second edition. Cambridge: Cambridge University Press.

Axelrod, Rise B and Cooper, Charles R. 1986. *The St Martin's Guide to Writing*. New York: St Martin's Press.

Bauer, Laurie and Trudgill, Peter (editors). 1998. *Language Myths*. London: Penguin.

Beswick, Wayne A. 1996. *The Pleasure of Being: Culture, Dialogue and Genre*. Canberra: unpublished doctoral thesis.

Blake, Gary and Bly, Robert W. 1993. *The Elements of Technical Writing*. New York: Macmillan.

Blamires, Harry. 1997. *Guide to Common Errors in English*. London: Cassell.

Bloomfield, Leonard. 1933. *Language*. New York: Holt, Rinehart and Winston.

Brooks, Cleanth and Warren, Robert Penn. 1972. *Modern Rhetoric*. Shorter third edition. New York: Harcourt Brace Jovanovich.

Burchfield, Robert W. 1985. *The English Language*. Oxford: Oxford University Press.

Burchfield, Robert W. 1992. *Points of View*. Oxford: Oxford University Press.

Burchfield, Robert W (editor). 1996. *The New Fowler's Modern English Usage*. Third edition. Oxford: Oxford University Press.

Butt, David; Fahey, Rhondda; Spinks, Sue; Yallop, Colin. 1995. *Using Functional Grammar: An Explorer's Guide*. Sydney: Macquarie University.

Carter, Ronald (editor). 1982. *Language and Literature: An Introductory Reader in Stylistics*. London: Unwin Hyman.

Chalker, Sylvia and Weiner, Edmund. 1994. *The Oxford Dictionary of English Grammar*. Oxford: Oxford University Press.

Clanchy, John and Ballard, Brigid. 1994 [1981]. *Essay Writing for Students: A Practical Guide*. Melbourne: Longman Cheshire.

Collerson, John. 1994. *English Grammar: A Functional Approach*. Newtown: Primary English Teaching Association.

Collinson, Diané. 1986 [1982]. *Writing English: A Workbook for Students*. Aldershot: Wildwood House.

Collinson, Diané; Kirkup, Gillian; Kyd, Robin; Slocombe, Lynne. 1992. *Plain English*. Second edition. Buckingham: Open University Press.

Crystal, David. 1995. *The Cambridge Encyclopedia of the English Language*. Cambridge: Cambridge University Press.

Crystal, David. 1997. *A Dictionary of Linguistics and Phonetics*. Fourth edition. Oxford: Blackwell.

Cutts, Martin. 1996. *The Plain English Guide*. Oxford: Oxford University Press.

Deese, James and Deese, Ellin K. 1979. *How to Study*. Third edition. New York: McGraw Hill.

Edwards, Mary. 1985. *Dictionary of Key Words*. New York: Macmillan.

Eggins, Suzanne. 1994. *An Introduction to Systemic Functional Linguistics*. London: Pinter.

Evans, David. 1999 [1995]. *How to Write a Better Thesis or Report*. Melbourne: Melbourne University Press.

Fabb, Nigel. 1994. *Sentence Structure*. London: Routledge.

Flexner, SB (editor in chief). 1987. *The Random House Dictionary of the English Language*. Second edition, unabridged. New York: Random House.

Fowler, HG and Russell, N. 1960. *A Wealth of Words*. Melbourne: Macmillan.

Fries, Charles Carpenter. 1952. *The Structure of English: An Introduction to the Construction of English Sentences*. New York: Harcourt, Brace and Company.

Gilman, E Ward (editor). 1989. *Webster's Dictionary of English Usage*. Springfield, Mass: Merriam-Webster.

Glaser, Joe. 1999. *Understanding Style: Practical Ways to Improve Your Writing*. Oxford: Oxford University Press.

Gowers, Sir Ernest. 1982 [1948]. *The Complete Plain Words*. Second edition, revised by Sir Bruce Fraser. Harmondsworth: Penguin.

Graddol, David; Cheshire, Jenny; Swann, Joan. 1994. *Describing Language*. Buckingham: Open University Press.

Green, Pamela. 1992. *A Matter of Fact: Using Factual Texts in the Classroom*. Armadale, Vic: Eleanor Curtain.

Greenbaum, Sidney. 1988. *Good English and the Grammarian*. London: Longman.

Guiraud, Pierre. 1975. *Semiology*. Translated by George Gross. London: Routledge & Kegan Paul.

Halliday, MAK. 1994. *An Introduction to Functional Grammar*. Second edition. London: Edward Arnold.

Halliday, MAK and Martin, JR (editors). 1981. *Readings in Systemic Linguistics*. London: Batsford.

Harris, John. 1993. *Introducing Writing*. London: Penguin.

Hawkes, Terence. 1983. *Structuralism and Semiotics*. London: Routledge.

Herman, Jeff and Adams, Deborah M. 1993. *Write the Perfect Book Proposal: 10 Proposals That Sold and Why*. New York: John Wiley & Sons.

Hornby, AS. 1954. *A Guide to Patterns and Usage in English*. Oxford: Oxford University Press.

Jakobson, Roman and Halle, Morris. 1956. *Fundamentals of Language*. 's-Gravenhage: Mouton.

Jespersen, Otto. 1924. *Philosophy of Grammar*. New York: Henry Holt.

Jespersen, Otto. 1962. *Growth and Structure of the English Language*. Ninth edition. Oxford: Blackwell.

Kennedy, Chris. 1982. "Systemic Grammar and Its Use in Literary Analysis". *Language and Literature: An Introductory Reader in Stylistics*. Edited by Ronald Carter. London: Unwin Hyman.

Leech, Geoffrey. 1981 [1974]. *Semantics: The Study of Meaning*. Harmondsworth: Penguin.

Lyons, John. 1995. *Linguistic Semantics: An Introduction*. Cambridge: Cambridge University Press.

Martin, James R. 1984. "Language, Register and Genre". *Children Writing*. Edited by F Christie. Geelong: Deakin University Press.

Martin, James R. 1992. *English Text: System and Structure*. Amsterdam: John Benjamins.

McArthur, Tom (editor). 1992. *Oxford Companion to the English Language*. Oxford: Oxford University Press.

Millward, CM. 1988. *A Biography of the English Language*. New York: Holt, Rinehart and Winston.

Neman, Beth S. 1983. *Writing Effectively*. London: Charles E Merrill.

Nunan, David. 1993. *Introducing Discourse Analysis*. London: Penguin.

Pearsall, Judy and Trumble, Bill (editors). 1995. *The Oxford English Reference Dictionary*. Oxford: Oxford University Press.

Quirk, Randolph; Greenbaum, Sidney; Leech, Geoffrey; Svartvik, Jan. 1985. *A Comprehensive Grammar of the English Language*. London: Longman.

Renton, Nick E. 1990. *Metaphors: An Annotated Dictionary*. Melbourne: Schwartz and Wilkinson.

Richards, Jack; Platt, John; Weber, Heidi. 1985. *Longman Dictionary of Applied Linguistics*. London: Longman.

The Right Word at the Right Time: A Guide to the English Language and How to Use It. 1985. London: The Reader's Digest Association Limited.

Salkie, Raphael. 1995. *Text and Discourse Analysis*. London: Routledge.

Simon, Rachel. 1997. *The Writer's Survival Guide*. Cincinnati: Story Press.

Simpson, John A and Weiner, Edmund SC (editors). 1992. *The Oxford English Dictionary*. Second edition. Oxford: Oxford University Press.

Skeat, Walter W. 1882. *A Concise Etymological Dictionary of the English Language*. Oxford: Clarendon Press.

Steinmann, Martin and Keller, Michael. 1995. *NTC's Handbook for Writers*. Lincolnwood: NTC Publishing Group.

Stern, George. 1994. *Choosing Your Mark: A Guide to Good Expression and Punctuation*. Canberra: Australian Government Publishing Service.

Stern, George. 1995. *Spot On! Correspondence and Report Writing with Guidelines on Plain English*. Canberra: Australian Government Publishing Service.

Stern, George. 1997. *Using Grammar in Your Prose*. Canberra: Australian Government Publishing Service.

Stern, George. 1998a. *An Outline of English Grammar: with Practices and Key*. Canberra: Australian National University.

Stern, George. 1998b. *Applying for Jobs and Winning at Interviews*. Canberra: Australian National University.

Stern, George; Bolitho, Robert; Lutton, Russell. 1993. *The Guide to Australian Usage and Punctuation*. Melbourne: Collins Dove.

Stuart, Cristina. 1988. *Effective Speaking*. Bury St Edmunds: Pan Books.

Style Manual for Authors, Editors and Printers. 1994. Fifth edition. Canberra: Australian Government Publishing Service.

Swan, Michael. 1995. *Practical English Usage*. Second edition. Oxford: Oxford University Press.

Thomas, Owen. 1965. *Transformational Grammar and the Teacher of English*. New York: Holt, Rinehart and Winston.

Turner, GW. 1986 [1973]. *Stylistics*. Harmondsworth: Penguin.

Vallins, GH. 1957 [1956]. *The Pattern of English*. Harmondsworth: Penguin.

Vallins, GH. 1960. *The Best English*. London: Andre Deutsch.

Wardhaugh, Ronald. 1993. *Investigating Language: Central Problems in Linguistics*. Oxford: Blackwell.

Williams, Geoff. 1994. *Using Systemic Grammar in Teaching Young Learners: An Introduction*. Melbourne: Macmillan.

Wren, CL. 1966 [1949]. *The English Language*. Norwich: Methuen.

Index

The numbers after the entries refer to chapters and sections.